To Brian

with deep appreciation

and best wishes

Lawrence E. Walsh

The Gift of Insecurity
A Lawyer's Life

Lawrence E. Walsh

Foreword by Nina Totenberg

Cover design by Andrew Alcala, ABA Publishing
Cover photograph by Elson-Alexandre

The materials contained herein represent the opinions of the authors and should not be construed to be the action of the American Bar Association unless adopted pursuant to the bylaws of the Association.

Nothing contained in this book is considered as the rendering of legal advice, and readers are responsible for obtaining such advice from their own legal counsel. The book is intended for educational and informational purposes only.

Copyright © 2003 by the American Bar Association
Chicago, Illinois. All rights reserved. Printed in the United States of America. No part of this book may be reproduced in any form or by any means, electronic or mechanical, including but not limited to, photocopying, recording, or by any information storage and retrieval system, without written permission of the Publisher, except where permitted by law.

Library of Congress Control Number: 2002109271

ISBN: 1-59031-133-7

www.ababooks.org

CONTENTS

Dedication

To J. Edward Lumbard, Jr.

Inspiring leader, teacher, and friend.

Foreword

In 1969 I was a very green, young reporter for the staid *National Observer,* and I went to meet the staid senior partner of Davis Polk & Wardwell, Judge Lawrence E. Walsh. I had talked to him several times on the phone and hadn't gotten much out of him, so I thought maybe if I went to see him, it would help. He was then the chairman of the American Bar Association's Judicial Screening Committee, and I was a nobody—new to the legal beat in Washington, a non-lawyer, and, worse yet, a woman.

By then I had grown used to being dismissed by men, patted on the head, or in some cases just hit on. So you simply cannot imagine my astonishment when I was ushered into a large office and greeted warmly by this rather austere-looking gentleman in a three-piece suit, who then proceeded to engage me in a lively conversation about the role of his committee, how it conducted its business, the problems it faced, particularly in getting honest assessments of Supreme Court nominees—oh, and did I have any thoughts about how the process could be improved? As I would learn in the decades to come, talking to Lawrence Walsh is *always* worth a reporter's time, but you don't find out anything you could call a scoop. You just understand the dimensions of what you are covering much better. That was true on that day, as it has been on many days since in the 33 years that I have known Judge Walsh. What astonished me on that day was that this very senior Wall Street lawyer in such a hidebound-looking place treated me not as some silly girl but as an equal. What has astonished me as I have grown older is his ability to understand the role of the press, even when we made his life rather unpleasant.

A case in point was the day in 1987 when I called him at home in Oklahoma. I had been phoning around trying to figure out who would be appointed the Iran-Contra independent counsel. I won't bore you with the path that took me eventually to the conclusion that Walsh had been chosen, but I finally had enough information to place a call to him and ask. He laughed and said he really couldn't help me. I wheedled. He refused to take the bait. But my sources were good and I was sure enough to write a story. The next day the *Los Angeles Times* said it had confirmed my story. And then . . . silence. Nothing for days, as I (and Ron Ostrow from the *L. A. Times*) chewed my (our) fingernails. Finally, the announcement came, and I called Walsh again. "What was that all about?" I demanded to know. Well, he explained, it hadn't been a done deal yet, since he was still being checked out when I called, and he could tell I had enough to write a story, and if somebody had some reason to oppose him, it would be better if it came out, and the only way it would come out was if his name was out there.

Now, that is a remarkably sophisticated assessment of the situation he faced when he got my call. It is also a reflection of his long-held view that a major nomination should not be made until the press and public have had a little time to stir the pot. I think he came to that conclusion after his experience as chairman of the ABA screening committee when G. Harrold Carswell was named to the Supreme Court. In hindsight, he clearly felt that the ABA had wrongly given Carswell its stamp of approval, and he persuaded President Nixon, for a short time at least, to let the ABA vet potential nominees before their names were publicly announced. So I thought it kind of nice that he applied the same standard to his own nomination, even though it gave anyone who didn't like him plenty of time to sink his prospects.

In the years that followed, of course, Judge Walsh acquired a goodly number of antagonists. His role as Iran-Contra special prosecutor won him few friends in the Republican circles in which he had long traveled; nor were his critics all partisans. I think he did care, but not enough to compromise what he viewed as "the rule of law." In the end, he was very angry about the pardons President George H. W. Bush granted to the men Bush had served with in the Reagan Administration. But the rest of the hurdles that defeated much of the Walsh investigation—the court rulings making it so difficult to prosecute, and the court rulings that invalidated the hard-won convictions—were all things he knew were possible when he took the job.

I remember the first interviews I did with him at the beginning of his tenure. Even then, he was worried about how to deal with classified information, how to overcome the objections of the not exactly disinterested intelligence community. Even then, he was worried about how to prosecute while congressional hearings were ongoing. Even then, he worried that getting the information he needed from foreign banks would take years, putting his investigation in political jeopardy. I remember thinking that the problems he alluded to were overblown, that it would somehow work out. But in hindsight, I think he knew he could be thwarted, and simply tried his best not to be.

What I have learned about Lawrence Walsh over the years is to respect his judgment, even when it seems a little wacky. I remember one time during the Nixon Administration when I got hold of a list of potential Supreme Court nominees, and I called Walsh trying to get a third confirmation on it. He was on vacation on Cape Cod and said he would call me back. The next thing I knew I was talking to this Lion of Wall Street, former federal judge, former deputy attorney general of the United States, and I could hear cars and trucks in the background! He told me it would be inappropriate for him to comment on my list, but that I should keep pressing, I was on the right track. And I said, "Where are you, with all that noise in the background?" And he told me he was using a pay phone somewhere near his house because he didn't trust his phones not to be tapped. I, with all the wisdom of my 26 or 27 years, rolled my eyes, thinking he was a little paranoid. Just a few years later, we learned that the Nixon Administration had tapped lots of people it suspected of disloyalty. So he wasn't paranoid after all—just careful.

That judgment has served him well over the years. As we learn in this book, it is a judgment born not of confidence but of insecurity, of being a C student not from the social elite. As Walsh puts it, it was "the Gift of Insecurity" that led him down so many nontraditional paths in his life—a life that took him from seafaring jobs aboard freighters and ocean liners in his college years to prosecutorial jobs in pursuit of the mob as a young lawyer working for District Attorney Tom Dewey. Indeed, the jobs Lawrence Walsh has held during his life have been incredibly diverse—from Wall Street litigator to deputy U.S. negotiator at the Paris peace talks with North Vietnam, from counsel to the New York commission charged with cleaning up the waterfront to Iran/Contra independent counsel, from federal judge to deputy attorney general in the Eisenhower Administration. For me, one of the most fascinating and charming chapters was about his years as No. 2 in the Justice Department, for his tenure covered the desegregation of the Little Rock schools, his relationship with southern senators as he sought to shepherd through the Senate judges pledged to uphold civil rights, and some other perhaps more marginal, but quite entertaining events—such as his meeting with President Eisenhower to explain why the Administration really could not champion the suppression of D.H. Lawrence's *Lady Chatterley's Lover*. It seems that the postmaster general had appealed directly to the president on this question, giving Ike a copy of the book with the offending passages underlined, and it fell to Deputy Attorney General Walsh to explain to the president of the United States why the Justice Department was not going to appeal a decision by a lower court allowing the book to be sent through the mails.

Eisenhower, like many others over the years, decided to respect Walsh's judgment.

As a reporter, I have not always agreed with Judge Walsh, and have on occasion told him so. What astonishes me now, more than three decades after I first met him, is that he can take a healthy disagreement. He welcomes it as an opportunity to rethink a position, and if he continues to disagree, he expects you to be able to take it too!

—Nina Totenberg
Legal Affairs Correspondent
for National Public Radio

Preface

The title of this book is that of a speech I gave the third-year class of the University of Miami School of Law when I was president of the American Bar Association. Invited by Dean Soia Mentschikoff, a former classmate who knew of my academic shortcomings, I decided to pitch my remarks to the C students, who needed encouragement. I told them that the law review members and other outstanding students would quickly be hired by leading law firms and led into a lifetime of narrowly specialized practice, whereas the C students, if they were sufficiently opportunistic, would have both a more varied and enjoyable practice, and in the end, perhaps even more success than their classmates. "The Gift of Uncertainty" would have been more accurate; it was that meaning of "insecure" that I had in mind, not something more precarious.

The lure of extracurricular activities diminished my academic performance but never left me. At first, because I had no other choice, I immersed myself in the excitement of public office. Then when I did have the option of a more secure calling, I nevertheless kept returning to public activities—the extracurricular activities of law practice. As a result, my experience in unusual litigation and the controversies of public office led to high state office, an early judgeship, high federal office, and a prestigious partnership, culminating in 25 years of highly successful practice defending private clients in controversial cases and finally directing a government investigation of the president of the United States.

As an unexpected but all the more valuable benefit, I was, at various levels, an insider and witness to the transition of the reform Republicans to the moderate Republicans who formed the centrist party of the mid-twentieth century. Either leading the way or supporting other reform-minded groups, this wing of the Republican party could claim much responsibility for balanced periods of economic progress and gradualist reform, beginning with the election of Governor Thomas E. Dewey to the governorship of New York and ending with the downfall of President Richard Nixon. I am also proud of accumulating some interesting adversaries along the way, among them Fritz Kuhn, president of the anti-

Semitic German American Bund; Anthony "Tough Tony" Anastasia, intimidator of the New York Waterfront; Governor Orval Faubus of Arkansas, a leading opponent of school desegregation; and even respected leaders Senator Bob Dole and President George Bush, who used their offices to block prosecution of political colleagues.

Once near the beginning of my career, a good lawyer told me not to be one of those lawyers who wandered back and forth between private practice and government office. I meant to follow his advice, but I'm glad I failed. I've enjoyed the variety, and each type of practice has helped broaden and sharpen my insights into the others. At least for those of us at first tagged as B or lower, I offer this story of 60 years of practice, which I can honestly say has never been dull.

Because I have been blessed with a long life as well as an active one, this story also reaches back to the living conditions of small Nova Scotian communities, which, when I was born, more closely resembled Anglo-Saxon communities than those of today. In a single century, scientists have outdistanced all their predecessors in controlling disease and in improving community conditions of life, but the hazards of unregulated living conditions and old-time diseases which they have overcome have been replaced by the more frightening dangers of environmental disaster and of mass destruction which they have created, from which we have all received the challenge of insecurity in its more usual sense, a lack of safety.

Acknowledgments

Acknowledgments for an autobiography could easily become a lifetime list of benefactors. I have been remarkably well treated. Those for whom I have worked and my associates have been generous and supportive. Those who have reported my activities have been accurate and perceptive. Those who have criticized them have usually been fair and helpful.

I am particularly grateful to my longtime associates, Guy Miller Struve, Leon Silverman, Rick Ford, Judge Miriam Goldman Cedarbaum, and Professor John Barrett, for reading early drafts and for their thoughtful suggestions.

The basic editing and advice of Donald Lamm, former president of W.W. Norton & Company, Inc., has been generous beyond measure and has led to a treasured friendship.

My secretary, Marla White, drawing on her own editorial experience, has contributed her research, judgment, and advice in the course of her long hours of work.

Finally, Adrienne Cook and the American Bar Association publications team have generously exposed our effort to the light of day.

Chapter 1
IMMIGRANTS

In the spring of 1763, a ship carrying a small group of New England younger sons, their families, their cattle, and their possessions made its way through the twisted, silted channel of Yarmouth Harbor at the southwesterly end of Nova Scotia, where the Bay of Fundy meets the Atlantic Ocean. Each family had received a grant of land from the colonial governor, who hoped to cultivate this rugged headland. Two years before, an exceptionally severe winter accompanied by illness and death had driven back a similar group of New Englanders. The earlier French settlers, for the most part, had avoided the exposed mouth of the Bay of Fundy, settling farther up the bay at Fort Royale (now Annapolis Royal) and then spreading down river valleys directly across the Nova Scotian peninsula to the ocean.

Even in hardship, the new colony flourished. With the few roads still uncleared of stumps and almost impassable during the spring thaw, farmers as well as fishermen became boatmen, relying of necessity on water transport. Conversely, fishermen managed small farms to support their families. The new arrivals included two pairs of my mother's great-great-grandparents, all fourth- or fifth-generation descendants of early New England settlers: Joseph Pitman of Beverly, Massachusetts, and Joseph Sanders[1] of Salem, New Hampshire, and their wives and children. A year later, Joseph Sanders wrote his brother, describing the ground as fertile and the orchards abundant, and urging him to join them.

---

1. Joseph Sanders was one of many descendants of Joseph Saunders, an Englishman, who arrived in Salem, Massachusetts, in 1637. The family spread to Haverhill, Massachusetts. When the boundary between New Hampshire and Massachusetts was redrawn, the farm of Joseph Sanders' parents, Henry Sanders and Mary Mitchell, was on the New Hampshire side of the line.

During and after the American Revolution, wealthier loyalists moved to Nova Scotia. In 1784, after the war had ended, another ancestor, William Moses of New York, reached Yarmouth. He became a shipbuilder and a ship owner. As others like him arrived, Yarmouth boomed and became the second largest city in Nova Scotia. Breakwaters were inserted to keep the outer bar from closing the harbor. Dredging cleared the channels. Inexhaustible lumber fed the shipyards. Nova Scotian ships became world famous. Not quite matching the beautiful Yankee clippers, they were nevertheless trim, well built, well manned, and expertly commanded.

My mother's father, Captain Edwin Sanders, William Moses's great-grandson, rose to command ships at an early age. He was known as a deeply religious ship's master who, in decent weather, mustered his crew amidship each Sunday for prayer service. More than one Nova Scotian learned to use a prayer book from him. He and his wife, the former Ellen Maria Pitman, built their home in Port Maitland, a small, new settlement 12 miles up the coast from Yarmouth. My grandmother raised three children there while her husband's worldwide voyages for English and Canadian owners sometimes kept him away for a year or more at a time. Once, before the children were born, she had moved to London to be with him. There, their first child was born and died. On occasion she would travel to Montreal or some other seaport to meet him.

My mother, Lila, was born May 14, 1879. An admired, beautiful child, she finished the 12 grades of the Port Maitland school, taught school for a year in a one-room schoolhouse, and then graduated from the school of nursing of the Somerville Hospital, just outside Boston. For several years she nursed patients at home, in a time when extended nursing was often a necessity.

In 1829, James Walsh, son of Lawrence Walsh and Eleanor Walters of Bilarnon/Ballynamarra, Wexford County, Ireland, was shipwrecked as his vessel, bound for St. John, New Brunswick, too closely skirted the Nova Scotian coast off Ledges, near Port L'Hebert. Rescued, he joined an already existing Irish community in Liverpool, Nova Scotia, where he married Margaret Phelan, who had been born there 20 years earlier. They had nine children, the third of whom was my grandfather, William James Walsh. After completing school, he worked as a lumberman in Jordan Falls, a tiny community where trees cut during the winter were floated down the river and milled for the shipyards of Shelburne, nine miles away.

Although a Roman Catholic, my grandfather married Rosanna Swanberg, a devout Methodist and a descendant of a Hessian farmer who had received a royal land grant and a Scottish mother, whose parents had immigrated to Nova Scotia during the Highland Clearances.[2]

Young William Walsh bought a half-cleared farm of approximately 140 acres. He and Rose had five children who were raised in their mother's religion, although they adopted their father's Conservative Party politics. Their second child, Cornelius Edward, my father, like all of the children, walked to a one-room schoolhouse two miles from home. After the eleventh grade, his teacher persuaded his parents to let him complete the twelfth year at the Shelburne Academy, nine miles away. To do this, he worked for his room and board.

The circumstances of the family had never been easy, but they became desperate when my grandfather's right hand was cut off in a lumber mill accident. After he was carried home by his fellow employees, the children watched from the edge of the kitchen while the doctor completed the amputation, with the blood spurting up to stain the kitchen ceiling. My grandfather and his wife nevertheless worked the farm and supported themselves and their family without help—probably due to the fierce determination of my grandmother, who did a man's work as well as her own. The children also worked. Because he was the strongest and the best able to handle tools, my father did more than his share. Determined to be a physician, he accumulated funds by teaching school in Clarke's Harbor, Nova Scotia; selling stereopticon viewers and slides on Cape Breton Island; and then working in Boston for a few years as a railroad auditor. At about 23, he enrolled in the medical school of Dalhousie University, in Halifax, where he pitched pennies for lunch and, in winter, studied in an unheated room with an oil stove between his legs and his books on top of it. At the end of the year, he transferred to McGill University and completed his four-year medical education, working for his meals but concealing this activity from his classmates.

In 1906, after graduation, he accepted the invitation of an older doctor to open a practice in Port Maitland to serve the area between Yarmouth

---

2. Her mother, Mary McKay, was first cousin to Donald McKay, the noted designer and builder of record-breaking clipper ships, whose father, her uncle, also immigrated to Nova Scotia after completing his service as an officer of the Black Watch regiment. Among McKay's most famous ships were the *Flying Cloud,* holder of the record for the trip around Cape Horn from New York to San Francisco, and the *Lightning,* which logged over 400 miles in a single day, with an average hourly speed of over 18 knots, a feat unequaled by any nineteenth-century vessel under steam or sail.

and Cape St. Mary 25 miles away. He fell in love with my mother, he said, because he so liked the "brambles" that she supplied at a Methodist church picnic. They were married in June 1910. I was born 19 months later on January 8, 1912. Captain Sanders noted my arrival as though making an entry in a ship's log. "It looks as though it is going to blow from the east. Lila *(my mother)* and infant *(me)* are doing well."

Port Maitland, where I spent my first two and one half years, was a small fishing port. Its harbor consisted of a weathered, wooden, L-shaped breakwater and a shorter supplementary pier inside a submerged reef known as Trinity Ledge. It protected a 15- or 20-boat fishing fleet on the otherwise exposed coast of the Bay of Fundy. The boats I remember were 20- to 30-foot open motor boats that had replaced earlier sailing craft. The putt-putt of the one-cylinder motors was the sound to which I went to sleep at night as, depending on the tides, the fleet sailed out in the evening and returned the following morning with its catch.

The unpaved shore road from the piers climbed up a modest hill past racks of curing fish and lobster traps to the unpaved post road half a mile inland. The four corners offered a general store, a dry goods store, the post office, and the Ellis House, a two-story hotel for traveling salesmen and summer vacationers. Perhaps 60 houses, some with small farms and pastures, spread out from the crossroads. From her sewing room with a large bay window, my grandmother overlooked the four corners and, in the other direction, in the distance, the sea.

My parents' house was on the post road, midway between the general store and the two churches and the blacksmith shop. In back of its barn, pastures rolled down to the sea. The front room was my father's office, where I said goodnight to patients on the way upstairs to bed. There was no central heating, refrigeration, or indoor plumbing. A kitchen pump drew water from a well. Wood stoves heated downstairs rooms lit by kerosene lamps.

In some ways, the little hamlet epitomized security. There were few strangers. There were hardly any automobiles. Transport was by slow-moving oxcart and occasional horse-drawn buggy or carriage. The railroad had bypassed us in favor of a shorter inland route. The nearby blacksmith's shop was the best show in town. As soon as I could walk, in spite of spankings, I ran there at every opportunity. No one in Port Maitland drank much; temperance laws forbade the sale of liquor. No one was truly wealthy. Most were hard-working and few were in debt. There was no crime. Although fishing was always a hazardous occupation, the fishermen were skilled and sensible. I heard of only one who was lost at sea. A sudden storm had washed him overboard without warning. It was a religious community, not in the sense that everyone went to church, but in its respect for the Sabbath. When my mother took me to the shore on Sunday morning, the only sound would be the church bells, usually the deeper Baptist bell, which reverberated through the lifting fog across the meadows and fields.

As the son of a respected father and a popular mother, I grew up in a happy home. My father necessarily made house calls, sometimes quite distant, but he was home more than most fathers and was almost always there for dinner in the middle of the day and supper at night. As the younger of two doctors, he had the most distant patients. He visited the back areas where French families and communities still remained. An oldest daughter of one of these families lived with us and helped my mother. No one used the word *servant*. Daughters of large families helped smaller families. Similarly, a daughter of a nearby neighbor looked after me. It was, however, the French girl to whom I became most attached. She taught me a few words of French. I took the name Douglas Lombard and told all who would listen that I was her brother.

My early feeling of security ignored matters beyond human control. The unpredictable ocean, weather and crops, life and death required faith, for there was no human recourse in the event of failure. There were no protective government programs and most would not have wanted any. The closest hospital was Yarmouth, 12 miles away by horse-drawn conveyance, even more remote for my father's more distant patients. Emergency operations were performed on kitchen tables with kerosene lamps and without nurses. Antibiotics had not yet been invented. There was a vaccination for smallpox and an inoculation for diphtheria, but its life was so short that it was not given until the first child of the family became ill; then the other children would be inoculated but the first child would die.

My father's fee was one dollar for an office visit and two dollars for a house call, but only one dollar if he was called in from the road as he was passing by. Sometimes a family would wait all day with a sick child, hoping that he would pass by, and then send word to him in the evening, when he would set out with one of his two trotters—probably Dolly, who would always bring him home, even if he fell asleep. His treatments were more successful than most because he was an expert diagnostician and because he was conservative about performing operations. Although he himself suffered from appendicitis, he would not risk an operation. When an attack flared up, he would simply go to bed until it went away.

After he concluded his eighth year of country practice, he was ready to move. He enrolled at the Post Graduate Hospital in New York City to specialize in the treatment of problems of the eye, ear, nose, and throat. He and my mother were then 35. I was two and a half, a beginning reader, a big talker, and always poised to run away to the blacksmith shop or the general store. As we embarked for Boston, we did not realize that a world war was about to start and that gradually the young men of Port Maitland would be gone—enlisted in the Canadian army for four years of bitter trench warfare.

We moved into a temporary home on the first floor of a small apartment house in the Bay Ridge section of Brooklyn. It faced north and was dark most of the day, but for the first time we had running water, inside plumbing, and electric lights with gas lamps as a backup. With my father away from early morning until evening, there was little to do. A three-year-old could not run loose. Occasionally older children took me to play under the clotheslines in a backyard shared with surrounding buildings. My mother regularly visited a Nova Scotian friend, but that was worse than staying home. I tired of looking at the same books in a corner while they repeated the same stories and agreed on the same views. Although a teenage son occasionally took me to the library, I was expelled for playing with a wonderful, clicking turnstile that alerted the librarians as patrons entered and left. Each evening I watched the lamp-lighter light the gas street lamps. As I fell asleep, I heard men whistling on nearby doorsteps or strolling in the street. Before radios and gramaphones, women sang or played the piano and men whistled. On Sundays, my father stayed home and took me to buy the newspaper. He read me the funny papers and in the afternoon took me to Sunset Park to watch the older boys fly kites.

In the summer of 1915, after completing his postgraduate work and being licensed to practice in New York, my father successfully passed the Dominion examination and was licensed to practice in all of Canada. Unexpectedly, however, he was offered a practice by a retiring doctor in Flushing, Long Island. We said goodbye to his trotters and sold our Port Maitland home. From then on, when I visited Nova Scotia each summer, I stayed in my grandmother's house.

Our trips to Nova Scotia took two nights and parts of three days. Coastwise passenger vessels then linked East Coast cities from Savannah, Georgia, to Bangor, Maine. Because my mother was prone to seasickness, we frequently avoided the rough water of Buzzard's Bay by taking one of the nightly large, paddle-wheel steamers from New York to Fall

River and an early-morning rail connection to Boston. The *Commonwealth*, with its lounges, dining room, and string quartet, was the largest paddle-wheel steamer in the world. Our overnight trip to Boston connected with another overnight service across the mouth of the Bay of Fundy to Yarmouth, where a horse-drawn stage to Port Maitland and rival railroads to Halifax, back to back, awaited passengers.

The *Prince Arthur* and the *Prince George*, running between Boston and Yarmouth, differed from those comfortable steamers designed for protected waters. Relatively small, built in England in 1898 for cross-channel service, they were twin-screw, ruggedly seaworthy but spare in comfort—no running water, no ventilation except portholes, which were not usable in bad weather. We carried our sandwiches to avoid the dining room. After passing Cape Ann, the boats rolled and pitched to ocean swells. One crossing, during a full gale in 1922, was so rough that the main deck was awash. With an otherwise desirable stateroom at the entrance to a cross-deck passage, we heard the water continuously slosh from one side of the vessel to the other as she rolled. In the middle of the night my father was summoned to treat a passenger in the stuffy accommodations below decks. With no ship's physician, he had been identified as a doctor from the passenger list. He stopped the passenger's heavy nosebleed but, although never seasick, he admitted to feeling "a little queasy."

Each summer we also visited my father's parents in Jordan Falls, midway between Yarmouth and Halifax. The Yarmouth-Halifax train averaged about 20 miles an hour. It was said that on a long upgrade, the conductor could hop off the first car, pick a cup of blueberries, and get back on the last car before it passed. It also stopped frequently. Soft coal dust blew through open windows as I squirmed on the green "plush" seats that prickled bare legs.

My grandparents' farmhouse was more rudimentary than our Port Maitland home. While it was heated by wood stoves in the kitchen, dining room, and parlor, there was no kitchen pump. Water was drawn from a deep outdoor well and poured into a bucket that was kept in the "summer kitchen," in back of the real kitchen. Drinking from a gourd dipper that hung from the wall, we believed the water the best in the world. That unheated kitchen was the only refrigeration, except for a root cellar under the house, for barrels of apples, turnips, and potatoes.

The real kitchen was the center of family activity. On a long window bench just inside the kitchen door and beside the stove, my grandfather would slice plug tobacco for his pipe and visitors would sit and talk.

Behind it, the children had scratched their initials into the windowpanes as they had played checkers and with their few toys. Although we had our meals in the dining room, the parlor was unused except for when my grandmother occasionally sang hymns, accompanying herself on an organ that she pumped with her feet. If the ground-floor bedrooms were occupied by others, my father and I climbed a ladder to sleep in the attic on a wonderful feather bed where my father and his brothers had slept. In winter, he said, they had to break the ice in the water pitcher so they could pour it into a basin to wash their faces.

There were usually no children to play with. My only young friend was Gibby, my grandfather's helper, a descendant of runaway slaves who had settled in East Jordan. I followed him around as he let me help him with his work. One day, working in a potato pile, I became so full of dirt that my mother scolded me and gave me a bath in a washtub in the center of the kitchen, with everyone looking on. As I protested, my mother said she had to do it so the dirt would not rub off on the pillow at night. I looked over at Gibby and asked if his black rubbed off on his pillow and he shyly said, "No." My mother yanked me out of the tub and gave me a long-remembered spanking, for "hurting someone's feelings." Lack of intent, she explained, was no excuse.

During summers I tried unsuccessfully to learn to swim along the pebbly beach of the cold river. My father swam the breast stroke. He kept telling me to swim like a frog, not realizing that I had never seen a frog swim and that I really didn't like frogs. The most exciting feature of the farm was the railroad, which cut through just between the cleared portion and the wooded portion. Each day, as we heard the warning whistle, someone would grab me and run to the road, so the engineer could wave as he passed. Even if we were on the river beach over a hundred yards from the railroad, we still made the effort. The problem was the freight train, which was unpredictable and sometimes required someone to get me up during the night.

As far as I remember, my grandparents had no horse or conveyance. My aunt had a bicycle that she used to get to her music pupils. Everyone else walked. When we visited the farm, we carried our suitcases from the railroad station, over two miles from Jordan Falls or one mile from East Jordan. The shortest route from the post office and the Jordan Falls station was across the railroad bridge over the Jordan River. Passenger trains usually ran on schedule but there was always the danger of meeting the freight train on the bridge. My father instructed me that if this happened, I was to jump into the river, even though I could not swim. He said that he would rescue me. I was never sure that I would do this, because the swift-flowing river looked a long way down. In my own mind, I thought that I might hang over the edge from one of the ties and hope that I could get back up after the train passed. If I couldn't, dropping into the river would be no worse than jumping.

The move from Bay Ridge to Flushing precipitated a new level of filial defiance and consequent punishment. My father never took a taxi in New York. He was fascinated by the transit system and never tired of telling friends in Nova Scotia and elsewhere how far he could travel for five cents. Although there were some circumferential trolley lines: the basic pattern of New York's public transportation was to bring everyone into Manhattan and then back out. Loaded with suitcases and packages, we traveled to Flushing on three trolley lines: the first from Bay Ridge to the foot of one of the bridges to Manhattan, the second to Queensborough Plaza in Long Island City, and the third to Flushing. The second leg of the trip was in a summertime, open trolley car, without sidewalls or windows. There was no central aisle. The seats ran across the car and the conductor had to slide along a running board on one side of the car to collect fares. I had never before seen an open car. I was so thrilled by my first ride in one that I refused to get off and gripped the back of the seat in front of me so stubbornly that my father had to pry my fingers off of it. Then, while on the station platform, I received another memorable spanking, one of the few executed by my father. The rest of the trip was an anticlimax in a smelly, closed car on a line that ended about a quarter of a mile from where we were going to live.

We were to be the first residents in a row of small, identical homes erected on the edge of an apple orchard. On about a 25-foot plot, each house had a kitchen, dining room, living room and front hall downstairs, three bedrooms and a bath upstairs. Only the house on the corner had a garage. My father had not decided to apply for United States citizenship. We had not bought a house or a car. When we spoke of *home*, we meant Nova Scotia. We were still immigrants.

Chapter 2
ASSIMILATION

Less than 20 years before our arrival, Flushing, along with all of Queens County, had been incorporated into the Greater City of New York, but it had not changed very much. The subway system had not reached it. People commuted on the Long Island Railroad or by the trolley lines that interlocked the Queens County communities.

It was an old community, founded in the mid-seventeenth century by Dutch nurserymen. They were followed by Quakers, who left a meeting house built in 1690, and the Bowne House, built a year or two later. Because of its fertile soil and its history as a nursery, it claimed to have a larger variety of trees than any other community of its size. Among them were five Cedars of Lebanon and a giant weeping beech, whose branches covered a quarter of an acre. We believed it was the largest tree in the world. The town hall had become a courthouse for magistrates and municipal court judges, and across the town square the Company I Armory was a continuing reminder of Flushing's contribution to the Union Army during the Civil War. At one end of the square was a fountain with Neptune and sea nymphs, but in front of the armory stood the Civil War monument to which most children came on Decoration Day with bouquets of flowers, for which they received a small pin of recognition. Civil War veterans still marched in the Decoration Day parade, although the older ones rode in automobiles.

The two-lane main roads, Broadway and Sanford Avenue, were paved with asphalt and lined with elms that arched over them. Most of the smaller streets were lined with maples and still had a dirt surface, hardened somewhat by annual summer applications of a heavy oil to seal the dust. Roads on which trolleys ran were paved with Belgian paving blocks. There were few automobiles. Almost everyone walked. Deliveries of ice and milk were by horse and wagon, and the daily garbage and ashes from coal-burning furnaces were collected in an open wagon, drawn by a slow-moving horse accompanied by a kindly, bearded garbage man, continuously smoking a stubby pipe. The community's major blemish was a long-standing project to fill the marshy meadows on the far side of Flushing Creek with ashes collected from Brooklyn's thousands of coal furnaces. The inevitable accompaniment of organic garbage required constant burning. A few times a year, when burning coincided with unfavorable winds, Flushing would endure the odor.

Nova Scotians did not cluster in communities, unlike immigrants who did not speak English. They sought each other out individually, but they mingled more readily with existing residents. For children, this sometimes precipitated minor clashes. Most of the remaining houses of the row in which we lived were taken by second- or third-generation Irish families. I was the oldest and most assertive of the smaller children. As a loyalist who listened to my parents' regular recitation of British and Canadian excellence, I expected a similar response from the Irish, whose country was, in my father's atlas, colored the same pink as all the other parts of the British Empire. Trying to ingratiate myself one morning with Mrs. McInerny, as she was hanging out clothes, I started out by saying, "Now Ireland belongs to England, doesn't it?" She turned on me with something very close to fury. "It certainly does not, young man." She sent me home, telling me never to come back talking such foolishness. I checked my position with my father at noontime dinner. I rechecked the atlas, but I did not press the point because Mrs. McInerny's daughter was my principal playmate. Nevertheless, from then on, I was known as John Bull whenever I attempted to assert my seniority among the smaller children or engage in arguments with the older children.

My first fear of government occurred when a uniformed police officer called and told my mother that I had vandalized the back porch of a nearly finished neighboring house. My friends and I had found a pot of brownish paint on the doorstep and had repainted it. As we were all rounded up, my friends claimed they had only used sticks; I had used the only brush. After first considering flight, I had to confess. A forgiving owner spared me.

Religion was the next testing point. In Port Maitland there had been only Methodists and Baptists. There was little for a child to choose between them. The Methodist church was on higher ground and overlooked the hamlet and the sea. The Baptist church had a higher steeple and a better bell. In Flushing, we never joined the Methodist church, although for a while I went there to Sunday school. My father was a

Mason and belonged to two church men's clubs, but he was not a churchgoer. My mother followed my father. He had agreed to join the Methodist church if its treasurer beat him at checkers. In a series of 20 games, my father won 19; the twentieth was a draw.

Flushing offered many more denominations. We regularly passed a small Episcopal church on the way to the grocery stores. When I asked to go there, my mother snapped at me, as though I were teasing for something I knew I could not have. When I insisted on a reason, she simply walked a little faster and said that Episcopalians were peculiar.

A more serious conflict arose when I decided to become a Roman Catholic. Jimmy, a neighbor's nephew, who spent the summers in Flushing to avoid the heat of his East Harlem apartment, told me that if I became a Catholic and he blessed me, it would protect me from being struck by lightning. I asked a few questions and then accepted on the spot. He first crossed himself, mumbled something, and then blessed me. I went home to noonday dinner and happily told my mother that I had become a Catholic. She slammed down whatever she was doing, warning that my father would deal with me when he came home to dinner. When he did, he was at first gentle. Avoiding theology, he insisted that Jimmy could not deliver on his promise. As I defended Jimmy, my father asked if I was going to believe him or Jimmy. After a little hesitation, I said that I would, of course, believe him, but I argued that it was unnecessary to face that issue. Let me accept Jimmy's blessing for whatever it was worth. If I were still in danger of being struck by lightning, I was at least no worse off than I was as a non-Catholic. Hurrying to get back to the office, he resorted to authority and told me that I could not become a Catholic and to tell Jimmy right away. Jimmy was generous. He said he would let the blessing stand although he doubted that it would be of much value to a non-Catholic.

The neighborhood's one Jewish family, a later arrival, was noted less for its religion than for its twin infant sons. They were too young to walk, let alone play, yet my friends and I visited them nevertheless and observed approvingly the twin baby carriage, go cart, and other solutions to the two-infant problem. We also pondered the differences in non-identical twins. The father, a hairdresser, unexpectedly cemented our family relationship by lending me a wig to wear in a school play about George Washington and Betsy Ross. While the boy playing George Washington had been given a real wig, the rest of us wore caps of fluffed cotton. The night before the final rehearsal, he simply dropped in and said he did not want me to be out-dressed by others.

Medical science seemed almost as baffled in Flushing as in Nova Scotia. Listening to conversation of visitors, I heard of one doctor's family fighting for a son stricken with pneumonia during the summer. With no antibiotics and no air conditioning, they played the garden hose on the bedroom window all day and all night to try to drop the heat. More frightening was the polio epidemic that swept New York in the summer of 1916. My father sent my mother and me back to Nova Scotia for the entire summer because the epidemic climaxed during the hot weather. When we returned, we found that a boy across the street had been crippled, as had another boy from Vermont, who had spent the summers with an aunt who lived on our street.

Still more alarming was the influenza epidemic that started in 1918 after the United States had entered the world war and continued into 1919. Neighbors returning from Manhattan told of the number of funerals they had passed on the way to the city. As many as seven might be met while crossing Queensborough Bridge. Parts of the city had run out of coffins. People were being buried in pine boxes. The cemeteries that now exist along Queens Boulevard, between Manhattan and Kennedy Airport, were filled during this period. The first time I saw my father really worried was when he realized that my mother had contracted this illness. My Grandmother Sanders was brought from Nova Scotia to take care of the house and me while my mother was confined to bed. Without effective medicine, survival depended upon nursing care.

By now, my father had bought a secondhand Buick four-cylinder touring car. On Sunday afternoons, he would often drive us to the Mineola airfields, where we could watch aircraft taking off and landing. On one Sunday, halfway there, he turned around and returned home over my strong protest. As a favor to her parents, he had been taking care of Mary Theiman, a teenage neighbor, and he was afraid that she was in danger of death. That night she died, and the next day I watched with some fear as her older brother came to have my father sign the death certificate. I was afraid that he might be angry about the outcome, but he was gracious, though grief stricken. This was the first death of someone close to me. The boy across the street who had contracted polio was older and had never played with us. Mary, on the other hand, was more easygoing. She had played with us and taken us shopping with her.

When I went out to play two mornings later, our street was lined with a row of horse-drawn carriages behind a horse-drawn hearse. I had never seen anything like it. The children of the neighborhood collected on Mrs. McInerny's steps as one of the older girls explained what was happening. The hearse was white and Mary's casket was white because she was a child. Behind it was the carriage for the flowers, then a carriage for the priest, then Mary's parents, then her brothers, followed by relatives from out of town. My father and mother were in the eighth carriage with other neighbors right behind them. As the cortege pulled away and diminished and disappeared down our tree-lined, unpaved street on its way to St. Michael's church, its elaborate logic was satisfying to me and to the other children. The consensus was that although we had lost Mary, she was in good hands. Later, I listened as my parents told my grandmother about the funeral, my mother explaining to her, with my father's agreement, that she envied Catholics who had faith because they seemed to get such assurance and comfort from their religion—a long step for someone who had been brought up as a stern Protestant, apprehensive of Catholicism.

Except for croup, I was relatively healthy. My first serious illness was measles. With a temperature of over 104 degrees, I fought off my father's attempt to give me castor oil. I no longer believed his promise that, the way he fixed it, I couldn't taste it. My father angrily handed the medicine to my mother and told her, "If he doesn't get this, he will die." He then put on his hat and left the house. I took the dose for my mother. She never tired of teasing my father about his cop-out, but his performance had been impressive. His threat of death was more believable than a promise of tastelessness.

School came next. I did not start until I was six. My parents, who did not believe in kindergarten, taught me to read at home. In a large and bright corner of our kitchen, I had my desk and blackboard and my books and toys. My mother was usually there cooking. Since my father would not eat "bought" bread and we had a coal range as well as a gas stove, mother baked most of the time; white bread, brown bread, rolls, muffins, and cake. When she made mince pie, I ground the meat, suet, and apples. Having run a one-room schoolhouse, she had no trouble keeping her eye on my activities as I drew and read and wrote. On my first day at school, in the first grade, I already knew the sound of the letters and the spelling of the words with which the class was dealing. After a few hours I was moved to the second grade. I had no trouble with the lessons, but I had never learned to keep step. Each day, the entire class would march around the room. Those who kept step were permitted to sit down, and those of us who couldn't kept on marching. More than once, I was the last person marching around the room.

Our school, the old Jefferson School, had been renamed Public School 22 of Queens. It was in the outlying, rapidly expanding part of Flushing as hundreds moved from Manhattan to avoid the congestion from the high peak of immigration in the early twentieth century. The school was overcrowded. In grades just behind mine, it began part-time operation so that the same room could be used by two grades. Supplies were short. Ink was diluted with water, and some geography books were outdated because of boundary changes after World War I. There was pressure to move students into higher grades as quickly as possible. Accordingly, I skipped the first half of the third grade and the first half of the fifth. This created no great difficulty as to my studies, but being one or two years younger than my classmates began to embarrass me. Further, my mother did not like the clothes my classmates wore, especially knickers that bagged down from the knees. She dressed me as though I were in Nova Scotia, with a nice, blue suit made from the less shiny parts of one of my father's. If someone untied my flowing bow tie, I could not retie it. This sometimes provoked fights, but these early problems came to an end when we moved to an older section of town. My mother surrendered. I was assimilated into a group of boys my own age and became more completely Americanized.

The neighborhood to which we moved was then at the very outskirts of Flushing's residential area, but it was about to be engulfed in a building boom. On a hill near the end of a streetcar line, ours was the last house before a large, wooded area and not far from working farms. By walking a quarter of a mile to one of the highest points of Long Island, we could see the buildings of Manhattan. Our "back sitting room," behind the parlor, became the family room. There I did my homework and had my bookcase of boys' books; my father had his radio, which he had built himself and which he kept improving; and my mother came there to do her sewing.

I easily established myself among the boys of the neighborhood, but from time to time I was expelled by our autocratic leader when I debated some of his rulings. For five or six years, relationships fluctuated as new houses were built. Neighboring groups merged and expanded to enable us to form baseball and football teams. Radios were not available to children. We exchanged boys' books, mostly adventure stories about young athletes in boarding school and college. From the public library, two miles away, we read books of an earlier vintage about Horatio Alger's hard-working heroes, as well as stories about the Civil War. Booth Tarkington wrote about boys like us, and Sax Roehmer was our source of information about the evils of the Orient and Near East. The *Book of*

Knowledge was our standard reference. Zane Grey and Kipling and Stevenson came later.

Our school linked four or five small neighborhoods. Except for the few who were delivered by horse-drawn stage from outlying farms, all the students walked home for lunch. We all had the same "childhood" illnesses—whooping cough, mumps, chicken pox. I also contracted scarlet fever. At 12, most of the boys became Boy Scouts. Some went to summer camp, but I missed this because of other family activities. Several of us attended Sunday school at the First Presbyterian Church, the church closest to the school. A former University of Iowa football player, the head of a prospering New York brokerage firm, became our teacher, and proved a significant influence less with the weekly lesson than with stories about football and his discussion of current athletic and other activities. But he induced class perfection in memorizing basic tenets by rewards of trips to Manhattan movie theaters.

My father was strict about Sundays. No cards, checkers, movies or athletic events. We collided when he tried to force me to listen to Dr. S. Parkes Cadman's Sunday afternoon broadcast from Brooklyn's Bedford Avenue YMCA. I claimed that Sunday school was enough and that he wasn't a very good preacher. We compromised: I refused to listen but my father would not let me do anything else while Dr. Cadman preached. If something was wrong with the car, my father repaired it on Sunday, sometimes drafting me or a friend of his to help. This could lead to vehement profanity, usually emphatic variations on the word "damn," and occasional bursts of rhetoric such as, "If you do that again I will knock the devil out of you in ten different ways."

On March 17, 1921, my sister, Dorothy, became the first American-born member of the family except for Laddie, an Airedale puppy. He had been born on November 2, 1920, Election Day and President Harding's birthday. In 1922, with some sadness, my father became an American citizen and I became a citizen derivatively. Our immediate ties to Nova Scotia ended as my grandparents died within a few years of each other. My father's practice increased rapidly, and he was called upon as a consultant by doctors in communities farther out on Long Island. After he upgraded our car to a Hudson Super-Six and we took longer trips on Sunday afternoon, he showed us and all visitors the beautiful homes in Manhasset, Port Washington, Roslyn, and beyond. My father had now become an enthusiastic citizen of a new country where a person who worked hard could become a millionaire. It wasn't clear how I was to do it, but I sensed what was expected of me.

The recession of the early 1920s struck some neighborhood parents and also some Nova Scotia friends. Unemployment insurance did not exist. Traveling salesmen who called on the trade (drummers) suffered most severely. Children overheard adult discussions but did not embarrass their playmates. Similarly, in a community where parents rarely separated, fatherless children inevitably stood slightly apart. Without government assistance, community sympathy softened but also marked the distinction. I dreaded such a tragedy. I kept my head down as I passed the children peering through the gates of St. Joseph's Orphanage, and I also felt the same helplessness when I was sent to deliver messages to the well-behaved but unattended children of Mrs. Featherstone, our widowed cleaning woman.

Anticipation of the extension of the New York subway system to Flushing caused a real estate boom just ahead of the great stock market boom. Broadway became Northern Boulevard, a major conduit to northern Long Island. Its elms were cut down and uprooted. The beautiful lawns of old homes were cut back as the road was expanded to four lanes. Finally, old homes began to give way to apartment houses. One of the homes was converted into Flushing's first family restaurant, the Amber Lantern Tea Room, but frugality and my father's preference for home-cooked meals prevented us from participating in its popularity. The community celebrated as Abramson's dry goods store was expanded to a million-dollar department store. St. George's Episcopal Church and churchyard, which had been the dominant feature of Main Street, was somewhat diminished by two large moving picture theaters at each end of the street. As open areas between Flushing and Long Island City were filled in with new real estate developments, such as Jackson Heights, Flushing increasingly became a part of the greater city.

Security seemed to have arrived when my father built a new house. It was a white stucco, red-tiled, eight-room house with enclosed sun porches at each end, in the center of the newly subdivided McCreery Estate. For insulation, its walls, under the stucco, were a new type of cement block developed in Germany that permitted the air to circulate horizontally as well as vertically. It was a success. The house was cool in summer and heat loss was reduced in the winter. For the next year, we were happy there. A grand piano found its way to one corner of the large living room. My father's radio, with its speakers and batteries, was established in another. Stoddard's Lectures, The Harvard Classics, Green's *History of England,* and a set of Shakespeare filled one bookcase and the Encyclopedia Britannica and other books filled another, with a large fireplace between them, over which hung a painting of my grandfather's bark *Stella* in an 1870 North Atlantic hurricane. My books were upstairs, but the sun porch on the south side of the house, in many ways the new family room, held my father's collection of *National Geographic* magazines and maps, which I studied again and again.

Undercutting the complete joyousness of the new house was the obvious fact that worries during its construction had aged my father. He had been in a constant struggle with the contractor to obtain everything that was specified. After leaving his office in the evening, he would use a flashlight to check the work that had been done during the day. If the cellar floor was specified to be four inches deep, he would make secret chalk marks at various points on the wall before the cement was poured so that he could check its actual depth. He became noticeably grayer and also more short-tempered.

When we no longer returned to Nova Scotia, he indulged his love for boats. His first, a 41-foot sloop, the *Acadian*, was too big for him to sail alone and I was not much help. After a year, he sold her and bought a 38-foot raised deck cruiser, the *Novia*, and charts for a trip to Nova Scotia. In the summer of 1926, as a test run, we sailed her to my uncle's summer house in Touisset, Massachusetts, across Mt. Hope Bay from Fall River. Delayed by fog, the trip took most of three days. In the fog I plotted our course with parallel rulers and dividers. We narrowly avoided an accident because we had not adequately corrected for the engine's deviation of the magnetic compass. Sitting at the bow of the boat, I saw a disturbance in the water immediately ahead of us. I shouted to my father. He turned the boat away and we skirted a large, rocky outcrop just below the surface of the water. In the fog, we had wrongly identified a nearby buoy.

The return trip was even more exciting. First we had to disentangle our anchor from my uncle's mooring. For security, my father had used both. In a cove of a small river, the tide and the river current had turned the boat in circle after circle each day. My father was strong enough to pull up both and finally disentangle them and replace the mooring. Then the weather turned bad. At the mouth of Narragansett Bay, the sea was too rough for us to chance the 21-mile unprotected run from Point Judith to Watch Hill, so we put back into Newport and started again the next morning. The weather was still not good, and just as we reached the exposed entrance of Long Island Sound, I happened to look back. The clouds had taken the oily, hard cast that foretold heavy wind, and I could see the beginning swells of an ugly, following sea. When I warned my father, he said he'd already seen the gathering storm and hoped I hadn't noticed it. As the Sound became rougher, we took shelter in Duck Island Roads, behind a tiny uninhabited island with a lighthouse and two breakwaters forming an angle of protection.

After waiting three days for the storm to blow itself out, we started for home. We passed New Haven and had reached a point just east of Bridgeport when the engine spluttered and stalled. In less than a minute we broached to and began rolling heavily, with dishes sliding out of their lockers and breaking in the cabin as we drifted rapidly toward the shore. My father went below to see if there was dirt in the carburetor. Not finding any, he touched the starter. The engine spluttered. On deck, I immediately pushed the throttle up full, the engine roared, and I threw the engine into gear and started the circle to head back into the waves, away from the shore. My father came up in time to finish the maneuver, with the *Novia* almost ready to pitch-pole as she leapt over the breaking waves, and we headed for open water. Turning back to New Haven, we could find nothing wrong but we did fill the gasoline tank, which we had been unable to do since Newport. My father ultimately found the problem: the outlet for the gas tank was at its forward end and not in the middle. When the level of gas was low, the pitching of the boat broke the flow of gas and caused the engine to stall out. The remedy was to put a small tank between the big tank and the engine so that the small tank would always be full and assure an even flow. While my father continued to talk about our next trip to Nova Scotia, I was beginning to have doubts. The Bay of Fundy might not deal as mercifully with amateurs.

That trip on the Sound was really our last experience together. In early October, my father developed paralysis on one side. A few days later he was unable to shave himself. A McGill classmate, a neurologist at New York's Presbyterian Hospital, immediately hospitalized him. Although he lived for another three months, I never saw him again. My mother visited him daily but, hoping for recovery, she did not want me to see him disabled. At first doctors talked of sleeping sickness, then ultimately brain tumor. From listening to my father's earlier conversations with other doctors I knew what that meant—probable blindness and death. On Sundays, when my uncle drove my mother to the hospital, I went with them in case I should be invited in, but I waited downstairs in the car. My mother's daily weekday trip was exhausting: a mile walk to the subway station, then changing to the elevated over Queensborough Bridge to 57th street and another train to 63rd street, followed by a walk over to Lexington Avenue and then the same route in return. Even after she told me that my father could no longer recognize her and no longer knew that she was there, she kept up her visits and I continued to be hopeful that somehow he would not die. I had a short prayer that I said each day, usually in study hall, about the fourth period. One day, as I was leaving study hall for a class, I realized I'd forgotten to say it and then I asked myself why was I praying at that time, when my worst courses of the day were over. And then, of course, I realized.

That afternoon, the house was empty when I returned. My sister was at her playmate's, a few houses away. A little later, however, my Uncle Alvin arrived. He seemed disconcerted and told me that my father was very, very sick. I told him that I knew that, but that I hoped he'd get well. I tried to carry on a casual conversation with him or return to whatever I had been doing. A little later my mother arrived, accompanied by a woman I had never seen before. When she came in she hugged me and said that my father was not going to get well. I patted her and tried to encourage her and said that people were always getting better after doctors told them they wouldn't get better. Finally, I asked her, "Is he—is he dead?" and she said that he was. The lady who was with her had been his nurse and had come home to stay with my mother that night. I kept my composure. I just felt as though everything had dropped through the floor. I went over to the neighbor's to get my sister and bring her back for supper. Somehow my mother and the nurse put a meal together. That evening my uncle gave me a little note promising his everlasting support. He kept his promise. My sister did not know for several weeks that her father was dead. He had idolized her; I'm not sure she could ever know how much. When she was told several weeks later, she took it matter-of-factly. Mother heard her talking with her playmate. She told him that her father had been sick and that he had gone to live with God. They decided that was a good thing.

A strong-willed mother can hold a family together, but trying to survive the loss of the unquestioned family head was, on a much larger scale, like a boxer trying to stay on his feet to finish out the round after a savage knockdown. For the first time, my mother was going to handle money matters and take responsibility for ultimate family decisions. Old friends and new friends helped. My father's lawyer helped her invest the modest estate in small real estate mortgages. The doctor who bought my father's practice became a family friend and, in a way, reached out to me to replace a son he had lost. Dentists took care of us. No one sent a bill. More subtle support came from teachers, scout masters, Sunday school teachers, my friends, and the parents of my friends. Our immersion in the community was clear. My mother became a citizen in her own right.

Yet misfortune did not end. That summer, Laddie, my dog, who chased automobiles, was run over and killed. That night, without mentioning it, three girls from the neighborhood dropped in to teach me to play auction bridge. Then in January, my father's brother died of a stroke as his train was arriving in New York for him to be with us on my birthday.

While my parents were popular, we had never entertained or visited very much. My father had evening office hours six days a week as a convenience to patients who commuted daily to Manhattan. Most men we knew worked six days a week and their wives had limited help at home. Sunday afternoon was the most popular visiting time. Refreshments were simple and nonalcoholic. After my father's death, these occasions gradually became somewhat less frequent.

During the Christmas holidays before my father died, I had started delivering orders for grocery stores. My best job started a few months later. For three nights a week, I ran the coat-check room at the YMCA. Saturday was the big night when there were basketball games or other entertainments. On other nights I could study, although I was always being interrupted. Still, without my father's oversight, my schoolwork was deteriorating. Although I stayed in the school's honor group, I dropped close to the bottom of it. My father's hope that I would be an engineer was jeopardized by my indifferent grades in the sciences and an especially poor performance in math. Out of a basically good faculty, I consistently drew the one hopeless math teacher who was bored with her subject, drearily waiting for her retirement, and thus easily distracted into irrelevant retrospection by smart alecks. I regularly flunked her midterm exams and then pulled back up by getting a high grade on the state regents' exams at the end of the term. In plane geometry I reviewed for the exam with another teacher, and in intermediate algebra and trigonometry, I reviewed with a friend of my mother's who taught math in another school and who supplied me with a set of review books, one containing all the questions previously asked on regents' exams and the second showing the solution to each question. It only took one or two nights with her to enable me to understand how to reach solutions to the problems and gain high grades. But simply passing the examinations did not give me much depth in these subjects. Finally, I graduated and received a $200 scholarship from the Good Citizenship League of Flushing.

As I approached high school graduation with no prospects of a postgraduate year in a boarding school, my mother, uncle, and friendly advisers somewhat erroneously concluded that Columbia University would be the cheapest solution, because I would be able to live at home and commute the one and one half hours each way. My regents' grades were good enough for admission. I passed the required comprehensive examination without trouble. Learning to dance for the senior prom at school was more uncertain. Without realizing that Bea Feinberg, who sat across the aisle from me, was one of the most popular girls in the class, I invited her as my partner. Taken aback, she nevertheless accepted, but to avoid disaster, she enrolled in the dancing class that I and many others were attending. When she observed the archaic steps it was teaching, she took me aside and taught me the basic square. I took my first taxi to pick her up an hour before the prom began, but at her wise suggestion, we waited at the nearby YMCA to avoid being the first lonely arrivals.

During the prosperous 1920s, religious and racial differences did not significantly affect school relationships. Young Catholics had to go to confession on Saturday, which posed a minor scheduling problem. Many Jewish children then did not observe religious holidays. Unaware, I had tried to recruit one for my Sunday school class. In high school I tried to recruit another for Hi-Y, a young people's club located in the newly opened YMCA. While Flushing High School, the outermost high school for northern Queens County, exposed us to more varied ethnic groups than our elementary school, there was little meanness. When two friends and I looked for a table in the lunch room where we could sit together, we found one where a black student was at first sitting alone. As we joined him, we were followed by others, forming an interesting combination of religious and national origins: Italian, Japanese, Canadian and German, Catholic, Protestant and Jewish. Throughout four years, our table never had a vacancy. In fact, it was usually crowded. One student became a track star, another finished third in the class academically and was runner-up for president of the student body, another was an all-city football end, another an all-city tennis star.

Several of us applied for admission to Columbia University. When we received our preliminary Admissions Office evaluation to enable us to decide whether to apply elsewhere, we were all in relatively favorable groups, but for the first time, we were classified by religion or national origin: Anglo-Saxon Protestants were in Group I, Italian Catholics in Group II, and Jews in Group III. As we compared notes at our lunch room table, we felt shame. Those "favored" by the grouping, I believe, felt the shame more deeply than the others. In the end we were all accepted, and we understood that Columbia, in the heart of New York City, then had quotas on Jews and perhaps all city residents as it was trying to increase recruiting from outside the city. This was our first exposure to a deep-seated problem. Its impact was double-edged. As white, Anglo-Saxon Protestants, were we secure because we were "favored," or insecure because we could not win in open competition?

Travel-hungry at a time when long-distance travel was still exceptional, I had dreamed of going to Europe, and my father had planned to take us after my high school graduation. My Uncle Alvin, who had maritime associations, produced a substitute, a job as assistant steward on the United States Line steamship *America* sailing for Plymouth, Cherbourg, Southampton, and Bremerhaven, Germany. Having been allocated to the United States as part of World War I reparations, the 25-year-old coal-burning vessel, once briefly among the largest ships in the world, now provided slow but comfortable passage to two classes of passengers, cabin and tourist. In our excitement over our first day on board, two other students and I stopped moving accumulated luggage on the foredeck as the ship moved down the Hudson River. While I was pointing out landmarks in lower Manhattan, a gruff voice sounded from the bridge telling us to get on with our work. I kept looking over my shoulder as we slid through the Narrows, past Ambrose Lightship, into the open sea. After one afternoon as a bellboy, I was assigned to the tourist dining room headwaiter as busboy because I did not have blue trousers. Although losing tips, I then enjoyed the same food as the passengers. Following behind a storm, we met rough weather. For the next two days, when off duty, I would be on the foredeck, notwithstanding the spray, fascinated by the heavy seas. I felt proudly bonded to my ship, half shrouded in fog, with black smoke pouring off to one side as she impassively and impressively rose and dipped through seas that looked 30 feet high.

Ten days later, after dropping some passengers at Plymouth and Cherbourg, we tied up in Bremerhaven, the port for the city of Bremen. We had only one day off, little money, and no clear idea of what to do, so a couple of other students and I bought third-class railroad tickets to Bremen and marveled at the neatness and intensity of cultivation of the farms we passed. On advice of shipmates, we singled out for gruesome attention a large church known to have a crypt so dry that bodies committed there mummified. We made only one acquaintance as we walked through crowded streets. One of my friends, thinking that only we spoke English, remarked that a girl ahead of us had a "nice ass." When she turned and said, "Thank you very much," we invited her to lunch. She was from Cincinnati. Returning to the ship with my friends, I had my first drink, a glass of wine. Feeling a little silly, I was sure that I was growing up.

It was shipboard experience, rather than my hasty foreign visit, that moved me. On our return voyage, after passing the chalk cliffs of Dover, picking up passengers in Southampton and Cherbourg, and loading passengers brought to us by a small steam tender while we lay anchored among the deep green hills outside the harbor of Cobh, we had a relaxed Atlantic crossing. Unlike the vacationers we carried to Europe, our westbound third-class passengers were immigrants from Ireland, Poland, and Central Europe, a few in native costumes, including felt shoes. Shy and self-effacing, some children at first cleared their tables after eating in the dining room. I explained that it wasn't necessary; that was my job. A friendly fireman took a bellboy and me into the fire room where the great, roaring, coal-burning furnaces created the steam to drive the ship. While stokers with coal-dust rimming their eyes continuously dumped wheelbarrows of coal in front of the line of furnaces, the firemen spread it evenly in the firepits. The blast of heat from the firepits was breathtaking. I watched from a few feet away under a ventilator, suppressing my excitement as the chief engineer passed by. He was the legendary Paddy Brennan, said to have beaten men and to have killed a man, one of the toughest of a tough calling. We were told that Paddy Brennan was so hated that in some ports he could not safely go ashore. The way he wore his cap signaled those in the engine room. If the cap rested on the back of his head, fine, but if the visor were pulled down over his eyebrows, watch out!

The day before we reached New York, my friends and I unexpectedly decided to quit. The headwaiter was angry but even after a short voyage, we had "channel fever," the indescribable urge to go home—a phenomenon given its name by English seamen nearing their home port. Home did seem wonderful, but after a week or two my mother let me know that she had not expected me to quit. My uncle again solved the problem. The S.S. *Coamo*, of the New York and Porto Rico (1928 spelling) Steamship Line, needed a bellboy. I made two two-week round-trips from New York to San Juan and Santo Domingo City, my first experience in the tropics. From the open half of the gunport next to the bell station and the entrance to the dining room, I watched flying fish and porpoises as they played just below me in the ship's wake and the bright blue sea. In the crew's quarters, however, cockroaches and bedbugs flourished side by side, disproving the belief of some seamen that cockroaches kill bedbugs. Each night I took my bedclothes up to the boat deck to avoid the marauding insects. Except for tropical showers that drenched without warning, I slept well.

Shore trips were secondary, one day in San Juan on each trip. After visiting El Morro, the sixteenth-century fortress from which the Spaniards had repelled Drake's effort to invade the island, I spent the afternoon in the salt-water pool of the recently completed Hotel Condado-Vanderbilt. That evening an older bellboy and a couple of stewards tried to expand my knowledge of life by taking me, unknowingly, to a house of prostitution. Shocked, I quickly left, with the girls ridiculing me from the door and windows. On my second trip, the elderly chief bellman and I took a ramshackle bus to Caguyas, speeding through the mountains while my companion kept shouting in Spanish to slow down. Caguyas was an unspoiled small city; its plaza in front of the cathedral was said to be the most beautiful in Puerto Rico. On the trip, however, we also passed rural and poorer areas, and, poignantly, the men of a family walking along the edge of the road to a burial with a coffin on their shoulders followed by a few sad women and children.

The bellboys' job was lucrative. The standard tip was 25 cents, the equivalent of a few dollars today. By my second trip, I was the high earner. But my greed led to a new experience. An officer of a sugar company, who tipped well, urged me to give up plans for college and work for his company, a chance to start earning immediately instead of seven years later. Although I had declined, on the last night before arriving in Santo Domingo, he sent for me. Somewhat drunk, he wanted a homosexual relationship. I had no difficulty in avoiding him, and the embarrassment ended when the chief bellman, having noticed my absence, came to the room.

For the most part, the older members of the crew were protective. A few days before we reached New York, the assistant purser, for whom I had frequently delivered mail and telegrams, sent for me to pick up something from his stateroom. Obviously brooding, he urged me not to go to sea. When I told him that I planned to go to college, he congratulated me. I thanked him and left. That night he shot himself. Shocked by the thought of his body stored in one of the ship's refrigerators, I wondered how I could have helped him. I had begun to learn that sometimes an older person will talk more freely with a young person than with someone his own age.

Not having time for a third trip, I registered at Columbia in the third week of September. My entering physical examination found me five feet eight inches tall and weighing 110 pounds. To graduate from Columbia, it was necessary to swim the length of the 75-foot pool in a heavy sweatshirt, and also to jump or dive from a 10-foot tower. I swam the pool but I didn't know whether to dive or jump from the tower. Deciding to dive, I landed absolutely flat with a smack that convulsed all spectators. Hardly an illustrious beginning.

Chapter 3
IMMATURITY

While many others had been admitted to Columbia as young or younger than I, their precociousness usually reflected intellect, or at least a commitment to scholarship. My under-age arrival reflected an overcrowded elementary school. The excessive enthusiasm of persistent immaturity characterized my college days. Sometimes it was manifested by reckless challenges to older students and other times by recklessly cutting corners in my studies. My brashness sometimes attracted favorable attention, sometimes older-brother-like assistance, but also displeasure. My academic interests during this last great opportunity for generalized learning were subordinated to extracurricular activity and part-time work.

Columbia University, in 1928, was the largest private university in the country, but its undergraduate college was the smallest of the Ivy League, with approximately 1,200 students. Tucked in a quadrangle at the southeast corner of the university campus, most of its classes, its library, and its common room and lockers for commuters were in Hamilton Hall at one end; its dining rooms and the centers of student activity were at the other end, in its tallest dormitory, John Jay Hall. Abutting the quadrangle was South Field, once the varsity athletic field from which first-baseman Lou Gehrig hit homers through dormitory windows, but now relegated to freshman teams and intramural sports after a recent gift had built a new stadium, said to seat 40,000, and a new varsity athletic center at the northern tip of Manhattan Island, 100 blocks uptown.

The indoctrination address of the chairman of the student board, the elected leader of the student body, hardly mentioned academic excellence. It emphasized similarities between the traditions of Columbia and other Ivy League colleges. My childhood reading of Frank Merriwell responded as I looked forward to fun-filled rivalry between classes, the privilege of sitting on a certain fence, and some modest hazing of freshmen by sophomores. Columbia, like many other institutions riding the stock market boom, was an exuberant center of optimism where a modest amount of work would assure graduation and contacts with alumni a successful career. In 1929, the *Columbia Daily Spectator* carried a sarcastic editorial suggesting that there be a doctorate for "contacts." My objective was not a Phi Beta Kappa key, but a varsity "C." And I was not alone. So strong was the interest in extracurricular activity that notwithstanding its small undergraduate student body, Columbia was consistently first or second in Ivy League baseball, basketball, swimming, water polo, fencing, and crew. Its poor performance in football was about to be corrected. Our freshman team could beat the varsity, and when Coach Lou Little moved from Georgetown to Columbia two years later, he led Columbia to a Rose Bowl victory in three years.

Columbia was then at its never-to-be-duplicated pinnacle in the rowing world. The Glendons, a Cape Cod family, the father coaching at the Naval Academy and two sons coaching at Columbia, had developed a long, powerful stroke that carried Columbia to victory in the intercollegiate regatta at Poughkeepsie in 1927. Columbia missed the championship by one-eighth of a length in 1928, with one oarsman still recovering from an appendectomy, and was about to win in 1929. Even a lowly position in this championship group could enrich a lifetime. Undersized and in no sense athletic, I set out to be coxswain of the freshman crew, even though this added an hour of commuting to my regular three-hour round trip. In the culminating race of fall practice, my crew was defeated by less than a length by its rival, and we were still in contention for the spring.

Crew practice began again immediately after January exams. First on rowing machines and with cut-out oars in the swimming pool, then on the Harlem River and then on the ice-cold Hudson, it occupied the entire spring. I was included in the squad that moved into the Manor House, a large old home that had once housed the owner of Baker Field, the new athletic center. Alternating between the first and second freshman crews, I was able to form friendships, not only with my own class, but with admired upperclassmen. But my prospects as a coxswain became grim as I grew taller and heavier. I reached 125 pounds, the absolute maximum even for a varsity coxswain, despite giving much of my food to oarsmen and running two miles each evening in sweat clothes. I coxed the first freshman race against Kent School and three more against other schools, but a newly arrived freshman coxswain who weighed only 95 pounds eliminated me from intercollegiate competition. When the crew moved to Poughkeepsie for the intercollegiate regatta, I was replaced even as substitute coxswain.

My exuberant immersion into campus activities brought a few invitations to join fraternities. Once I saw two blue-and-white-tipped oars hanging on the dining room wall of the Beta Theta Pi house, including the 1927 oar of the current crew captain, my decision was made. My mother dubiously agreed to the extra expense.

I could not have gone to Poughkeepsie in any event, because my uncle had found me a job for an around-the-world trip on the Dollar Steamship Line. I signed on as an ordinary seaman as the S.S. *President Monroe* was about to leave for a side trip to Boston, preparatory to her 'round the world run. She was a 502-foot combination cargo and passenger vessel built for service during World War I. With jobs easy to get in the summer of 1929, many seamen quit after every trip, spent their money, and then took another job. We made the trip to Boston undermanned, with only a few of the old crew and me to handle the ship's heavy hawsers and trim cargo booms, departing and arriving port. Our crew was replenished on our return to New York by seamen who had just quit the S.S. *Leviathan*, the largest ship in the world. Some of them were more than a little wild. In Havana, our first port of call, many got totally drunk. Preparing to sail at midnight, I watched them stagger back on board and fall prostrate on the covered hatches. With a few sober seamen, I again helped handle the lines as the vessel let go from the pier and we squared the cargo booms for sea. The *President Monroe* had nine hatches, an unusually high number, with about 15 pairs of heavy metal booms pivoted on king posts (double masts on opposite sides of the ship) that had to be secured in their cradles.

Approaching the Panama Canal, we met the beautiful *Tusitella*, one of the last full-rigged sailing ships in regular service, on her run from Hawaii to New York. With every plain sail set, she epitomized grace. Crew and passengers lined our rails. Our ship dipped its ensign in respect. Then the Panama Canal offered a new thrill as I watched the Canal's expert line handlers and donkey engines called "mules" conduct our vessel through the locks. Between the locks at each end of the canal, the ship threaded some narrow passages, the most dramatic being the Culebra Cut piercing the central ridge of the isthmus. After leaving the canal, we painted steadily to show off the ship in its home port, San Francisco. During the 12-day run up the Pacific coast we could, at times, see the mountains of Central

America, Mexico, and Southern California. Alongside the ship, we were accompanied by porpoises, swordfish, and sometimes sharks, and at a greater distance, an occasional group of whales.

I was atingle as we passed between the steep hills of the Golden Gate. There was no bridge. San Francisco was only a small city, but it was a storied place that filled an easterner's imagination with covered wagons, the 1849 Gold Rush and the great clipper ship *Flying Cloud* bursting through this very channel with her long unbeaten record voyage from New York. Moving slowly to one of the innermost piers, we passed alongside the Embarcadero, the notorious waterfront street, once a brawling seaman's paradise. Most piers were occupied. Japanese and Chinese vessels loading and unloading and those of the Matson Line bespoke the Orient and the Pacific islands. The cargoes on our pier smelled different from those on the East Coast. The city had a bustling quality. I walked to the foot of Market Street, where speedy ferries carried commuters across the bay to the commercial center and to the system of trolley cars and connecting cable cars up Nob Hill and into Chinatown. Even Alaska was brought closer by a few remaining sailing vessels and a handsome scrimshaw walrus tusk I found in a pawn shop window and bought for one dollar.

By the end of our third day in San Francisco, I began to look for dinner and a movie. The ship's food was terrible. A cafeteria was the best I could afford. With the tables full, a somewhat subdued, middle-aged man joined me. As we talked, I concluded that his wife had probably just died. He later disclosed this and said that, in a word, he was lost. Not knowing what else to do, I invited him to come with me to see the Marx Brothers in *A Night at the Opera*. He had never heard of them but at the movie, he enjoyed himself, even commenting on the Italian style of Harpo's fingering of the harp. Leaving the theater genuinely happy, he gave me his card and urged me to call him if I ever returned to San Francisco. My ship left the next day.

On sailing day, I was assigned to the bridge on the eight-to-twelve watch—shining brass, cleaning brightwork, or painting in the morning and standing lookout at night. More important to me was the opportunity to steer the ship one half hour each morning and each evening while the quartermaster went below for coffee. (The *President Monroe* was still steered by hand.) While our watch was under the fourth mate, my immediate boss was the quartermaster, Eddie Shaw, from Erie, Pennsylvania, an excellent seaman, a veteran of several years on the Great Lakes, and the best helmsman on the ship. Great Lakes crews prided themselves on their ability to get into and out of a port in a few hours and to thread narrow waters without reducing speed. They demanded helmsmen who could keep a vessel precisely on its course, sometimes pointing to a mark ahead, sometimes blotting out a mark behind with the ship's funnel. The fourth member of the watch was a cadet my age also making his first trip and intending to return to school. Because we were both amateurs and beginners, we were called the "goofy watch."

Trying to keep awake while standing lookout was a problem. I drank cocoa on my mid-watch break, which probably made me more sleepy. With only eight hours between my watches, I could never get more than seven hours' sleep unless I gave up breakfast or dinner. Standing at the very bow, I would watch the stem of the vessel descending and then ascending from the swells; I paced the fo'c'sle head; I sang to myself; but if I sat down, I would doze and then have to struggle back to pacing the deck. Sometimes other seamen kept me company. Required to respond to the half-hourly bells rung from the bridge and to report every light I saw by ringing the big ship's bell, the mate could tell how sleepy I was by the time lapse of my response. Finally he had me stand the last half of the watch walking up and down on the flying bridge over the wheel-house, with the cadet at the bow. If I stopped walking, he would come up to see if I'd gone to sleep.

Steering was monitored by a clock-controlled, circular graph in the chartroom. The central line for each watch was the course to be steered. An inked needle showed every deviation. On most days, unless there were heavy seas, we tried to keep within one degree on either side. The secret was, according to Shaw, to get the wheel "on fast" and "off faster," before the vessel overreacted. I was competitive enough but there was no way in which I could match Shaw, and he persistently complained that the cadet and I were spoiling the record of the watch, even though our watch's record was better than that of either of the others.

Shaw, the cadet, and I almost always went ashore together. Shaw's plan for sightseeing was to walk up and down the "main drag," get "laid," and if he had time, a decent meal and then return to the ship and save his money. The cadet and I stayed with him except for the second part of his program. While he was engaged with a prostitute, we explored a little more by ourselves. Honolulu, our first port together, was then a very small city and territorial capital. As we arrived, I first heard Hawaiians sing "Aloha" and watched them bedeck visitors with leis. At Waikiki Beach, the Royal Hawaiian was the only hotel. Its beautiful, flower-filled grounds and its casual, relaxed, uncrowded ambience, the sparkling harbor and the view of Diamond Head seemed to close out all strife and even the whole world from its enclave of enjoyment. Cold and polluted waters were forgotten as we swam in the sparkling surf. Then, that evening, at sunset, as passengers dropped their leis off Diamond Head, we began one of our longest stretches at sea, 13 days to Kobe, Japan.

The seamen's fo'c'sles were just under the poop deck and just over the noisy steering engine at the very stern of the ship. In the afternoon they were hot, so trying to catch up on my sleep in order to stay awake on watch, I started to lie out on a relatively unused part of the deck with just a pair of shorts. Before long, I learned another old saying of the sea: "If you can't get a girl, a clean old man or a nice young boy will do," as I had to fight off some tough and horny shipmates who wanted bodily contact—something more purposeful than schoolboy wrestling but not amounting to attempted sodomy. I had grown strong and agile enough to resist, but I didn't get much sleep. Even at night I had to sleep lightly clothed, regardless of the heat. The two other ordinary seamen who stood watch shared my fo'c'sle. Both were tough. One boasted a dishonorable discharge from every branch of the service and more than one stretch in prison. Although the other had also served time and claimed to have been an excellent pimp, the first was the harder one to repel. Fortunately, however, he always seemed satisfied if he could simply win the wrestling match.

This rough-and-ready education contrasted with the reticence of parents and teachers in the 1920s. On the day we sailed from New York, my uncle had vaguely warned me not to let older seamen mistreat me, and the chief mate had, in a kindly way, told me to let him know if I were mistreated, but they were so vague that I really did not know what they meant. The Kinsey Report had not been written; the "pill" had not been invented; there was no television; moving pictures were restrained by the industry code; and high school and college hygiene courses were primarily concerned with the common cold and the value of exercise. Even at Columbia, which required a course in hygiene, my professor was so abstruse and elliptical that at times I did not understand what he was talking about. When, in the opening class, he asked all of us who had not masturbated to raise our hands, I didn't know what the word meant. So I thought probably I hadn't. I started to raise my hand, but I noticed that a majority kept theirs down, so I pulled mine back down. Then he laughed, "Ha-ha! I'm glad to see there are so few liars in the room." Baffled, I finally made an appointment with the younger instructor to get a more matter-of-fact discussion. He was refreshingly explicit, perhaps even a little ahead of his time. To him, abstinence was the worst possible course to follow and having a well-treated mistress the best. I knew only a few girls and I didn't think any of them would want to be a mistress, so I had just concentrated on becoming the freshman coxswain.

The most memorable part of the trip was a glimpse of the Orient as it was before the rise of Japanese militarism, Chinese communism, and the post–World War II economic explosion. Entering Japan's Inland Sea on my evening watch, we tied up in Kobe Harbor just before midnight. Japan was a friendly, bargain hunter's paradise. Early the next morning, Japanese salesmen were on board to sell us very fine, made to order, monogrammed broadcloth shirts for a dollar apiece, ten dollars a dozen. Enjoying our first rickshaw ride, we loaded up with presents to bring home. Without any plan for sight-seeing, we simply mingled with the crowds in the busiest areas. Only a relatively few Japanese wore western clothes. Their own dress seemed far more becoming—kimonos, obis, thonged, sometimes stilted slippers. That night we passed through the Inland Sea between the three major islands of Japan and into the Yellow Sea. Because of abrupt turns and the sometimes narrow channel, Shaw steered the entire first four hours. From the ship's bow, I could see, outlined in the dark, softly lit homes and terraces on either side, beneath the background hills and mountains.

Shanghai, three days later, in many ways resembled a foreign colony, with different parts governed by different European countries. It was hot. Some Europeans wore pith helmets believed necessary to avoid sunstroke. The cadet and I did too. Shaw always wore a cloth cap. We wore suits, but Shaw, like many seamen, would never wear a necktie. With two afternoons to look around, we began with the handsome shops on Nanking Road, the principal street in the International Section, and explored some sidestreets, but the big city, its sidestreets, and Chinese shops seemed less attractive and less hospitable than Kobe. The many beggars left our ears ringing with their chant, "No mama, no papa, no chow-chow, poor little son of a bitch." At its berth, parallel to the Bund, our ship attracted "bum-boats," sampans sculled by one oar at the stern, in which whole families lived and begged for scraps of garbage from the ship. Much more cheerful and pleasant than those on shore, they would throw up a line and let us pull up a bucket in which to put whatever we could find for them. They then washed the utensils in the polluted water of the harbor and returned them to us.

After three more days at sea we passed between island mountains to enter the beautiful harbor of Hong Kong. Although I did not realize it at the time, this was the climax of the trip, the breaking point between eager exploration and homesickness, the halfway mark, and the beginning of the long journey home. More than any other city, Hong Kong fulfilled my dreams of the Far East. It was still a small city of less than 100,000, a city of mostly small shops and rickshaws. Unlike the muddy river water of Shanghai, its harbor sparkled like the ocean and teemed with activity, with Chinese junks, large and small, entering and leaving, and steamships anchored at roadsteads awaiting a pier. We tied up at Kowloon, on the mainland opposite the city. For the first time in many years, I was again in a British colony at the very peak of the expanded British Empire. Somehow we sensed the expertness of British colonial administration. Shortly after we docked, a large Canadian Pacific liner tied up across the end of an adjoining pier. Our crew, working in undershirts, watched the sprucely uniformed crew of the Canadian ship, responding to whistles of the mate and bo's'n, drop the ship's headlines to the waiting longshoremen on the pier. Although we smirked at this somewhat starchy performance, I realized that this was in its way a ceremony, part of "showing the flag," a policy that had helped hold together the world's greatest empire and create the myth of British superiority so that British ships and British businessmen were always the first in and the first out, whether dealing with harbor officials or with native merchants. With only one afternoon ashore, we took the ferry to the city and used rickshaws to shop.

As we started on our "downhill" voyage for home, we began to count the days and our sight-seeing began to diminish. Manila still reflected its former Spanish status, but also that of an important American military base and an American colony. Curious about Philippine tribesmen, during an afternoon's walk around the city, I bought a dress machete in a leather scabbard, which I was told the tribesmen carried. Two days later in Singapore, just one degree above the equator, we returned to the "Far East," as I thought my grandfather knew it. For four days we loaded tin, while several of us were assigned to watch cargo to be sure that it wasn't stolen. We took pride in our heavy cargo. As our ship's water line submerged, we felt part of a successful enterprise. On our afternoons off, we took rickshaws into the city and, without guidance, looked around the business section and the Chinese section. With a population of less than 200,000, there seemed to be more Chinese merchants than Malaysian. The Raffles Hotel was still in its heyday, set in ample grounds and surrounded by a broad veranda, with a shaded, cool bar and rotating fans. I thought of sea captains relaxing with each other or with their ship's agents.

After proceeding up the Straits of Malacca to load more tin at Penang, we passed the tip of Sumatra into the northern edge of the Indian Ocean and to Ceylon. I regretted missing Calcutta. In Colombo, while admiring the well-kept Victoria Gardens and the well-administered city, we could not visit Kandy or the older communities. Somewhat ashamedly, we began looking for an ice cream soda. Asiatic improvisations became as interesting as our sightseeing. That evening as we passed between the harbor breakwaters, we began another 13-day stretch across the Arabian Sea through the Gulf of Aden and the Red Sea to Suez, where we anchored overnight to wait our turn to enter the canal. Although we passed Aden at night, we could from time to time see other coastal areas and the high, sand-colored cliffs of the Arabian peninsula.

The trip through the Suez Canal began on my watch. Shaw steered the entire four hours through the narrow waterway. There were no locks, simply a large ditch through the Isthmus of Suez with a lake in the middle. While passing caravans of camels in the nearby desert, we were hit with a short sandstorm that plastered the side of the ship. That evening in Port Said, I was on watch and could not go ashore. In Alexandria, at the mouth of the Nile, having to stand watch in the morning, we did not have time to go to Cairo. Sadly, we lacked information to explore Alexandria itself, the most ancient place that we would visit. On the way to Naples we could see the loom of the mountains and the narrowness of the passage as we passed through the Straits of Messina in the night. We spent our one free afternoon in Naples at a cafe overlooking the city and Mount Vesuvius. Our visit to Genoa was equally brief. After a few hours to walk around the streets we left for a few hours to do the same in Marseille, still a seaman's town, dusty from the summer winds from the Sahara Desert.

The trip from Marseilles to New York was another 13-day stretch but it was broken by passing along the cliffs of the Spanish coast with their ancient watchtowers. The great Rock of Gibraltar was silhouetted against the night sky as we passed it on my watch. Twelve hours later, while I had the wheel on the morning watch, I noticed a disturbance ahead, very like the one I had noticed when my father and I nearly hit a rock in Long Island Sound. I hesitated for a moment, afraid the mate would ridicule me if I told him that we were in danger of hitting something, but I had no choice and I shouted to him. He came out of the chart room, took one look, and then ordered me to port the helm 10 degrees, which, in those days, meant to go to the right.[1] As we were about to pass the disturbed water, a funnel cloud reached down and sucked it up into the sky and it became a waterspout, with its enormous column of water just off our port side. We would have hit it head on. As the waterspout passed, we were drenched with sheets of water, but no damage was done. After passing the Azores and another week at sea, we finally entered New York Harbor and found our pier in Jersey City, next to the Erie Railroad yard.

My final problem was how to get all of my souvenirs home. Shaw had sold me an enormous, solid leather suitcase that he bought in Japan. It was so heavy I could hardly lift it empty, but as I filled it with my ivory tusk, machete, and other memorabilia, as well as sea boots I hadn't needed, I could barely lift it with both hands. Nevertheless, with it and my old suitcase full of my clothes, I started for home, walking 50 feet and resting, another 50 feet and resting again, all the way down the pier, across the long bridge over the freight yards to the Hudson and Manhattan tubes, then to the Long Island Railroad. By the time I arrived in Flushing, I had given up trying to carry them, and for the second time in my life I took a taxi, arriving home just in time for dinner.

My sophomore year at Columbia started happily. With over $100 saved from my summer's work, my mother agreed to let me live on campus in the Beta House. My two roommates were seniors. One was the president of the chapter. Unwittingly, I had cast the deciding vote that elected him, voting for him so that he would not be defeated too badly. Easygoing, they shared their neckties and finally gave me my first shave. As the youngest in the house, I answered the doorbell and the telephone and wound the phonograph. While our fraternity's national goals called for high scholarship, our chapter was not as concerned. A few steps away was Johnson Hall, the dormitory for women graduate students. Its dietitian had three Beta brothers and it had the best food on the campus. I worked there two hours a day for my meals. Most of those working with me were graduate students. As we ate all our meals to-

---

1. The "helm," like a tiller on a small boat, is moved in the opposite direction of the rudder, which it controls. To go to starboard (to the right), the helm is directed to port. In the 1930s, these antiquated directions were replaced on merchant ships, as they had been earlier on naval vessels, by directions prescribing the movement of the *ship,* not the *helm*, for example, "right 10 degrees" or "left 10 degrees."

gether, they formed a sort of second fraternity of older friends. Many of them were midwesterners and southerners attending Teachers College. Two were law students. Some were straitlaced, others open advocates of promiscuity. More or less patiently, they sandpapered my brashness, made somewhat worse by the self-confidence generated by my summer's trip.

At 140 pounds, I wanted to row, but Hugh Glendon dryly pretended concern that I "might bend a rigger," so I helped out as coxswain, not to compete, but just for the pleasure. Columbia's squad was small, with only a few full crews. Individual oarsmen who were left over rowed in what was called a "pickle boat," a mixture of oarsmen light and heavy. In the fall I coxswained that boat. Then I started swimming regularly as part of a gym teacher's program to develop intramural swimming and possible junior varsity competition. But there were three underlying problems. I was still a pre-engineer, carrying 18 points with some very heavy courses. Then the stock market crash threatened these normal activities.

In October 1929, as highly respected corporate bonds began their steady decline, preferred stocks dropped precipitously, and some foreign countries and cities repudiated their bonds, the value of my mother's meager investments sagged. The Flushing real estate market had broken even before the stock market, and my mother had had to sell our house below its peak value; she then had to take it back and resell it below cost after the first purchaser went through bankruptcy. By spring, I took a second job working three to five hours a day in the university bookstore for 50 cents an hour. Guided by a graduate student, I passed calculus; coached by a friendly laboratory assistant, I passed chemistry. Although harshly attacking the concept of a state relief program, I did well in the economics part of contemporary civilization. Strong in English history, I passed the combined course of history and literature, but when it came to French, I flunked and had to repeat the semester, which killed my chance for the scholarship I now badly needed. After upperclassmen sent me to Walter Fletcher, a friendly Beta alumnus and partner in one of New York's leading firms, on his advice, I switched from pre-engineering to pre-law.

That summer I made three voyages to Hamburg, Germany. Jobs were harder to get, but with four months' experience, I was hired as an ordinary seaman, this time for the United States Lines ship *President Harding*, a ship similar to the *President Monroe* but larger and faster. One of a class known as "535s", she was 535 feet long, had seven cargo holds and carried over 200 passengers at a speed of about 18 knots. Only those in the steward's or purser's departments had contact with the passengers. Fewer jobs had made some seamen resentful of students doing summer work, but I was befriended by the older and better seamen, primarily those from Baltic countries to whom Hamburg had once been a home port.

The ancient Hanseatic port was a true seaman's town. The Reeperbahn was for them the main street; its St. Pauli cabarets were home; and the regular prostitutes, subjected to weekly health tests, met them on each trip, not as strangers but as friends. As a college student novelty, they took me with them and proudly introduced me. Lindbergh then being the great American hero, they jokingly called me "der kleine Lindbergh"—the little Lindbergh. While their friends offered to educate me free of charge, I passed up the opportunity and instead we took them sailing on Lake Alster, in Hamburg's great central park. Each time the ship sailed, some of the girls would come down to wave farewell to their friends on the crew, including me.

Sight-seeing did not amount to much. On my first trip, another student and I took an overnight train to Berlin, trying to sleep on hard third-class benches which, after a couple of hours, became crowded as the train filled. Sleepily, we walked up and down Unter den Linden, took a guided tour through the imperial palace, and returned to Hamburg. More and more, it was the time at sea, watching the sunsets and the deepening evening colors of the sky and sea, that I enjoyed. On each trip departing Cobh, we skirted the Irish coast in the late afternoon and evening with the sun setting over the green hills, a climax of the voyage.

My junior year, my first full year as a pre-law student, I dropped my bookstore job and showed modest academic improvement, closer to a B level with even an A in an advanced course in government. I also received the first and only recognition for my extracurricular activities, as one of 20 selected to be founding members of the Junior Society of Blue Key. Most of the other members were prospective team managers or varsity team members, so I performed most of the society's responsibilities. Greeting visiting teams and other campus visitors at every opportunity, I was recommended for a varsity letter by the chairman of the student board, but the awards committee would not approve. My roommate had for two years worked part-time for a lawyer. Street-smart, he advised me on dates and introduced me to a downtown tailor who sold decent clothes at bargain rates. Buying from the manufacturers lightly basted, ready-made clothes that could be extensively altered, this tailor's suits were almost custom made. Yet the prices were amazingly low: for a suit, $25; for a tuxedo, $30; a full dress suit for $38; and $19 for a top coat.

In the fall of 1930 the fraternity chapter required more time as the deepening Depression endangered its existence. The graduation of two large delegations left the chapter undersized. Some members did not return and some couldn't pay their dues. I was in charge of rushing. To help in rushing and to keep an eye on our finances, we began to draw on our younger alumni, among them a young lawyer, Frank S. Hogan. He lived near Columbia. Like many young lawyers at the time, he had left a large firm after two or three years to go into partnership with another lawyer his age, and he had developed secondary activities to serve the public and as a possible source for clients. With old Columbia acquaintances and their friends, he was trying to dislodge the Democratic Party assembly district leader, Andrew Keating, a satellite of Jimmy Hines, the leader of the adjoining assembly district and one of Tammany's most powerful figures. The Beta House fitted easily into his schedule. He and one or two other alumni kept the chapter alive and financially sound even though the Depression must have endangered his small law firm. He became a generous adviser and friend.

That summer, I made two trips to the east coast of South America as a seaman on the S.S. *Southern Cross* of the Munson Line. The two-week stretch to Rio de Janeiro was broken by a short stop in Bermuda, where we swam from the side of the ship anchored just outside the harbor. Entering the harbor of Rio de Janeiro at sunrise, we watched the play of color and light on Sugarloaf Mountain as we skirted it and then upon the more distant mountains encircling the city. With little free time, we explored the main avenues with colored designs on the sidewalks and took the cable car to the summit of Sugarloaf. Then, after brief overnight stops at Santos, the port for São Paulo, and at Montevideo, at the mouth of La Plata River, we spent three days in Buenos Aires, cold and wet. While some of us dutifully walked the principal boulevard past the plaza to the capitol, most evenings were spent in bars drinking hot toddy, which was mostly hot water with deceptively little whiskey. Then the unfortunate discovery of wine at 19 cents a bottle produced a near murderous hangover. This was the first trip in which I drank past my limit. Prohibition was in such disrespect that drinking had become commonplace at fraternity dances. While I was a sophomore, two seniors had taken me to a speakeasy to indoctrinate me. They became drunk and I had to bring them home. Convinced of my capacity to drink, I thereafter readily tested myself against others, including the seamen with whom I was working.

Although a sister ship of the *President Harding*, the *Southern Cross* carried a much reduced but excellent crew, only 10 able-bodied seamen and one ordinary seaman. One of the best seamen, who had started on square-riggers, befriended me and taught me to do more demanding work. In New York, between trips, I passed the Coast Guard examination for able-bodied seamen (A.B.) and the bo's'n promoted me for my second trip. This meant I worked aloft, in the masts and rigging. My friends were protective as I lowered myself in a bo's'n's chair to paint upright booms and stays. To paint the smokestack, seven other seamen and I had to hitch along the rim of the stack, trying not to look down into its cavernous gas- and smoke-filled cavity, and then lower ourselves down the outside of the stack in bo's'n's chairs. I was given the easiest section to paint, in the middle of the side with the fewest obstructions. My friends could not help me, however, when in Santos I was assigned to the chain locker, to stow the heavy anchor chain ("ship's cable") when it was hauled up by windlass from the excrement-smelling river bottom. Standing on the heavy chain as it clanked in and flaking it to avoid kinks, I could not help thinking about what would happen if the brake on the windlass slipped and the anchor accidentally dropped.

Free to elect courses for my senior year, I was impressed by a sociology course taught by Professor Casey during his first year at Columbia, illustrating by parable the sensitive differences among long-standing social groups and the folly of shallow evaluation or imitation. That fall I was six feet tall and weighed over 150 pounds. I rowed in both fall and spring, not as a competitor, but simply for the pleasure and exercise. A graduate student who had been a track and boxing coach at a small college encouraged me to try out for winter track and also to let him teach me a little bit about boxing. Although I had a good stride, I really was not a promising track candidate. When spring crew practice began, I reverted to my favorite sport but then, for the first time, I recognized an academic priority. I gave up rowing to catch up in the accounting lab and I actually received an A in the course. I also met Maxine Winton, a petite, pretty, and vivacious Barnard undergraduate who had transferred to Columbia's School of Business. At first just looking for a date for the year's last fraternity dance, I fell enthusiastically in love with her, while she was more dubious about me. Unsophisticated but persevering, I began a four-year, ultimately successful courtship by taking her to a matinee of my first Broadway musical, the revival of Jerome Kern's *Show Boat,* with Paul Robeson.

Graduation ceremonies were large but, except for listening to medical students take the Hippocratic oath, uninspiring. The college graduates were a small part of the university ceremony. President Nicholas Murray Butler, imperious as he often was, presided, but I don't remember the commencement speaker. At an earlier class day ceremony just for the college, I listened uncomprehendingly to our valedictorian and salutatorian, neither of whom I knew or now remember. A few days after graduation, I returned to the Dollar Line as an A.B. on the S.S. *President Jackson*, another sister ship of the *President Harding*. Now in the very pit of the Depression, there was no available ordinary seaman's job, and I found myself uncomfortable as an A.B. out of practice and somewhat afraid. Most of this crew seemed unfriendly, young, tough, able, and West Coast. Only one other seaman was hired in New York. The crew was then assigned work over the side, on the ship's hull, that in previous years would have been left to shore gangs. My first day was spent in a lifeboat, spot-painting rust patches along the water line. Those working with me dropped hand over hand down a line hanging from the deck. Never having done that, I did not try to match them. I used my legs as well to shinny down the line. For coffee break, they pulled themselves up the same way, while another seaman and I remained in the lifeboat. That evening, I climbed back up the line, but again used my legs as well as my hands. When they went ashore, instead of going over the gangway, they simply went down the ship's lines, hand over hand, to the pier. I again used my legs, but that put me in the awkward position of having my legs higher than my head as I reached the sag in the lines near the pier.

The second day, the crew worked on stage planks hung over the ship's side to paint the white upper part of the hull. Teamed with the other new A.B., Glen Corbin, I told him that although I knew how to do it, I had never worked on a stage plank before. He was friendly and showed me how he intended to rig his end of the stage and make fast and release the line by which it was lowered and suspended. Painting on a stage plank was less secure than in a bo's'n's chair. At the ends of the plank, one could hold onto the suspending line and feel secure even when standing, but when it became necessary to work in the middle of the plank, there was nothing to hold onto. By lowering the plank in small stages, we avoided standing in the middle. Finally, after we finished one fleet (succession of drops), we had to climb back up the supporting lines to the deck and pull our stage up behind us without messing up the paint that we had just applied, and then move to a new fleet. We worked safely for two days. If either end of the plank had let go, we both would have been dropped 30 or 40 feet to the cement pier below. (A few months later, after I had returned to school, Corbin was killed in such an accident.)

The chief mate who had hired me had also been the chief mate on the *President Monroe,* but he left the ship in San Francisco. The new chief mate was out to make a name for himself by upgrading the condition of the ship. Consequently, we holystoned the decks each week and were in the rigging a lot, chipping encrusted paint off king posts, stays, and booms. Entering and leaving port, we did much of the covering and uncovering of hatches and readying of cargo booms for use by the longshoremen. To cover the hatch, it was necessary to insert a heavy steel beam across the middle of its mouth and then lay the wooden hatch covers between the beam and the outer hatch combing. Although commonplace work, there was always the danger that, if improperly handled, the weight of the hatch cover could pull a seaman 30 or 40 feet down into the hatch or that he could be forced to drop it into the hatch below. The trip was testing throughout. I was apprehensive each time the bo's'n entered the fo'c'sle to hand out the day's assignments.

The Far East was a less friendly place than on my first trip. Japanese militarists had already started hostilities in Manchuria. We had less time ashore in Kobe. In Shanghai the crew could not go ashore at all because of a cholera epidemic. Between Shanghai and Hong Kong, one of the hottest stretches of the trip, we painted the skylights over the engine room, under a scorching sun, as some of the crew had to quit to avoid passing out. We sailed through the tail end of a typhoon between Hong Kong and Manila. On the return trip to Kobe, because we had been in Shanghai, the Japanese kept the crew onboard and forced us to use containers to avoid discharge of any waste in Kobe Harbor.

During the long stretch across the Pacific from Japan to Hawaii, a Philippine third-class passenger died of pneumonia. Without family claims or resources to return the body home, he was buried at sea. The bo's'n arranged with the storekeeper and my friend Corbin to sew the body into a shroud of canvas weighted with shackles and bits of old iron. Their compensation was a bottle of whiskey. At about 11 o'clock at night, they placed the body on an extra hatch cover near the stern of the ship. Those of us who volunteered lifted the hatch cover and placed an end on the rail and held it while the chief mate grimly read the burial service. The always-present wind, the soft sounds of the sea movements under the arching sky merged with the rhythms of the ship to match the soaring quality of a cathedral, but the loneliness, without a congregation, left us feeling eerie and isolated. Reverent yet unskilled, we tipped the hatch cover and slid the canvas sack into the sea. It did not enter silently because air contained in the canvas shroud momentarily resisted submersion, but it sank. The propellers were supposed to stop for a moment out of respect and to avoid sucking the body to them. I'm not sure they did, but there was no misadventure.

The unhappy climax of the trip was being fired in San Francisco. While I had been marginally filling my job, I also had been reckless. I could not avoid extracurricular activities, as well as other silly incidents. I had been observed by the chief mate when I had, with a few others, slipped ashore for a case of beer in a small village where the ship was docked opposite Shanghai, and I had led others in a Sunday afternoon mid-ocean party with liquor bought in Japan. The party was a social success as we spiked coffee with alcohol. Becoming ever more joyful, shipmates broke out better liquor from their lockers; and eyes teared as a young Irish ordinary seaman with a pleasant tenor voice sang "Mother Machree," "Danny Boy," and other Irish songs. Finally, the two seamen who had sewn up the shroud of the dead Philippine passenger produced their bottle of whiskey. After the party, several of us stretched out on the foredeck hatches in full sight of the bridge. Never mentioning these incidents, the chief mate simply said that he wanted to hire a seasoned seaman who had formerly served under him. Confronted with the problem of getting back to New York in time for the opening of law school, a secret I had previously kept from most because of the prejudice against students, my friends advised me to swallow my pride and apply for the job of an ordinary seaman who had quit. The chief mate agreed, so I reached New York on schedule. Unfortunately, this sobering lesson was not enough. A far more drastic lesson awaited me as I started law school.

Before then, however, one more demonstration of the catlike balance of old sailing ship sailors cheered me. Off Cape Hatteras, following one day behind a hurricane, the seas regularly broke over the foredeck and left it awash. I was one of several sent into hatch number four, just forward of the bridge, to secure cargo. The West Coast longshoremen had stowed cargo three decks high into the hatch's forward "tween-decks," leaving the square of the hatch empty. They had too lightly braced the cargo. As the ship pitched, the stacks of cargo bulged out and threatened to break loose. Working beneath this threat, we helped the ship's carpenter construct heavy braces and lay them against the most dangerous bulges. Then my mouth dropped open as I watched our elderly Estonian storekeeper and Finnish bo's'n, without handholds, simply run up the almost 45-degree slope of the new braces and force them down into place by the weight of their bodies as a downward pitch of the ship eased the bulging cargo back in place.

Chapter 4
THE TURNING POINT

"So little Rollo came up the steps of Kent Hall," leered Karl N. Llewellyn, Columbia's Betts Professor of Jurisprudence. Drooping both hands like claws, he drummed on his desk as though he were about to devour us and started the first of his introductory lectures based upon his book, *The Bramble Bush*. Of all his warnings and suggestions, I was hit hardest when he singled out those who had slid through college but were now determined to become good scholars. On the blackboard he wrote a great big 67 percent as he predicted that 67 percent of these new converts would flunk.[1]

Determined to be an exception, I had moved from the Beta House to a small third-floor room on the Broadway side of Furnald Hall, in which the screech of each halting 10-car subway train and the grinding accompaniment of trolley cars clanging their way to the crest of Morningside Heights simply intensified my determination to concentrate. I grasped at each bit of Llewellyn's advice like a farm boy learning to sail a boat. Long hours of daily study, weekend review; a once-a-month weekend "bender"; stop skip-reading as though reading the *Saturday Evening Post*; footnotes may be more important than the text; don't abstract individual case reports until you have read the whole assignment and understand what is pertinent. Don't be discouraged; after a month or two the significance of the case reports and other material would emerge. I continued to work at Johnson Hall but cut all my friends. My only deviation was a nightly

1. The former dean of the Harvard Law School was even more severe: "Gentlemen, look at the person on your left and the person on your right. Only one of you will be back next year." But Harvard was easier in admissions than Columbia, which was one of the first to administer an achievement test before admission.

telephone call to Maxine and a weekend visit to her Greenwich Village apartment, which she shared with two other girls, as she finished her last year in the Columbia School of Business.

Nevertheless, extracurricular activities found me. A second-year law student whom I had known in college persuaded me to assist two independent candidates for the state supreme court who were opposing nominees agreed upon in a deal by Tammany Hall and the Republican county leader. Too young to circulate petitions, I was assigned to assist Professor Elliott Cheatham, who was soliciting signatures from an empty store on Broadway. Reporting to him, I almost laughed outright as I observed his courtly reticence, trying to buttonhole passers-by. When one did stop, he was so earnest in his presentation that he would miss several others. From passers-by, I recruited a young man to help me and then a young woman art student to paint a sign for us, "Nominations"; we pasted newspaper editorials and clippings to the front window; we lined up empty telephone booths as a wall near the front of the store to hide the dirty interior, and then we moved Professor Cheatham off the street into our newly created office while we drew passing pedestrians in to him. As the line of prospective petitioners extended out into the street, others read the clippings on the window. Professor Cheatham was impressed. More than once, during my later difficulties, he generously repaid my few days of brash assistance.

After a few weeks of uninterrupted study, trying desperately to read faster, I did fairly well on short preliminary trial tests. Then I was again drawn off course by another college friend who wanted me to join a newly organized moot court and argue a case for it. Each moot court was required to field two teams against different opponents, one on each side of a hypothetical criminal case in which the reckless operator of an automobile was convicted of assaulting a blind person whom he endangered even though the blind person was unaware of the assault. Six points were at stake, and only rarely did the judges give more than a four-to-two division. My friend hoped that if my partner and I could avoid a default and hold two points, the other team, with the stronger side of the case, would win a four-to-two division. With a friend, a former varsity lightweight oarsman, I argued for affirmance of the conviction and wrote most of the brief. We not only won but received a high award of four and one quarter points, but at a cost of too much time diverted from my studies.

Then, when the university offered to buy our 117th Street fraternity house, I was drawn into the controversy of whether to move or not. Our house was remote from the center of college activities around which most of the other fraternities had their houses, but it received free heat from the university in exchange for an easement permitting steam pipes to pass under its basement to neighboring faculty buildings. When a more centrally located fraternity closed and offered its house for sale, I was among those who urged the move that might improve our participation in extracurricular activities. With the financial help of a few alumni, the new house was attractively renovated. Unhappy with my dormitory room and to help fill the house, I moved into a quiet room on the top floor. But distractions followed when we could not pay for coal, burned rolled newspapers in the fireplace, and took cold showers in freezing weather to get warm. Eager to get some regular exercise, I renewed boxing. To preserve a very important relationship, I extended my weekends with Maxine from one evening to two.

Meanwhile, the Depression, worsening month after month, was wiping out many who had optimistically invested in the stock market after the first crash. My uncle's government job had been eliminated. After failing to find employment on shore, he had returned to sea as a purser on a freighter. While my mother continued to husband her slowly diminishing assets, we had avoided debt. We still felt allied with the creditor interests. We regarded the election of Franklin D. Roosevelt as a new threat. New York state, under Governors Roosevelt and Herbert H. Lehman, had already restricted deficiency judgments against defaulting mortgagors. The Democrats, we believed, always tinkered with the tariff and now would devalue the dollar to ease payment of debts and perhaps even eliminate the gold standard. On election night, with a hard-working young couple from Port Maitland who looked up to my mother, we grimly listened to the radio broadcast election returns.

With only two final examinations in January, Contracts and the Development of Legal Institutions, I should have done well, but the night before the contracts exam my moot court partner, a commuter, lacked time to go home and insisted on sleeping with me in my single bed. Without much sleep, I was so nervous that I could not concentrate and I expected the worst. Sure of an F in Contracts, I went to see Professor Llewellyn to see if I could take another exam. Sympathetically, he told me to wait and see. He also told me how to avoid nervousness: follow the example of baseball pitchers—chew a wad of gum. Walter Fletcher, who had advised me to switch from engineering to law and who I hoped might someday help me get a job, took me to lunch and told me not to worry, that grades were not that critical. Then, unexpectedly, my Contracts grade turned out to be a B. In contrast, I expected a B on my Development of Legal Insitutions exam. But when the grade arrived in February, it was a D.

Spring final examinations, however, were a true disaster. Property, fortunately, was first. Then, on successive days, came Civil Procedure, Criminal Law and Torts, and finally Legislation. Contrary to the strong advice of Professor Llewellyn and others that cramming could not make up for lack of regular study and review, I went all out to cram, taking caffeine pills night after night to stay awake. As a result, I did badly in Torts, in which I should have done well. When the grades came in, I had dropped below the level necessary to stay in school, but not far enough to prevent readmission. B in Property and C in Civil Procedure helped, but the D's in my last three examinations added to the one I received in February put my overall average for the year below the required C-minus. I was readmitted on condition that I repeat all of the courses in which I received D. To graduate on time, I would have to attend two summer sessions.

A C in Torts would have saved me. The course was given in two segments, one by Dean Young B. Smith, the other by Associate Dean James P. Gifford. Gifford gave me a B on his half of the examination, but Smith gave me an F on his. A D from him would have meant a C for the course. The difference between a D and an F on Smith's half of the paper turned upon my answer to one question that was a dichotomy, requiring an answer in the alternative—if a particular factor were true and a second answer if that factor were not true. In my grogginess, I had left out the word "not" for the second half of the answer so that read literally, I was giving two inconsistent answers for the same alternative. When I showed Smith this obvious inadvertent omission, he said he could not overlook it even though there was no way in which my answer could be read sensibly unless he did. As a teacher he was perhaps right. If I had skimmed through the year, I might never have learned the lesson I had to learn.

To break my persistent distraction by college affairs, I was required to give up my meal job and live at home. Because of the long commute, this was a severe punishment. There were, however, a few bright spots. That summer Llewellyn taught Bills and Notes, a course he did not ordinarily teach. The following summer, Harvard's Professor Edward Morgan gave the course on Evidence, which, on the advice of Kitty, the law school elevator operator, I took in order to avoid a more abstract and less useful course taught by the regular Columbia professor. In my second year, except for B's in Torts and for my one-point essay for Professor Richard C. Powell in Trusts and Estates, all of my other grades were C. During the month between the end of my first summer session and the regular fall term, I worked as an able-bodied seaman on the S.S. *Veragua* of the United Fruit Line. The chief mate came from Nova Scotia. The trip, which served United Fruit plantations in Costa Rica, Panama, and Jamaica, allowed little time ashore.

The Depression by now, a year after my college graduation, was still worsening. Except for those of us who attended graduate school, my college class seemed to have disintegrated. Some well-liked classmates simply disappeared. Law school graduates, good students, could not get jobs. Some began to work for managing clerks and in other nonprofessional capacities. Although a graduate of Columbia's School of Business, Maxine worked for an investment banker for $10 a week, at times filling in as a secretary and telephone operator. When I visited her, she and two traders and the president and vice president and a handful of others were huddled in one corner of an immense office running a full city block; row on row of desks were all empty. Reminiscent of Edward Hopper's *Nighthawks*, my last stop after leaving her apartment for my long subway trip home would be an all-night White Tower restaurant, which served coffee from grounds already used at the Waldorf-Astoria Hotel. The attendant proudly told me that the Waldorf-Astoria only used its coffee grounds once before selling them. While I often fell asleep on the subway train and sometimes found myself riding back to New York, usually someone woke me up at the end of the line.

The most comical episode at the end of my second year was my trip to Tampa, Florida, to visit Maxine's parents and get their permission to marry their daughter. Without funds, I worked my way to Tampa as a seaman on a Moore-McCormick Line freighter sailing from Philadelphia. Hoping for a workaway's job, to my surprise I was hired as an able-bodied seaman assigned to the 12 to 4 watch as helmsman. While I had not steered in close waters, I thought I could handle the job because I had become fairly competent with a gyro compass. At midnight, as we left the pier, I was dismayed to find that there was no gyro recorder but only a slow-moving magnetic compass. As I looked for some point to steady on, the second mate relieved me and sent me to get a helmsman from another watch. Thereafter he had me practice steering by marks during the night, by lining up a part of the ship's rigging with a star.

In Tampa, at the stern of the ship, after handling the hawsers as we warped the ship into our pier, I slid down the lines to show off for Maxine, who was waiting on the pier. To visit her parents, however, I had to get cleaned up. On most ships, the crew did not have fresh-water showers. Each seaman had a bucket, which he kept clean. In it he washed his clothes and with fresh water he washed himself. There was no running hot water. The bucket was filled with cold water and then heated by inserting a steam pipe. In Tampa, it was so hot and muggy that I was perspiring faster than I could cool myself with buckets of cold water. Worse, because of the importance of the occasion, I had brought my only blue suit, which was winter weight. Neither the Wintons' house nor their car was then air-conditioned. My discomfort was so apparent that Mrs. Winton finally asked me to take my coat off.[2]

I certainly enjoyed the visit but, returning to the ship, we found that she had moved to another berth at Port Tampa, several miles away. Maxine got me there as quickly as she could, but with no passengers and no precise schedule, the ship was already singling up her lines, preparing to go to sea. With only one line left, the stern had begun to swing away from the pier. A seaman threw me a line, with which I scrambled up the side of the vessel and was pulled onto the deck. My best blue suit was never the same.

By now the whole crew knew I was a student visiting my fianceé, and they seemed to enjoy being part of the venture. Ascending the Mississippi River toward New Orleans, my mind was still on Tampa, and at one point I turned the wheel the wrong way. Although I quickly corrected this, the second mate, of course, noticed it. When we arrived in New Orleans he told me that he was going to replace me with an old friend of his who happened to be out of a job. He had been so generous in overlooking my shortcomings, I couldn't blame him. I agreed to return to New York workaway, as I had originally planned. Assigned to day work on deck, I worked hard to square accounts. When we lost an ordinary seaman in Baltimore, I was given his job for the short trip to Philadelphia.

Dean Gifford permitted me to return to the campus. He was very supportive. He authorized a low-rent room, then awarded on a semi-scholarship basis, and he waived an increase in tuition, also an award on a semi-scholarship basis, but he would not allow me to renew my meal job.

It was a good year. I roomed with a college senior who held a scholar-

2. Dr. Winton, a Tennessean, was a leading surgeon and among the first to support group health insurance—for Cuban cigar workers. He had married the daughter of the mayor of Tampa, a Dutch immigrant sent by his family at the close of the Spanish-American War to invest in Tampa real estate, who decided to stay in Tampa after falling in love and marrying Flora Newcomb, a visitor from Wellfleet, Cape Cod.

ship and was trying for Phi Beta Kappa. We kept the door locked. I still shortchanged my library work, but at least I read my casebook and footnotes. Through my roommate I met Soia Mentschikoff, an outstanding first-year law student who ultimately would marry Professor Llewellyn, become a professor of law at the University of Chicago and dean of the University of Miami School of Law. Her excellent outline of the course on Criminal Law brought me a B. Dropping to C's only in two two-point courses, I received B's in all the others. As a side benefit, my roommate exposed me somewhat to his study of philosophy and the classics. At least he made me realize what I had missed. Still deep in the pit of the Depression, he was a single-tax advocate, a follower of Henry George, and uncertainly fending off communism. He led me into one serious, time-consuming distraction by asking me to defend the fraternity chapter treasurer from charges of misconduct. To do this I had to cross-examine Frank Hogan, who supported the charges. While I was vigorous, he had no trouble in brushing off my effort. After an adverse chapter decision, having lost by one vote, I spent many hours on an appellate brief to the national fraternity, which received commendation but no reversal.

Throughout the winter and spring, however, the most serious distraction was job hunting—one or two afternoons a week without success. While the Depression had begun to ease a little, several high-ranking students had not been placed before graduation. But this became more than a distraction. After graduation, it was almost a full-time occupation.

In 1935, the major firms of the country were concentrated in Manhattan near the corner of Broad and Wall Streets. The centerpiece of the community, surrounded by skyscrapers, was the small but handsome bank of J.P. Morgan & Company, the once-bombed headquarters of the late J.P. Morgan, Sr., who, for nearly 50 years, had personified the turn-of-the-century "Wall Street banker." Across Broad Street was the New York Stock Exchange. Across Wall Street was the United States Sub-Treasury, which had served as the country's first capitol. Spanned by fewer than 50 street address numbers in four directions were the leading financial institutions of the country, banks, investment bankers, and stockbrokers. Slightly farther away were the headquarters of the world's largest private corporations. A few steps more distant were the large casualty insurance companies. Interspersed around these major institutions were the service organizations that supported them in their activities.

Nearby were their lawyers. In one building next to the Morgan Bank were Davis Polk Wardwell Gardiner & Reed, lawyers for the House of

Morgan; Cravath de Gersdorff Swaine & Wood, lawyers for Kuhn Loeb and many industrial giants; and Milbank Tweed, Hope & Hadley, lawyers for the Rockefellers. Across Wall Street were Sullivan & Cromwell, negotiators of the sale of the Panama Canal, and White & Case, attorneys for Bankers' Trust. Nearby were Simpson Thacher & Bartlett, counsel for Manufacturers Trust Company, and the two offsprings of the firm of Charles Evans Hughes, which split after he became Chief Justice. More recently established firms, built around famed prosecutors and lawyers who tired of waiting for partnerships in older firms, included Winthrop Stimson Putnam & Roberts and Root Clark Buckner & Ballantine, and perhaps the most recent, Donovan Leisure Newton & Lumbard, and Debevoise Stevenson Plimpton & Page. Before fax machines and photocopiers, banking and legal documents were typed six carbon copies at a time and delivered by hand. Transactions were speeded by this proximity.

Around this concentrated community, the downtown heart of New York stretched along Broadway from the Customs House and Bowling Green to City Hall and the state and county courthouses north of it. The Federal Building was then the old Post Office at the apex of City Hall Park. Only a few stories high, it symbolized the relative insignificance of the federal government prior to the New Deal. It housed the federal courts, district and appellate, and the U.S. attorney, although some personnel had been crowded out and into the nearby Woolworth Building, which had just recently been surpassed as the tallest building in the world. Two predecessors to hold this distinction were on Park Row on the easterly side of City Hall, the recently deserted center of the city's newspapers and the principal thoroughfare to the East Side.

Along Broadway and in the narrow sidestreets were firms less tightly connected to financial activities. Lord, Day & Lord represented *The New York Times*; others specialized in trial work. Among them were prominent Jewish firms. This was a period of undisguised discrimination. Eleven Broadway, for example, housed two of the city's most prominent trial lawyers, Judge Joseph Proskauer and his firm, and Max Steuer and his. Steuer was perhaps the highest-paid trial lawyer in New York, demanding $2,000 a day even in the 1930s. It was said that when a woman asked him for legal advice at a dinner party, he gave the advice but the following day sent her a bill for $10,000. Just west of Broadway on Trinity Place was the firm of Engelhardt, Pollak, Benjamin Cardozo's firm before he was appointed a judge. These firms were respected by the financial law firms but there was never any thought of merging. John W.

Davis was a friend of Judge Proskauer. They handled a number of cases together and they very much liked each other, but neither firm disregarded the barrier. Acceptance of religion-based discrimination in secular affairs reflected not only a restraint on competition but also the stiffer religious views of the time and the fraternal attitudes then present in many universities, preparatory schools, college fraternities, and some much larger adult fraternal organizations. Law firms rarely exceeded 20 partners. Many partnerships had a family-like quality. Partnership selection and even recruiting of associates had a fraternal component. Only after the turn of the century had firms like Cravath begun to concentrate on recruiting the academically superior.

The uptown law firms tended to be smaller and specialized and to serve individuals and newer business enterprises.

Traditionally, job hunting began during the Christmas holidays before graduation. Without waiting for third-year grades, an applicant organized his visits a building at a time. No appointments were necessary; the receptionist would say whether the firm was interviewing or not, and how many were already waiting. In 1934 and 1935 even the largest firms were hiring only two or three new associates, and several none at all. As I exhausted the larger firms, I then turned to smaller ones. I did not visit the Jewish firms because I knew that a person below law review rank had hardly any chance there. For example, Charles Breitel, who later became Governor Dewey's counsel and ultimately chief judge of New York, and who had a high law school average, started with a solo practitioner at $10 a week when most of the large firms were paying $1,800 or $2,100 per year.

A half dozen lawyers that I knew before I started job hunting assisted me as references and also with advice. The youngest of these, Horace McAfee, who had worked with me at Johnson Hall and often despaired of my irresponsible conduct and poor grades, earnestly taught me the ropes of job hunting. As an associate at Simpson, Thacher & Bartlett, he permitted me to use his firm's directories. Exhausting the simpler directories of large firms, I ultimately turned to the more comprehensive directories that included smaller firms with excellent ratings.

My first interview was with Orrin Judd, a young partner in the firm of Davies, Auerbach, Hardy & Cornell. Having been first in his class at Harvard, he took one look at my record and told me that I should quit job hunting, return to the law school library, and get higher grades that would pull up my average. My record, he said, was hopeless, I would not get a job. I asked him whether other factors would not compensate, such as "personality" and "extracurricular activities." He laughed pleasantly and said, not really, those qualities were looked for *in addition* to high scholarship, not in lieu of it.

Disregarding this sound advice, I continued to make the rounds of the largest law firms, not expecting to be hired but for practice in responding to interviews and to get a feeling for the profession. Some firms were not interviewing. In others, I was interviewed by a young associate or a young partner but never brought back for further interviews. During the spring, as I expanded my visits, I sometimes surprised small firms that had rarely had a law student call on them. Taking McAfee's advice, I pursued interviews late in the afternoon when lawyers were often more relaxed than earlier in the day, as they waited for their secretary to finish some work or for their customary train to go to the suburbs. Some seemed to enjoy talking with me and to regard my problem as a challenge. They made suggestions of possible jobs elsewhere and invited me to report back to them for additional suggestions. In this way I came to know seven or eight partners in good midsize firms.

I developed two special targets: admiralty firms and a new general practice firm, Donovan, Leisure, Newton & Lumbard. Although I had originally hoped to specialize in trusts and estates, I had shifted my objective to trial work, because I understood that was the least popular, and therefore the most likely opportunity for employment. On one cold, damp day, after I had canvassed the law firms in the large office buildings, I entered 26 William Street. Unlike the austere lobbies of the newer buildings, its lobby was crowded and irregular. The smell of coffee from the lobby luncheonette reminded me of a ship's messroom, and I was not far wrong. It was the building that then housed the leading admiralty firms of the city. Columbia did not offer a course on admiralty law, but I had written my third-year required essay for Dean Gifford on the admiralty rule of negligence. In these firms I was welcomed because of my seagoing experience, and I was interviewed by several partners. While the Depression had seriously diminished their work, they sent me to former associates who were starting out on their own.

Colonel William "Wild Bill" Donovan had been the commander of New York's famous Irish regiment, "The Fighting 69th," and had received the Congressional Medal of Honor. He had also been the head of the antitrust division of the Department of Justice at a time when that position included the responsibilities of the later created post of deputy attorney general. His three senior partners had all served under outstanding U.S. attorneys, Emory Buckner and George Z. Medalie. J. Edward

Lumbard, Jr., the managing partner of the new firm, young, handsome, and elegant without being ostentatious, was one of the few senior partners who ever interviewed me. He noted my academic record but he was interested in other aspects of my background. With no opening for me, he nevertheless encouraged me to return from time to time and check in with him. When I did, on a monthly or bimonthly basis, he turned me over to a junior partner, Frank Brick, who happened to be a close friend of Frank Hogan and another Beta alumnus, John Sullivan.

After graduation and passing the June bar examination, I never really stopped job hunting. Frank Hogan, in the meantime, had closed his law office and taken one of the 20 law jobs on the staff of Thomas E. Dewey, the special prosecutor newly appointed to investigate organized crime in New York County. The competition for these jobs was so intense that I had not bothered to apply. A classmate, my former moot-court partner, had been given a clerical job, keeping track of witness subpoenas. He turned over to me his temporary work as an investigator for the firm of Nims & Verdi, which specialized in unfair competition matters. I conducted interviews to test the uniqueness of certain product features that were being imitated by competitors and I began to do a little legal research, but the managing partner warned me that while the firm appreciated my work, it was not going to hire a full-time associate, and that I should not be diverted from looking for work as a lawyer. Professor Cheatham believed I would do better in the Midwest or Far West. With his help, I had written a large number of West Coast firms, but even though I received invitations for several interviews, I was broke. My bank account contained $6.00 and, after taking the bar examination, I had returned home to live with my mother. Maxine, who had typed many of the letters for me, gave me an opal ring given her by her father, in the superstitious hope that it might bring a change of luck. I began to wear the ring with the opal turned inside so that it did not show.

Several weeks later, on Christmas Eve, halfway to the subway station for a course of further interviews, I realized that I had forgotten the ring. I walked over half a mile back home to get it. As I opened the front door, my mother called that Mr. Lumbard had been trying to reach me. Putting on the ring, I called his secretary and then rushed to his office. The receptionist, who by now knew me well, took me to see not Lumbard or Brick but a new lawyer, Joseph Graham Miller. Unknown to me, Governor Herbert H. Lehman had that day appointed Lumbard and Hiram C. Todd, a well-known New York trial lawyer, as special assistant attorneys general to investigate a scandal in the Kings County district attorney's office. Three murderers caught literally red-handed with a dead body and the victim's blood on their clothes had escaped indictment. After the scandal had been exposed during the 1935 district attorney's election, the governor had reacted to public pressure for an outside investigation. Joe Miller was helping Todd and Lumbard organize their new office.

One of the youngest disciples of the Republican reform movement of the 1930s, Miller had held a junior position in the U.S. attorney's office and served in previous special investigations of scandal. Overthrowing the encrusted Republican organization of the 11th Assembly District, which included Columbia University, he had seized the district leadership. Raised in an orphanage, a graduate of South Carolina Presbyterian College and Columbia Law School, he had just left his job in the New York City Corporation Counsel's office. He asked me about salary. I told him I was ready to work for nothing if I could work for Lumbard. After being interviewed by Todd, I was appointed a law clerk and my salary was fixed at $1,800 a year. The job was expected to last only four months. With a few inches of material to read, I was told to return for work at nine o'clock the day after Christmas.

From time to time, Walter Fletcher had let me believe that he would find me a job at Davis Polk & Wardwell, then probably the leading firm in the country. For over half a century it had been J.P. Morgan's lawyers and was now headed by John W. Davis, former U.S. solicitor general, former wartime ambassador to Great Britain, former Democratic Party nominee for president, and the country's outstanding lawyer. Fletcher and his equally young partner, Otis Bradley, had displaced the head of the firm's trusts and estates department. When I wrote my second-year essay on the surcharge and removal of trustees, I had hoped to impress Fletcher.

In retrospect, it was fortunate that there was no job, but I was naïve enough to be disappointed. Nevertheless, I made the best of what first appeared to be a bad bargain by establishing a drinking relationship that lasted 40 years—until Walter Fletcher died. Although twice married, he had no children. To break the tension of his work, I believed he enjoyed a young, admiring listener who would no longer rely on what he said. While I have, over the years, enjoyed a half dozen drinking partners, none equaled Fletcher. Starting in a Prohibition speakeasy in back of the Stock Exchange and, after repeal, moving through several of New York's clubs, our favorite spot, not the most prestigious but certainly the most cordial, was the Manhattan Club, then housed in Jennie Jerome's former Madison Avenue mansion and the gathering place of the elite of Tammany

Hall. I listened to one extraordinary story after another, sometimes caustic, sometimes informative, sometimes moving, almost always exaggerated and frequently untrue. We usually went home after he told me once more how he had been awarded the Navy Cross during World War I, when, as we both knew, he had barely finished training as a naval aviator and had flown routine patrols over the Panama Canal.

Chapter 5
UNINDICTED MURDERERS

In New York, the Great Depression brought renewed interest in civic affairs and political reform. In good times, New Yorkers largely accepted Tammany Hall's domination of city government and the accompanying corruption. More interested in prosperity, few wanted to take time off to clean up the mess. One outstanding exception was Emory Buckner, a brilliant Nebraskan who had worked his way through the Harvard Law School after serving as a court reporter in Oklahoma. As a New York state special assistant attorney general and as U.S. attorney for the Southern District of New York, he drew young lawyers into public affairs, lawyers who would ordinarily have started their careers in downtown law firms.

Similarly, George Z. Medalie, the last New York U.S. attorney of the Hoover administration, brought with him as his chief assistant Thomas E. Dewey and he appointed as head of the criminal division J. Edward Lumbard, Jr., who had served under Buckner. Rather than wait years for a possible partnership in a large firm, they had both formed small firms in the twenties and they had both turned to Republican Party politics as their secondary community interest. With Herbert Brownell, David Peck, Archie Dawson, and other aggressive young lawyers, several from the Midwest, they rejuvenated the New York Young Republican Club. With a broader group, they ousted the decadent Republican county leadership. Then, with the important momentum of Judge Samuel Seabury's City Fusion Party, they helped elect Mayor Fiorello H. LaGuardia. His clean city administration reinvigorated the police department as Tammany-controlled senior officers were gradually replaced by the best career officers along with earnest young men who, in a depression, sought the security of a city position. Gambling and prostitution, the traditional sources of municipal corruption, had become the protectorates of individual Democratic assembly district leaders as the central discipline of Tammany Hall disintegrated. But in the 1930s a new element was added. Murderous gangs allied themselves with one side or the other in the economic strife between employers and labor unions.

In the spring of 1935, the year I left law school, rival gangsters killed children on the sidewalk. Reformers filled Madison Square Garden to express outrage. A "runaway" grand jury expelled the Tammany district attorney and demanded a special prosecutor. Governor Herbert H. Lehman responded by superseding the Tammany district attorney and appointing Thomas E. Dewey special deputy assistant district attorney. A few months later Governor Lehman appointed Todd and Lumbard special assistant attorneys general to supersede the Brooklyn district attorney. On December 24, 1935, fortuitously, I had tagged onto these reform groups.

Todd and Lumbard were to investigate corruption growing out of a single crime. During this rough-and-tumble period, Meyer Luckman had headed a profitable flour-trucking business. A close friend of the president of the Flour Truckman's Association, and supported by trucking executives in other industries, he dealt harshly with prospective competitors and generously with public officials. In his tight organization, his nephew, Harry, was his chief operating officer and another nephew, Sam Drukman, was his financial officer. But Sam was a weak point, an insatiable gambler who stole from the firm to cover his debts. When discovered, he defied Meyer Luckman, threatening, if prosecuted, disclosure of Meyer's illegal anticompetitive activities.

To deal with this problem, Meyer Luckman called a Sunday evening meeting of Harry and Sam in the company garage. That bleak February night, the streets around the garage near the Brooklyn entrance of the Williamsburg Bridge seemed completely deserted as Drukman pushed open the already unlocked door to enter the deadly quiet, poorly lit, open area surrounded by the parked trucks of the company. He noticed however, one additional vehicle, a Ford roadster with a rumble seat, and he saw a stranger waiting with Meyer and Harry Luckman. The stranger was Fred J. Hull, a professional killer who, during Prohibition, had worked as a convoy guard for Dutch Schultz, a Tammany-protected leader of New York's criminal syndicates who, after running liquor during Prohibition, took over the numbers lottery in Harlem.

Hull, who had acquired a bar and grill in the Irish section of west Harlem, needed extra funds. Armed with a sawed-off, weighted pool cue, he wasted no time. He battered Drukman to death, but not until Drukman had put up an unexpected fight and covered his three assailants with his blood. To ensure a fatal outcome, after Drukman was subdued, two separate lengths of clothesline, slip-knotted around his throat, bound his wrists and ankles tightly behind his back, so that any movement assured strangulation. Dead or dying, with blood still pouring from his wounds, he was dumped into a canvas bag and thrown into the rumble seat of the roadster.

Before Hull could drive the body away, however, Detective Third Grade Tom McAuliffe and a half dozen patrolmen burst through the garage door and arrested the two Luckmans and Hull a few feet from the auto. Photographs taken within a few minutes recorded the scene and showed the three with blood-soaked clothes. The police had responded to a phone call from an unknown person with a frightened voice who said that a murder was being committed in the garage. The alarm-giver was probably Harry Kantor, Drukman's assistant. Before he could be questioned, Meyer's brother Ike took Kantor to a Chicago nursing home to recover from what was said to be depression. A few days later, he was found dead, impaled on a steel picket fence under his bedroom window. One other witness to the episode, not observed by the participants, was Frank Cieri, a homeless derelict who happened to be spending the night in the neighborhood.

The arresting officers were from the local 35th precinct, not the homicide division. Meyer and Harry Luckman were detained in cells at the station house and then moved to the Raymond Street Jail. Fred Hull, however, ended up in a hospital badly beaten, with broken ribs and multiple contusions. Someone had recognized him as a "cop killer." When he refused to talk, the police dealt with him the old-fashioned way, with a brutal beating, subsequently insisting that he had fallen down a flight of stairs. The murderers did not complain; they fabricated a defense that he and they, as well as Drukman, had been beaten by some unknown person who escaped before the police arrived.

William F.X. Geoghan, then district attorney of Kings County, handsome, white-haired, and congenial, was an ideal candidate of the John McCooey machine that then dominated Brooklyn Democratic politics as Tammany Hall dominated Manhattan. Easygoing, he had assigned the investigation and prosecution to a rising young assistant district attorney, who presented the case to the April 1935 grand jury. In two or three days the bloody clothes, the bloody canvas bag, the sawed-off pool cue, the photographs, and the police testimony presented an obvious prima facie case of murder, but then, instead of requesting an indictment, the presentation stopped, not to be resumed until mid-May with seemingly insignificant toxicological evidence and evidence of Hull's condition, as well as testimony by senior police officers who had little to do with the case. Then, surprisingly, the jury found "no bill." The defendants, unindicted, were released, their bloody clothes returned, and the case buried but for two things: the investigative reporting of Murray Davis of the *New York World Telegram* and the effort by a Columbia professor, Joseph McGoldrick, to contest the reelection of William F. X. Geoghan. Geoghan was reelected with a plurality of over 300,000, but the clamor aroused by the exposed scandal caused Governor Lehman to appoint Todd and Lumbard to investigate the murder and the possible corruption relating to it.

The morning after Christmas, our file clerk, who had previously worked on a Lumbard investigation, opened the investigation's new office, a suite of a dozen dark cubicles on the Cedar Street side of the 14th floor of the Equitable building. Hastily assembled office equipment created a stenographer's room, supplied desks for lawyers and law clerks, and opened telephone service. In over half of the cubicles, two desks were doubled up, facing each other. A few senior lawyers had offices to themselves. The staff was entirely male. Male stenographers, while no longer commonplace, were not unusual, particularly for night work. Some of ours were outstanding and ultimately became court reporters, but one was approaching senility and began sending us anonymous letters with his theories for investigation. Without simple copying machines, stenographers could make six readable carbon copies, sometimes one or two more. Additional copies required a mimeograph procedure—cutting a stencil, stretching it over an inked cylinder, and running off copies by rotating the cylinder.

While I read and reorganized the files, Joe Miller moved in as our immediate boss. Todd stayed in his law firm's office on an upper floor of the same building. Lumbard used his nearby office but frequently arrived in the afternoon and had dinner with us. Before New Year's Day, older lawyers began to appear, including some veterans of prior investigations. Most colorful was John G. "Steve" Broady, a lawyer, but more important, an outstanding private investigator. A big Westerner, full of energy and impatient, he added to the strain of nightly staff dinners by telling the waiter to bring all courses at once. By tipping superintendents of New York apartment houses over the years, he had a network of informants. He was daring in the use of phone taps before they were restricted by federal statute. He also was attractive to women. Somehow, he could persuade many to admit to knowledge they had previously denied. Under Steve was our acknowledged chief investigator, who played the part almost to a comic extreme. With a shifty look, wearing a camel's hair coat and a black derby hat, he radiated stealth. Franklin S. Pollak, scholarly, idealistic, but without previous prosecutorial experience, was our legal analyst. Often academic, he was increasingly disregarded by our hard-driving lawyers. Younger lawyers borrowed from Donovan, Leisure included Walter N. Thayer III, later publisher of the *New York Herald-Tribune*, and Walter R. Mansfield, later a U.S. circuit judge. Harry Hopkins, our accountant, unfortunately lacked criminal investigative experience. With funding for only four months, Todd and Lumbard had reached for senior lawyers who could come to work quickly with only a temporary absence from their private firms. In this way, our staff contrasted with the concurrent Dewey investigation, which had a two-year authorization.

The haste that had restricted the selection of staff now dominated our work. Fearing witness tampering, New York Supreme Court Justice Erskine Rogers, an upstate judge who had been assigned by the governor to conduct an extraordinary term of court for all our proceedings, quickly impanelled a grand jury. Not being a special assistant attorney general, I could not enter the grand jury room, but I was responsible for the attendance of witnesses. Using the judge's chambers as a witness room, I came to know them all as they complained about repeated appearances. The grand jury promptly returned a murder indictment. Trial was set for February 3. The lawyer who became my best friend was Richard P. Heppner, a law school classmate. We decided to room together, first as roomers in a large West End Avenue apartment, then for a weekly rent of $9 each in the once elegant, then shabby Hotel Albert, on the corner of Fifth Avenue and Ninth Street. From December 26 through the February trial, Heppner and I worked every day from 9 A.M. until midnight. After organizing the witness files, I digested testimony. Lumbard assured me that even if I spent the rest of my life drafting corporate mortgages, the experience of condensing five pages into one without losing any nuance would be beneficial. It also kept me abreast of the development of the case. After the murder trial started, the grand jury continued its daily sessions investigating the corrupt cover-up. Heppner and I shared the digesting.

Lumbard was generous in including both of us in the staff conferences as the lawyers had dinner together, usually at Delmonico's, a once-famous but by then rundown restaurant, and at lunch in a private room at the Crescent Athletic Club in Brooklyn Heights. With little to say, we soon began to evaluate the others on the staff. The basic trial team would be Todd, Lumbard, Miller, and a fourth person to handle the exhibits. Each lawyer had some special interest. While most first worked on the murder case, a few immediately began to investigate areas of corruption. Broady cultivated Dora Kantor, the widow of Harry Kantor. My special assignment was Ike Luckman, who had disappeared immediately after Kantor's death. Inasmuch as we never found him, my work really consisted of accumulating all of the facts relevant to him for the interrogation of others.

The courthouse was not air-conditioned. Our first-floor courtroom at its main entrance vibrated with noise. Trolley cars and elevated trains screeched around curves aboveground and subways rumbled underneath. The three avenues that intersected near the courthouse were among Brooklyn's busiest thoroughfares. To open a window for ventilation could almost drown the testimony of the witness.

Once the murder trial started, when I could, I slipped into the courtroom. The prosecution's case consisted mostly of police officers and the exhibits, the bloody canvas bag, the sawed-off pool cue, and photographs of the defendants in their bloodstained clothes. The derelict who observed the garage on the night of the murder, happily bathed and enjoying a new suit of clothes, testified that no one had left the garage before the police arrived. The defense did not call any witnesses. Fred Hull's counsel remained mute throughout the trial. Angry because Hull's lawyer began trying another case after our trial date had been fixed and afraid of witness tampering, the judge had started jury selection without Hull's lawyer present. The lawyer appeared on the third day and before the jury was sworn. The judge offered him an opportunity to then participate in the process of final selection, but he refused.

After a trial of three weeks, the jury, to our disappointment, returned a verdict of murder in the second degree. Although confronting sentences of 20 years to life, the Luckmans congratulated themselves on escaping the death penalty and did not appeal. Hull did appeal successfully, but ironically, on retrial a year later, he was convicted of murder in the first degree and sentenced to death. By then the case had been strengthened by evidence I developed showing that Hull had been in debt and had paid off all his bills just before the murder. Governor Lehman commuted his sentence to life imprisonment.

Taking a weekend off after the trial, we started work on the corruption phase of our investigation. This led to an indictment two months later, charging a conspiracy to obstruct justice by a prominent defense lawyer, a leading assistant district attorney, two grand jurors, and a homicide detective. One grand juror pleaded guilty and testified to accepting a bribe from the lawyer and persuading his fellow grand jurors not to indict. The trial lasted four weeks, until the end of June. In addition to abbreviated evidence of the murder, Charles Corbett, a homicide detective, testified to a bribe offer. While an excellent police officer, he was a difficult witness because he insisted that he had a talking canary, and this persistent claim made him the butt of ridicule. The jury remained out for 27 hours during one of the hottest days of the year. Miller and Heppner and I remained near the courthouse and did not sleep. In the early afternoon of the second day, the jury returned a verdict of guilty against the bribe-giving lawyer and second grand juror, but two jurors held out in favor of the assistant district attorney and the detective.

Without taking time to grieve about the disappointing split verdict, Lumbard assigned me responsibility for investigating the police beating of Fred Hull. Under Miller's supervision, I had previously prepared the police witnesses for the conspiracy trial. As to police brutality, however, I hit a solid wall of hostile witnesses. There was no deviation from the story that Hull hurt himself by falling down stairs. I gave Lumbard a memorandum summarizing the conflict between the circumstantial evidence and the live testimony. It supplied the basis for a grand jury presentment to the attorney general and governor.

After a month working at the library of the Association of the Bar of the City of New York on legal research for pending appeals, I was called back to assist preparation for the governor's hearing on a second grand jury presentment urging removal of District Attorney Geoghan on charges that he had failed to supervise his office and that, by his own open friendship with Brooklyn's leading professional gambler, Leo Byk, he encouraged his staff to cultivate that friendship and to accept money from Byk while investigating the Drukman murder. We could not prove that the transaction, said to be a loan, concealed a bribe to the assistant district attorney presenting the case to the grand jury.

The state constitution gave the governor power to remove a district attorney after a hearing. We were hopeful that Governor Lehman would remove Geoghan. Not a true Tammany adherent, a member of a prominent New York banking family, Lehman had been added to Governor Roosevelt's 1928 ticket to give it religious balance. In 1932, when Roosevelt was elected president, and every two years thereafter, Lehman had run impressively for election and reelection, so, we speculated, he might not be subservient even to the powerful Brooklyn Democratic machine that controlled the state's most populous county. In August, Miller, Heppner, and I moved to Albany, beginning an exhausting stay in the DeWitt Clinton Hotel, where, except for a few hours' sleep a night, we were together for a month preparing for the hearing, drafting witness sheets, and re-interviewing witnesses. The state capital was half deserted. The legislature had long ago adjourned. We were assigned the fourth-floor office of a state senator looking across the Hudson to the Taconic Mountains.

On a few occasions we dealt with Charles Poletti, counsel to the governor, to answer questions or obtain information. He was always pleasant. His office, with a single window, was long, narrow and gloomy, lined with the working library of a New York lawyer. We misunderstood his role, appraising him as similar to a judicial secretary. In fact, he was an important official and a rising star of the Democratic Party who had gained the favor of Jim Farley, President Franklin Roosevelt, and Governor Lehman when, at the 1932 Democratic Convention, he switched his support from Tammany candidate Alfred E. Smith to Roosevelt, and thus opened a split in the theretofore-solid New York delegation. Then a Davis Polk associate, on the advice of John W. Davis, he passed up attractive Washington appointments to concentrate his government activity in New York, where he intended to practice.

Miller, Heppner, and I were joined by others as the public hearing began. I painfully learned what it was like to be on the losing side of a case. In the impressive, high-ceilinged Executive Chamber on the second floor of the capitol, its walls lined with portraits of past governors, Governor Lehman, with two independent advisers, conducted the hearing from a huge desk at the center of one end, while his counsel, Poletti, occupied a smaller desk to his right and the stenographic reporter one to his left. Lehman seemed pompous and dependent on Poletti. He was not a lawyer and had little use for circumstantial evidence. To dramatize the forensic loss of the bloody clothes that the district attorney's office had returned to the murderers, Lumbard displayed the bloody canvas bag and contrasted the prosaic description in the police report. Lehman was unimpressed. He told Lumbard to "get that thing out of here." We thought he increasingly favored Geoghan. We had to admit, however, that Geoghan's lawyer, Lloyd Paul Stryker, one of New York's best, had been excellent in his cross-examinations, particularly of Detective Corbett.

With our old job of digesting hearing testimony, Heppner and I divided our time between our office in the capitol and the hearing room.

Notwithstanding the beauty of upstate New York and our early enthusiasm, we soon felt our lonely isolation in a small city where we were unpopular. It was worse than even our first few hectic weeks before the murder trial.

I had a special problem. I was delaying my marriage to Maxine, which we had planned for the Labor Day weekend, certain that the hearings would be over by then. But they were not. We decided to go ahead anyhow. A friend of Maxine's lent us her apartment for the weekend. During a lunch break in Albany, I bought a ring. On the Saturday morning before Labor Day, I caught an early train for New York, but it was behind schedule. Over an hour late, I fretted through the trip, arriving at Grand Central after 11 A.M., and rushed downtown to the city clerk's office, which was about to close at noon. Maxine had been waiting since eleven. The clerk's staff helped us get our license and off to Trinity Church at the foot of Wall Street, where a priest was ready to marry us in the chapel. Because of our uncertainty, neither of us had notified our parents until the last minute. My mother and sister were there and we received a belated telegram from the Wintons. Heppner, who would have been my best man, was covering for me in Albany, and an old Flushing boyhood friend stepped in for him and hosted a champagne lunch. Then Maxine and I were at last alone to embrace, while I tried to figure out what I would say to Lumbard about my absence. On Miller's advice, I had not mentioned my trip to New York.

By then it was clear that Governor Lehman was hostile and unlikely to remove Geoghan. The press, which previously had been favorable, now split, with a *New York Times* reporter writing one hostile story after another and conferring with Geoghan's counsel. Maxine and I postponed our planned honeymoon for another week and I returned to Albany Labor Day evening. On the train, who should I meet but Lumbard, himself, who gently asked what I was doing in New York. Ambiguously, I told him I had had some family trouble. For the three-hour trip, I squirmed in a false position. When I reported the encounter to Miller, he decided to tell Lumbard the truth. When the hearings ended later that week and Maxine came to Albany, Lumbard had us both to dinner and wished us well. The governor did not announce his decision at the end of the hearing but it followed shortly. Removal was denied.

In accordance with arrangements made by Maxine while the hearings were concluding, we took the Delaware & Hudson Railroad to Port Kent, midway up the west side of Lake Champlain, to spend a few days at a resort hotel, Trembleau Hall. Stopping at every station, the train had few accommodations. Arriving too late for dinner, we went directly to our hotel room. The following morning, however, we were the center of attention. We had intruded upon the regular post-season reunion of about 20 guests who grinned at us as one began to hum the wedding march. We quickly surrendered. They took us to Ausable Chasm. After enduring a softball game and a brief swim in the chilly lake, we spent the next day by ourselves, on the steam ferry round-trip to Burlington, Vermont, on the opposite side of the lake. After continuing on to Montreal, staying a few days at The Queen's Hotel overlooking the railroad freight-yard, we returned to New York. We found a $40-a-month apartment at 115 Montague Street, Brooklyn's first elevator apartment building. It was on the fourth floor, along one side of a narrow air shaft, hidden from the sun except when, in early morning, it briefly lit our bedroom windows. A friend of mine in the furniture department of R.H. Macy & Co. helped us buy some good-looking low-priced furniture.

After the Albany hearings, all of the lawyers left the investigation except Joe Miller and me. Mr. Todd stayed on as the head of the investigation, but Joe really ran it. I was promoted to special assistant attorney general and began to question witnesses before the grand jury, but, with a reduced support staff, I also did odd jobs like serving subpoenas in all parts of Brooklyn and Manhattan. Two older lawyers were hired. Frank Pollak returned at times to argue the appeals from the conspiracy case convictions. These convictions were reversed except for the grand juror who had pleaded guilty.

That fall I developed a perjury case against Louis Luckman, a nephew of Meyer Luckman, who had served as a courier delivering payments to corrupt the murder investigation. Having a lead that he had given money to Assistant District Attorney William Kleinman while Kleinman was recovering from an appendectomy in Israel Zion Hospital, I questioned several nurses, showing them a photograph of Louis Luckman, a short, stout person with challenging eyes, a pronounced chin, and a down-turned mouth clamping an ever-present, half-smoked cigar. Kleinman's night nurse immediately recognized him. His day nurse at first tried to protect Kleinman by denying recognition. The head nurse on the floor was sort of in between. By the time I was through, I had five witnesses. Joe Miller, taking over in the grand jury, finally pressed all of the nurses into a positive identification. One of them remembered urging Kleinman not to see Luckman at the time of his first visit and Kleinman saying, "It's all right. I have to see him." Both Kleinman and Luckman had denied under oath ever meeting each other. After trying Louis Luckman three times, with the first two juries disagreeing 11 to 1 for conviction, the third jury convicted him. I handled the exhibits at counsel table with Todd and Miller.

While working on the perjury cases, we also developed a case against Max Silverman, the president of the Flour Truckman's Association, who had assisted in frustrating the original grand jury investigation. He was convicted of conspiracy to obstruct justice. In this case, I questioned my first trial witness, putting some documents into evidence. Well-known defense counsel Caesar B.F. Barra would probably have conceded the information if he had not good-naturedly permitted me to carry out my determined presentation.

Working ever more closely with Joe Miller, I came to understand the constant distrust—insecurity, if you will—that pervades a special counsel's work. Most often working against well-represented persons skilled in corruption, while lacking close relationships with permanent government agencies, specially appointed prosecutors necessarily become excessive in their precautions. As the perjury cases were tried and retried, we had to be sure that our witnesses were holding to their testimony. Joe required interviews and re-interviews by me and sometimes by himself. By the time we were ready to try William Kleinman for his perjury, our witnesses had been interviewed, examined, and cross-examined, before the grand jury and at trial, over a half dozen times. They held up well but were exposed to inevitable trivial inconsistencies as to details. Kleinman himself was formidable, both as a witness and as a lawyer, as he delivered his own summation. He was acquitted.

When, in the fall of 1936, Governor Alf Landon of Kansas challenged the reelection of President Franklin D. Roosevelt, I at first paid little attention. My Republican loyalties were held in check by my realization that, in New York, a Democrat had better future prospects. Joe Miller ended my hesitation, however, when he slapped a card on my desk and said, "Sign this." It was an application for membership in the New York Young Republican Club. A few days later, he sent me to meet Chase Mellen, Jr., who had been the Young Republicans' first reform county chairman. While he had been later displaced, he was still an upper eastside assembly district leader and he needed help. As I started canvassing for Mellen, Joe also sent me to a west side leader. Undermanned as the Republicans were, I canvassed two city blocks on opposite sides of Manhattan and, on Election Day, served as "watcher" in both polling places, riding the bus back and forth. While my efforts were lost in the deluge, I received an early lesson on the dangers of overgeneralization when I tried to get a vote from an obvious Democrat, an old Irishman in a cold-water flat, by citing the anti-Roosevelt position of the Irish hero and long-time Democratic leader, former Governor Al Smith. "Out! Out!" the old gentleman shouted, "I'm no bloody turncoat."

By the fall of 1937, approaching my second anniversary on the investigation staff, I was home more often and actually began to read well-known classics that I had neglected, beginning with the Bible. Maxine and I moved to the top floor of our apartment house, with a narrow view of the harbor. When we dutifully slept with open windows, the crisp flakes of coal ash from surrounding buildings and coal-burning ships crunched under our feet like crusted snow. That fall, however, Thomas E. Dewey ran for district attorney against the Tammany candidate. My friend Frank Hogan, still one of Dewey's assistants in the rackets investigation, asked me to help in the campaign.

Dewey wisely did not depend solely on the Republican organization. He established an independent organization of his own with a team in each assembly district. Hogan had been given west Harlem and the Columbia University area. With Joe Miller's permission, Hogan assigned me to an election district between Broadway and Monument Avenue and between 122nd Street and 123rd Street, a district that had never gone Republican, even in the Harding landslide. My opponent, a Democratic state assistant attorney general who had grown up in the neighborhood, greeted me patronizingly on registration day as he laughed for the benefit of his neighbors on the bipartisan election board sitting around the table at the polling place. The regular Republican captain also was amused by the appearance of an outsider in his district. I nevertheless canvassed every tenement from top to bottom. Most residents seemed to enjoy my visit and I enjoyed talking with them. On Election Day, we carried the district overwhelmingly for Dewey and even narrowly for La Guardia. A few weeks after the election, Mr. Dewey fired all except two of the staff of the district attorney's office and began the selection of the 70 replacements. I was in the first group he selected.

Chapter 6
DISTRICT ATTORNEY DEWEY

"Crew, swimming, and water polo—what did you do that took brains?"

So opened my interview with District Attorney-Elect Thomas E. Dewey. Recovering, I grinned and answered, "I was coxswain of the crew. That took brains." Mr. Dewey laughed with me. The interview went well. Mr. Dewey hired me as deputy assistant district attorney at $3,000 a year. This was the first time I met Dewey in person. Contrary to what I had read and heard about him, he was relaxed, good-natured, and attractive. I knew that he was tightly scheduled and his manner confirmed this, but he seemed to want to enjoy the conversation within those constraints. Well aware of the professional value of working in his office, I now felt the lift of his dynamism. I single-mindedly wanted to work for him.

I next saw Mr. Dewey on New Year's Day. By chance, we entered the district attorney's office together, on our way to his indoctrination meeting with the staff. He was dressed formally—short, dark coat, striped trousers, derby hat—and carrying a cane, then still a feature of formal attire. In our nondescript building, he seemed overdressed, but I surmised that he had just come from his swearing-in before State Supreme Court Justice Phillip J. McCook. For over an hour, he explained to our group of 70 what he expected of us and his rules to guide us. He did not have to emphasize hard work. The obvious challenge of the assembled group told me that I would have to compete as never before. Among many shrewd observations for conduct in a prosecutorial office, he included guidelines for dealing with the press. Do not subpoena a reporter without top clearance. Do not discuss office matters with the press except through the office press relations officer or immediately after filing an indictment, with a statement not going beyond the text of the indictment. He warned us not to compete for insignificant publicity, that there was no value in being mentioned on page 17 "along with the Bulgarian news." He predicted that the member of the group who would ultimately become most prominent would not be one of the senior assistants but a then-unknown young lawyer.

Few really believed Dewey's prediction, but among the youngest in the room was an unknown, William P. Rogers, who later became attorney general of the United States and then secretary of state. Two others became chief judges of the state of New York; a dozen or more became state or federal judges; others founded important law firms or became partners in leading firms; still others became corporate chief executives.

At first some of Dewey's advice seemed extreme—for example, to avoid shaking hands with an unknown defense counsel in public or in the presence of a defendant because of the danger that the lawyer would claim to his client a personal relationship and even a "fix." Some lawyers, he said, would tell a client that a plea bargain resulted from a bribe. The point was that we were replacing a tradition of personal favors, and even corruption. The old Criminal Courts Building had a bar of its own and a seamy history stretching back to Boss Tweed's time. It was built upon the site of a filled-in lake in back of the "Five Points," a nineteenth-century center of crime that produced one dead body a night, usually floating in the lake. "The Bridge of Sighs," an appellation taken from the bridge that led from the Ducal Palace to the dungeon in Venice, extended from the massive old red building over an adjoining street to the Tombs, a dark gray granite, oppressive, barred-window structure reminiscent of pictures of the Bastille. Another bridge connected the building to the district attorney's office in an eight-story loft across another street. Inside were large-windowed courtrooms and chambers arrayed around a gloomy four-floor atrium that was cut off by the upper floors before it could reach outer light, and also darkened by the overhanging, black-iron-railed, ill-lit gallery corridors connecting the upper courtrooms. To first-time entrants among the stream of defendants, jurors, grand jurors, and witnesses, it must have conveyed a mysterious and frightening atmosphere, a place where insiders must be appeased at whatever cost.

Because of the great volume, routine cases were not followed to conclusion by an individual assistant district attorney. One bureau received complaints; another presented cases to the grand jury; another tried misdemeanors in the Court of Special Sessions; another tried felony cases in the Court of General Sessions. Appeals were handled by the Appeals

Bureau. Special treatment was given to homicides, rackets, and complicated business frauds. Each had its special bureau thar followed each case from start to finish.

Mr. Dewey brought with him the entire staff of his rackets investigation: the outstanding original 20 and also a group of "dollar-a-year" men who had worked without compensation. The Rackets Bureau, to which I was assigned, was under Murray I. Gurfein, who, after finishing second in his Harvard Law School class, served as Dewey's assistant in the U.S. attorney's office and later broke a major case in the rackets investigation. Gurfein was one of three chief assistant district attorneys. My teammate was a former dollar-a-year man, senior to me but with less experience in court or before a grand jury or even interrogating witnesses. We got along well, as he gave me a free hand in my work, but unfortunately he was unmarried and liked to work almost every evening. This was hard on Maxine, who was left alone, and hard on our finances because, at first, there was no reimbursement for working dinners.

The "racket" to which we were assigned, while carried over from the original rackets investigation, was not as rough as some of the others. It was a scheme in which the electrical workers' union supported the electrical contractors' trade association efforts to restrain competition, particularly from newcomers. Large jobs were allocated among the members of the association, who supported each other with rigged bids. Contractors breaking with the system could face sabotage. For example, the conduits built into the wall of a building for electric cable could be plugged by dropping in a nipple or a couple of bolts that would lodge in an elbow through which the cable was to be drawn.

Trying to get testimony from within the group, I developed a perjury case against a Brooklyn contractor. On Gurfein's advice, after having the contractor sworn before a grand jury, I warned him of his rights and the danger of perjury, and then questioned him minutely and extensively to avoid any ambiguity and to leave no doubt of intent. He was indicted for perjury in the second degree, a misdemeanor that did not require proof of materiality and was triable without a jury before three judges of the Court of Special Sessions. In this, the first case I tried alone, the defendant was convicted after a two-day trial and sentenced to nine months in the penitentiary. Arguing my first appeal, the Appellate Division of the Supreme Court affirmed the conviction, although one judge dissented because he felt that I had virtually entrapped the defendant. The New York Court of Appeals affirmed without opinion.

Gurfein then had me assist him in the trial of Assemblyman Edward

S. Moran, who, as chairman of the State Assembly's committee on insurance, had accepted a bribe. My Irish name was considered an advantage when prosecuting an attractive Irish defendant before jurors of Irish extraction. As Gurfein's only assistant, I prepared the witnesses and documentary proof. Gurfein tried most of the case while I introduced the legislative records and other documents. His opening address was outstanding and his summation good. After we spent a weekend at Gurfein's summer home preparing Moran's cross-examination, he did not testify. He was convicted on all counts and sentenced to prison.

Returning to the electrical contractors' case, my partner and I developed new perjury cases against the principal officers of a major company that was represented by Max Steuer. The contractors complained that their association had retained Steuer for $50,000 to represent them, but he had simply called them to his office and spoken two sentences, "Don't talk except before the grand jury," and "Don't talk unless you receive immunity." He then sent them away. When individuals were indicted, he explained that his representation of the association did not include the individuals. They paid an additional fee. Gurfein took over the cases but they both ended with pleas of guilty to perjury in the second degree.

Taking advantage of the Christmas holiday season, Steuer was impressive in his argument on sentence. He spoke, as he usually did, almost in a whisper, to compel judges or juries to strain a little bit to listen to him. His clients were given 30-day penitentiary sentences with permission to serve them one at a time, to keep their businesses going. After sentencing, Steuer took Gurfein, my partner, and me to lunch at Holtz's old German restaurant on Broadway, just south of Canal Street. I listened respectfully while he and Gurfein exchanged views and anecdotes. After one of the two defendants started to serve his sentence, both decided to cooperate. Two other contractors followed suit. We were then able to indict all of the leaders in the industry. They pleaded guilty to a conspiracy to restrain trade.

The indictment and pleas were approved by Dewey personally. A young staff member would see him when he approved a major indictment or other disposition of an important investigation.

During my first year, I saw Dewey two other times. Once we met leaving the office and he gave me a ride home in his car, questioning me steadily about the progress of my work. The other was on a Sunday when I was one of few working. He called in all of the lawyers present in the office to get their off-the-cuff reaction to his proposed recommendation for the sentence of Richard Whitney, former president of the New

York Stock Exchange, who had pleaded guilty to grand larceny. I believed it a fair and effective statement of the facts and reasons for imprisonment. A little flustered, I was extravagant in my praise but Dewey restated my position more accurately and thanked me. While I was there, however, I witnessed one of his few displays of temper as he tried to insert a change and found his pencil improperly sharpened. Then he found all of his pencils sharpened improperly. He broke each of them against his desk, saying, "Don't I have someone who knows how to sharpen pencils?"

Before completing his first year in office in 1938, Dewey ran for governor against Herbert Lehman. He lost narrowly, by 60,000 votes. Kenneth Simpson, the New York County Republican chairman, did not give Dewey his full support. The word was that he had tried to make a deal that, if elected governor, Dewey would appoint him district attorney to fill the vacancy. Dewey, of course, had refused. On election day, like many on the staff, I served as a watcher in an election district just north of "Hell's Kitchen," in the assembly district of Tammany's then-chief, John Curry. The Republican members of the local election board fraternized with the Democrats, one of whom stood next to the voting machine, telling black voters, "Vote all the stars, dearie." I persuaded watchers from the American Labor Party to join in my unsuccessful protest, even though their party opposed Dewey.

After the electrical contractors' case, Gurfein reassigned me to be the fourth and junior member of a crack team headed by Gurfein himself, to investigate Chief Judge Martin T. Manton of the U.S. Court of Appeals for the Second Circuit. Overextended by the Depression's battering of the real estate market, Manton had tried to hold his investments by taking bribes for his decisions as a judge. We had two difficulties. First, Manton's immediate associates were ready to face prosecution rather than tell the truth; and second, we were having difficulty finding evidence of a state crime that we could prosecute. His obvious crimes, which we were ready to prove, were violations of federal law, but they could not be prosecuted by a county district attorney. I did assist in a successful prosecution of one of Manton's "bag men" for perjury in the second degree. Although defended by two leading criminal lawyers of the day, he was sentenced to the penitentiary. As a federal investigation of Manton commenced, we made public a report of our evidence to the Judiciary Committee of the House of Representatives as a basis for impeachment. We also gave our information to U.S. attorney John T. Cahill. His prosecution was successful. Manton was convicted and sentenced to prison.

By the summer of 1939, I was again ready for reassignment. Stanley H. Fuld, an outstanding appellate advocate, who had been Dewey's respected legal expert during the rackets investigation and was now chief of the Appeals Bureau, invited me to join his staff. Although I assisted Fuld on one or two major briefs, I was most attracted by the large volume of routine matters that I could handle myself, including, in addition to appeals, almost daily applications for certificates of reasonable doubt to release a convicted defendant on bail pending appeal. While I was still slow and uncertain in my library research, I pleased Fuld with my ability to compress an effective statement of facts. In a criminal case, particularly relatively routine cases, the statement of facts was often the most telling part of the brief.

After I had successfully argued four appeals, Milton Schilback, head of the General Sessions Bureau, responsible for felony trials, asked me to assist Herman J. McCarthy in the trial of Fritz Kuhn, the national leader of the German-American Bund, an anti-Semitic, pro-Nazi organization that was growing among German communities in various parts of the country. As in the Moran case, my Irish name as well as my experience in the preparation of trials was perceived to be valuable in a case in which the defense might try to exploit anti-Semitism. Kuhn had been indicted for grand larceny, stealing from the Bund to support a mistress as well as other activities.

The single word that described McCarthy was "exuberant." Handsome and self-assured, with thick, red, wavy hair and a red mustache, he had defended many cases for the city of New York while an assistant corporation counsel. All he wanted, he said, was a chance to sum up last, because in New York civil cases, the defendant summed up first. Defending cases for the city, he had developed friendships with the police and other city employees, with counsel for the leading casualty insurers and also with counsel for Walter Winchell. He enjoyed drinking and he enjoyed having an understudy accompany him, sometimes with our wives, sometimes with other lawyers.

The key to the case was Fritz Kuhn's mistress. After we located her, she realized that she might be subject to prosecution if we proved her a party to Kuhn's theft or other activities. More important, she had broken with Kuhn and had no urge to defend him after he had left her. She agreed to cooperate.

Our next effort was to keep secret that we had found her. To this end, McCarthy and I misled witnesses before the grand jury as we questioned them about her possible whereabouts. Over telephone taps, we heard them chortle that we were "grouping" in the dark. How to keep a vivacious lady hidden and quiet? McCarthy had a friend, a powerfully good-looking New York police lieutenant, whom McCarthy characterized as a "stud." After arranging for him to be assigned as the lady's bodyguard, McCarthy persuaded another friend to let them reside on his Long Island estate until the case came to trial.

Next we had to get Kuhn to testify before he knew his mistress was cooperating with us. My principal contribution was to persuade McCarthy that we did not have to call her as part of our direct case. By using three telegrams that we had obtained from Western Union that suggested their relationship, and other proof of payments to her, we had enough evidence to defeat a motion to dismiss and get to the jury even if Kuhn did not take the stand. McCarthy took the chance. Our case survived the motion to dismiss, and Fritz Kuhn took the stand and denied any personal relationship with the lady. He claimed that she had been a Bund employee. Unknown to him, his mistress had given us all of his letters. McCarthy cross-examined him for two days on the inconsistencies between his direct testimony and what he had written. Kuhn was flabbergasted. His first answer was, "You have my letters." After compelling Kuhn repeatedly to admit that he had lied, we called his mistress in rebuttal and she convincingly clinched our case. Kuhn was convicted on all counts by a jury from which his counsel had purged all Jews.

The case was a daily sensation. Walter Winchell covered it in person and wrote a special column each day. In one about me, he overgenerously likened me to Jimmy Stewart, an extravagance that took me a while to live down. After Kuhn was sentenced, McCarthy let me handle a second-degree perjury case against James Wheeler Hill, the national secretary of the German-American Bund. In the Court of Special Sessions, without a jury, I would have had no problem in getting a conviction, but as trial was about to start, he pleaded guilty. I later tried and convicted Joseph McWilliams, a Yorkville anti-Semitic rabble-rouser, of disorderly conduct after he had previously escaped conviction by another assistant.

While I had expected to go back to the Appeals Bureau, I was now offered an opportunity to stay in the General Sessions Bureau and ultimately try felony jury cases. At first Schilback kept me as his personal assistant in "Part One." The Court of General Sessions' nine courtrooms were called "parts," each with its own judge and staff. Part One was for arraignments and pleas, Parts Two and Three for prisoners in jail awaiting trial, Parts Four and Five for homicides, and Parts Six through Nine for bail cases. The nine judges rotated through the parts on a monthly schedule. In Part One, I responded to motions and, in the state supreme court, to writs of habeas corpus. After a month or so Schilback began to let me handle some arraignments and plea bargains. I had a good record of dispositions. Defense counsel and the defendants tended to trust me. One month Schilback and I broke previous records with 125 dispositions.

Writs of habeas corpus to the state supreme court included both appeals from a denial of bail and also extradition matters, which sometimes required fact hearings. As the supreme court justices rotated the assignment every two weeks, I came to know many of them. I became particularly friendly with Justice John E. McGeehan, a cordial, former political leader from the Bronx, and also his legal secretary, who was then chairman of the Tammany Hall law committee. During a second two-week period with Judge McGeehan, his secretary, in a very nice way, told me that he would be glad to have me as member of his committee, which would mean turning Democrat and being in a favorable position for future advancement. We knew that Dewey would not seek another term as district attorney. After his narrow defeat for the governorship, he was a leading candidate for the Republican presidential nomination. Always worried about what would happen when his four-year term expired, I declined with some reluctance and said that I felt I was committed to the other side.

After his defeat in his first campaign for the governorship, Dewey continued to be preoccupied with politics as he sought the 1940 Republican nomination for president. At one point he attacked the lend-lease of U.S. destroyers to England while the United States was still a neutral. He also was an early—and perhaps the first important—advocate of a bipartisan foreign policy, supportive of the president. Senator Vandenberg adopted this proposal and later became its most prominent advocate. Again the district attorney's staff was excluded from political activity. We learned of Kenneth Simpson's final betrayal and Wendell Wilkie's sweep of the 1940 convention by listening to the radio, like everyone else.

Finally, in the summer of 1940, my great break came. I was assigned to Part Two to try jury cases during the summer under the supervision of John McDonnell, one of two Democratic holdovers, who had been kept on until he reached retirement because of his World War I service, in which he was awarded the Distinguished Service Cross. McDonnell's way of breaking in a new assistant was to "throw him in," which meant that he turned the case over to me and went out in the corridor and smoked his pipe. He was available if I got in trouble, but not otherwise. My first case was against a receiver of stolen goods, before Judge George Donnellan, who hated accomplices. He had become wealthy representing bootleggers during Prohibition and characterized cooperating accomplices as "Fagans," the name of the English agent who betrayed Robert Emmet, the young Irish hero who had led an early-nineteenth-century attack on Dublin Castle. Emmet had been hanged but only after delivering a stirring speech from the scaffold, urging just treatment of Irish Catholics and Irish nationalists. My principal witness was the robber who had sold the stolen goods to the receiver. While he was sometimes ridiculed in cross-examination, even by the judge himself, I secured a conviction. After that I had no trouble.

The year from October 1, 1940, to October 1, 1941, was perhaps the happiest of my many years of practice. Assigned to Part Three, I tried felony cases to juries, week in and week out. The cases in Part Three, although the defendants were imprisoned awaiting trial, were slightly more sophisticated than those in Part Two. For the first four months, with Tom Moore, who was my senior, we would each try a case a week. I prepared mine while he tried his. I had a good record during those four months, notwithstanding a double acquittal in one case of attempted burglary by two homeless men and a single acquittal in another. I learned to protect witnesses with difficult problems. I avoided an acquittal in a seduction case, and I obtained a conviction in an impairing of the morals of a minor case, handicapped by a hate-filled mother and a very young child. In another case, the complaining witnesses were prostitutes who refused to be extorted by a would-be pimp. The older of the two had complained to Frank Hogan, whom she had met as a prostitute witness against Charles "Lucky" Luciano. The defendant pleaded guilty during trial.

Tom Moore also broke the ice for me with the Irish Catholic court attendants, who originally distrusted a Protestant with an Irish name. After a few weeks, he arranged for the courtroom captain to have a few drinks with us at a bar near the courthouse. After I explained my Nova Scotian background and the absence of a Catholic church within miles of my father's home, the court attendants became cordial and I was welcome at wakes for members of their families. These attendants were valuable in many ways. The jury rooms were not soundproof; a cooperative court attendant could sometimes let us know what was happening while awaiting a verdict.

On February 1, 1941, I replaced Moore as the senior assistant in the part. My new partner was Bill Rogers, who had been working before the Court of Special Sessions, trying nonjury cases. As we first discussed the division of cases, it became clear to me that I was dealing with an astute young lawyer who was so shrewd that I would do better if, instead of debating the division of our cases, I relied on the laws of chance. We agreed to divide the cases by lot as they arrived from the Indictment Bureau, one for him and one for me.

Good-looking and self-assured, an editor of the *Cornell Law Review*, Bill had wisely married while in law school. His wife, Adele, also a law review editor, forwent her own law career as she and her family backed Bill, who, judging from his occasional comments, was much closer to them than to his own parents. With this help, he and Adele had brushed aside most of the grimy difficulties of living on a low salary and began raising children. This instinct for the important and the ability to rise above tedious distractions became characteristic of what was, in many ways, their joint career.

Except for an acquittal in one of his early cases, he and I had a perfect record from February to October, when I left. As we established our reputations for competence and fairness, defendants who had refused plea bargains in Part One began to plead guilty in our part, sometimes before trial but more often during trial. We set a new record for dispositions. Although we worked separately, sometimes if I were having a difficult trial, Bill would just drop in and sit at counsel table. His confident presence seemed to help with the jury. I would do the same for him. We each had good jury relations but the two of us together were even more effective. One of the judges told me that he hoped Bill and I would continue to practice together because we enhanced each other's effectiveness.

My last case was a good example. I was trying a second offender for robbery in the first degree. He and an accomplice had stolen a push truck of woolen fabrics in the garment center. While he had stood to one side, his accomplice used a broken revolver to threaten the messenger. They then sold the material to a receiver of stolen goods on the Lower East Side of Manhattan. After the accomplice was arrested for another crime, he cooperated and identified the receiver, and both testified against the defendant. The judge, who had once been the minority leader of the State Assembly, was cautious in all cases. He was particularly difficult in this one because he did not want to sentence the defendant, as a second offender, to a mandatory 30 to 60 years in prison, and he was somewhat deferential to defense counsel, the highly regarded James D.C. Murray. I had offered a plea bargain of attempted grand larceny in the second degree but it had been refused.

The case had at first not gone well. Having failed to realize that the receiver's transaction records had deliberately misdescribed the stolen goods as to color and pattern, I made a mistake in my opening address and in developing testimony. The records were, however, accurate with respect to quantity. The receiver admitted the deception and corrected his testimony. The accomplice was sincere and fair in his testimony but not very clever and an easy victim for cross-examination, particularly by the skillful Murray. But we received a few breaks as the case went along. The defendant, at times, smiled derisively at the accomplice during his cross-examination. At one point, on redirect, when the accomplice was describing how the defendant smiled during the commission of the crime, I was able to catch the defendant smiling and say, "Just as he is smiling now," and the accomplice's face brightened as he said, "Yes, just like that." Then the defendant and his wife staged a show as the jury was returning from lunch, weeping at the entrance to the courtroom. During my summation I reminded the jury of this performance and contrasted it with the other defendants they had seen quietly plead guilty and accept their punishment. Although defense counsel made an outraged objection and the judge struck that portion of my summation, the jury got the point. Throughout my summation, I tested the edge of permissibility and the judge interrupted me more than once, but I was forcefully effective, and I had the jury. Rogers sat at counsel table during parts of the trial and my summation. I welcomed his assurance as I took risks with the judge. The jury returned a verdict of guilty on all counts. After conviction, to avoid a 30- to 60-year sentence, I agreed to let the defendant plead guilty to grand larceny in the second degree and receive a mandatory sentence of five to 10 years.

While busy with my own cases, when I could, I would slip into a courtroom to watch Mr. Dewey or a chief assistant trying the most important cases in the office: Dewey trying political leader Jimmy Hines, the protector of Dutch Schultz; Gurfein trying Lepke for extortion in the garment district; Jack Rosenblum trying a murder case against the legendary Samuel Leibowitz. Leibowitz was perhaps the best-known criminal defense lawyer in New York, if not the country. While defending scores of murder cases, Leibowitz proudly boasted that no client of his ever went to the chair. To maintain this claim, and because of a problem between him and the defendant, he had tried to withdraw from this case, but Judge James Garrett Wallace, who as a prosecutor had, from time to time, opposed Leibowitz, denied his request. The case was strong against Leibowitz's client. A policeman had been killed as he interrupted a burglary. Leibowitz's client had held both a candle and the revolver before throwing it away. He wiped the handle of the revolver but, unnoticed by him, a drop of wax then fell on the gun and was impressed with his thumbprint. The case against the co-defendant was weaker, but a coat found at the crime had the same dry cleaner's mark as a coat found in the defendant's closet. Rosenblum did not disclose this until his summation, when he turned both coats inside out.

The Dewey district attorney's office and its alumni had a tighter unity than most large private law firms. Almost all of the lawyers were litigators, undivided by private clients. We were a team fighting common enemies, particularly organized crime and political corruption. Moreover, we were mutually dependent. Every four years the voters could decide whether to continue us in office. While, of course, there was rivalry among us, we vicariously shared the victories and defeats of our colleagues. Free of nepotism, paternalism, social demands, or other distortions, the competition was constant but fair. We were solid to the outside world. "Dewey man"[1] was a proud title, recognized with respect by political opponents as well as political friends.

Also, unlike most large private offices, our older advisers presented widely differing lore. Sol Gelb, later a judge of the Court of General Sessions, had grown up on the Lower East Side, graduated from a night law school without going to college, yet established himself as one of the best trial lawyers in New York. Older than most of us, short, heavy featured, he was powerfully ingratiating to jurors. After I began to try cases, I would get to the office early to join a half dozen or more younger lawyers who dropped into his office to hear him discuss cases or just the affairs of the day. Top scholars Murray Gurfein and Stanley Fuld were available to us when needed. Charles Breitel, head of the Indictment Bureau but once a sole assistant of a single practitioner, enjoyed getting the views of younger lawyers. Others like Joseph Sarafite, later a state supreme court justice, had been solo practitioners, with ready answers to questions regularly occurring in day-to-day practice. Frank Rivers, Yale Phi Beta Kappa and the first black accepted into the American Bar Association, gave shrewd advice softened by gentle humor. He became the first twentieth-century Republican to be elected to the New York City Court. Even the American Labor Party supported him.

While aware of our differences, we tried to bridge them. Tom Moore and George Monaghan (later police commissioner) arranged my election

1. There was, on our staff of 70 lawyers, a slowly expanding group of women, beginning with two: Eunice Carter, a black political leader, chief of the Complaint Bureau, and Florence Kelley, later the outstanding chief judge who revitalized New York City's Family Court.

to the American Fraternity Sons of Erin, to which many staff members of the office and the court belonged. Its permanent president was General Sessions Judge Cornelius "Neely" Collins, nearing 70, a former election district captain in the "gas house" district along the East River below 23rd Street, the personal assembly district of Tammany chief Boss Murphy. Notable for having 10 family members on the city payroll, including a younger brother as a state supreme court justice, he personified gruff cordiality. After corned beef and cabbage at a popular Irish West 23rd Street restaurant, the judge always opened discussion with a tribute to Robert Emmet, the martyred Irish nationalist leader. Looking at Irving Mendelson and me, the only two non-Catholics, he always explained that our organization was nondenominational, that respect for the memory of Emmet was universal.

During this period Maxine had changed jobs and received several promotions. Required to live in New York County (Manhattan), we moved from the fifth floor of a renovated tenement walk-up to a modern elevator apartment house on the corner of 59th Street and First Avenue, with a view across the city. We even had a part-time maid who, for $11 a week, worked afternoons and cooked dinner each night. We enjoyed weekend dinners with the Heppners and a few other friends. Having splurged on a $100 radio phonograph, Heppner and I, drinking together, would listen to symphonies until our wives would secretly have the elevator operator complain of the noise so that Heppner would go home.

Each summer Maxine and I vacationed in Wellfleet on Cape Cod. Through a second cousin, she had found a boardinghouse where, for $36 a week, we had a room and excellent food. To get to Cape Cod, we bought our first car, a used 1935 Plymouth, for $65. I had to learn to drive, because my family had never owned a car after my father died. I was at first uneasy about shifting into second gear. I repeatedly stalled, particularly when making a left turn. Much of one vacation was spent irritating other drivers as I practiced left turns through the lines of traffic on the outer Cape's two-lane main road between Wellfleet and Provincetown. In 1940, our third year there, Charles Breitel, with whom I had become friendly, spent a couple of weeks with us. This time together deepened our friendship, one that was to have critical importance to me.

While Dewey vigorously excluded the district attorney's staff from his political efforts, I had, on my own, become active in politics. I was the captain in my election district, between Second Avenue and the East River and between 58th Street and 59th Street. I was also president of the Ivy Republican Club, the political center of the old 14th Assembly District, which ran along the East Side from the 50s to 90s and included several ethnic concentrations—Irish, Italian, Czech, and German—as well as more well-to-do residents in the new apartments along the principal sidestreets. Enjoying calling on the voters in the tenements just as I liked talking to jurors, I helped switch my election district from Democrat to Republican, first for Wendell Willkie, who ran against Roosevelt in 1940, and held it for Republican candidates thereafter. In the fight for party control of New York County between Mr. Dewey and Kenneth Simpson, I helped carry the assembly district for Dewey. I was offered the Republican nomination for state assemblyman but, though Republicans were gaining, the assembly district was still predominantly Democratic and I did not have the money to undertake the challenge. The danger, as I was advised by Paul Lockwood, Dewey's executive assistant, was that a candidate, even though he knows he is simply trying to make a good run in a hopeless race, will ultimately think he has a chance to win, and then borrow money and get into debt in a vain effort to do so. I supported the nominee we selected but he proved the point. He did well, but not quite well enough. After the assembly districts were realigned a few years later, the Republican area in my district was added to another Republican area further south to form a strong Republican district. But before then Maxine and I had our first child and had moved to the suburbs.

As the summer of 1941 began, I received an unexpected phone call from Walter Fletcher. Two senior litigation associates had left Davis Polk and the firm needed someone who had trial experience and could assist Theodore Kiendl, the firm's principal trial lawyer. Kiendl and I hit it off from the beginning. When he heard that I had tried 36 complete cases and had started as many more that ended in pleas of guilty, he invited me to come with him as an associate. While he had other partners also interview me, it was clearly a matter of form, because he always introduced me proudly as someone who had tried a large number of cases. My salary was fixed at $5,000 a year. Davis Polk had never fired a lawyer. Security was in my hands at last.

Three months later, my district attorney's office colleagues also gained security. Through the intercession of General Sessions Judge John Mullen, a former chairman of Tammany Hall's law committee, Frank Hogan received the nomination of all political parties to succeed Dewey. He held the office together and served with distinction for many years.

Chapter 7
SECURITY—A BRIEF ILLUSION

In 1941, Davis Polk was the envy of most firms. John W. Davis, still under 70, was the country's leading appellate advocate. A former solicitor general, he had argued more cases before the U.S. Supreme Court than any other person since Daniel Webster. Judges were fulsome in their praise. Benjamin Cardozo, New York's great chief judge and later, Associate Supreme Court Justice, said that he always put a case aside for a day after hearing Mr. Davis's argument because his impact was so powerful. Not only an advocate, Mr. Davis was a reservoir of sound judgment and an ornament of grace. Returning to the United States after completing service as ambassador to Great Britain, he so impressed his fellow passenger Allen Wardwell, the then-senior active lawyer of the firm, that he wanted Davis as the new firm leader. The three senior partners of Stetson, Jennings & Russell, who had guided the House of Morgan for decades, died within a year of one another. The surviving partners invited Mr. Davis and Assistant Secretary of State Frank L. Polk to join them in a firm styled Davis Polk Wardwell Gardiner & Reed. Mr. Davis soon attracted large new clients, such as the American Telephone and Telegraph Company and the Standard Oil Company (New Jersey). A few years later he was the Democratic party candidate for president.

Mr. Polk, a descendant of President James Polk and a member of a well-established New York family, had been corporation counsel of the city of New York under the reform mayor John Purroy Mitchell. Although expert in public affairs, his principal field was trusts and estates. Mr. Wardwell continued to serve the Morgan interests. Mr. Gardiner and Mr. Reed, who had died before I arrived, had been strong forces in the expansion of the old firm.

The physical office at 15 Broad Street was unpretentious. At a time when other firms indulged in deep-carpeted, paneled reception rooms, Davis Polk's office displayed the functional simplicity of a true law office. The central feature was its extensive library, spread with oriental rugs, old plain tables, and straight chairs in each alcove, interspersed with deep leather armchairs. It had no walls other than its bookshelves, and it opened to a windowed area that broke through the row of partners' private offices that surrounded it. The reception room seemed like an afterthought, a sort of recess behind the receptionist, a few armchairs around a table on an oriental rug overseen by a poorly lit portrait of Grover Cleveland, who had been counsel to the firm during the four years between his two terms as president. On the other side of the entrance a handsomely curved staircase led to the offices on the 17th floor.

Facing the front door was an open area, set off by a low railing, from which the chief clerk and office manager, Mr. Bruder, and two or three assistants oversaw the running of the office. Ageless, with an almost military bearing, somewhat bald with close-cropped white hair and a stiff mustache, Mr. Bruder personified "no nonsense." While older associates addressed younger partners by their first names and some younger partners so addressed older partners, no one, to my knowledge, ever took such a liberty with Mr. Bruder. He saw everyone coming in and going out and, it was said, read every firm letter. When I was late in the morning, I felt that my misdeed would be recorded in his mind or in some black book.

The partner for whom I was to work, Theodore Kiendl, had, like me, arrived at the firm a few years out of law school. Serving on the Mexican border as a member of Squadron A, New York's elite National Guard Cavalry unit, he was a tent mate of Edwin S.S. Sunderland, the firm's expert on railroad reorganization. When Sunderland collapsed from exhaustion and exposure, Kiendl ministered to him. Sunderland later introduced Kiendl to the firm as the person to take over its unsatisfactorily handled Erie Railroad litigation. At that time, many large firms still farmed litigation to outside lawyers.

Handsome, powerfully built, with the grace of a natural athlete, Kiendl had been an all-American basketball player at Columbia and a baseball star. At graduation, he was offered a tryout with the New York Yankees but he decided instead to enroll in the law school. Having grown up in Brooklyn, a member of a large family, he first practiced with his father, as a small Brooklyn firm. Moving to Davis Polk, he may have felt the same strangeness that I did, but I am sure he was unfazed by it. He was a challenging person. Somehow, at least in my imagination, he never lost the stance of a star basketball player putting his eye on his opponent as he took his place on the court. At 50, with full, iron-gray hair, wearing perfectly tailored clothes, he made no pretense that he could pass unnoticed. Whether in court or in conference, whether before a judge or a jury, his self-confidence drew people to him.

Davis Polk was always a casual firm. When I came to work, no one introduced me and there was no place for me to sit. So I was moved into Allen Wardwell's large office in the senior partners' row while Wardwell was in Russia, arranging relief for the American Red Cross. As I sat uneasily at his desk with the door open, partners and associates hesitatingly looked in, much like the dwarfs when they first saw Snow White. Rumor spread around the office that I was an auditor from the Internal Revenue Service. Finally, Mr. Wardwell's son broke the ice and introduced himself. Then Andy Rogers, later an estates partner, and Amory Bradford, later executive vice president and business manager of *The New York Times*, invited me to lunch. While I appreciated their thoughtfulness, I was ill at ease under their polite but probing exploration of what kind of person I was with such an unconventional background. Both became valued friends. While I admired and even envied the social graces of my new associates, I decided against any false imitation.

Before I had an office, I had my first assignment. Mr. Kiendl represented the client of one of the estate partners in a child custody dispute. The parties were prominent and the newspapers were covering the litigation. With no background in domestic relations, I started my research. But as I worked through the digests, I began to notice faint checkmarks. Finally, I realized that either Mr. Kiendl or the estate partner had not relied on me alone. Someone else, never identified, had independently also reached my conclusions. The case was argued in chambers and the judge finally drew the lawyers and parties into negotiation, which led to a final settlement.

Before that case had ended, I was given a test case that would be tried by Kiendl in the municipal court and litigated through the appellate courts. The Commercial Cable Company, which had been acquired by our client, International Telephone and Telegraph Company, had a pension plan that was payable only out of profits. An elderly pensioner had been denied benefits because, after allowing appropriate reserves for depreciation, the company had suffered a loss. The issue was whether "profits" as used in the plan were to be determined before or after allocating income to reserves. Because of my solitary "A" in accounting I had a good basic understanding, but I drove the company treasurer to distraction as I probed him for all possible explanations and then cross-examined him repeatedly. While he became exasperated, Mr. Kiendl said he was the best-prepared witness he had ever questioned. Trying the case before a six-person jury in the municipal court, I was worried that Mr. Kiendl, with his undisguised pride as an important representative of the establishment, might create sympathy for the pensioner. I was wrong. The jury associated themselves with Mr. Kiendl and returned a 5 to 1 verdict for the defendant (five out of six being acceptable in civil cases.)

Finally the firm found a place for me to sit. Another new associate, who had replaced one of the firm's appellate experts, and I were given an alcove that had a window but no door. As the junior, I worked there on an old, brass-bound desk for the better part of the year while my alcove mate chain-smoked. I was somewhat humiliated when my friends from the district attorney's office came to visit me, especially if they had just left Charlie Breitel's pleasant office to which he had moved as an associate of Mr. Dewey when Dewey returned to private practice at the end of his term as district attorney.

Davis Polk had a large amount of litigation. I personally handled some relatively small matters, including defending a butler of one of an estate partner's clients, who had been arrested for soliciting homosexual company at Eighth Avenue and 42nd Street. The defendant had a previous record for the same offense. His case was tried before a magistrate at a time when the district attorney's office no longer manned the Magistrate's Court. The magistrate was both judge and prosecutor. It was awkward objecting to his leading the principal prosecution witnesses, and my difficulties peaked when the magistrate insisted on introducing my client's criminal record even though I did not put him on the stand. As my objections became less deferential, the magistrate found my client guilty but, graciously commending my defense, suspended the jail sentence and imposed a small fine.

My major case for Mr. Kiendl, in the spring of 1942, was a bitter will contest in which the collateral heirs of a wealthy Westchester widow challenged her bequest of most of her estate to the Church of the Heavenly Rest and to its rector. Walter Fletcher had drawn her will and he and Mr. Polk were her executors. Although a settlement was negotiated with one group of heirs, the widow's brother and his daughters were determined to break the will. They alleged that the widow was incompetent and under the undue influence of the clergyman. As Mr. Kiendl's principal assistant, I was responsible for locating possible hostile witnesses.

Steve Broady, who had worked with me on the Drukman investigation, was invaluable. With trial only a few weeks away, we had not found a maid who might have witnessed some of the meetings. Within 48 hours, Steve located her, had a copy of her statement to our opponents, and produced a new favorable statement. With the assistance of a leading Philadelphia firm, I had obtained the record of the contestant's divorce, which was based on his wife's accusation of cruelty and misconduct.

We had the burden of proving competence, the contestants the burden of proving undue influence. To anticipate the claim of undue influence, Kiendl wanted to put in a very strong case on competence, which would establish the testatrix's independence and strength of mind. He examined his partners, Walter Fletcher and Frank Polk, but he turned the rest of the assignment over to me. I put on 10 witnesses ranging from bankers to tradesmen and the postman, who all testified that without any doubt, the testatrix was an intelligent, strong-willed, and fully competent woman. When the contestants opened their case to prove undue influence, they depended upon the testatrix's brother and his daughter. In his opening statement John Nickerson, attorney for the contestants, had told the jury that the brother was a person of excellent character and reputation and that there was no rational basis for the testatrix to cut him off with a very small bequest. When the brother testified, he spoke well of himself and of the testatrix's high regard for him. Then Mr. Kiendl cross-examined him about the records from the Philadelphia divorce court. Startled, he first said, "You are not supposed to have that, that's secret," but Mr. Kiendl simply pressed his questions. As the contestant's case collapsed, Kiendl moved to dismiss the objections to the will, but the surrogate, Charles Millard, a likable recent political figure, was new at his job. Every time he had to make a ruling, he would amuse the courtroom by calling the court attendant and the court clerk to the bench and conferring with them before ruling. When Kiendl moved to dismiss, the surrogate unexpectedly and erroneously refused to consider the motion unless we also rested and relinquished our right to put in a defense.

He gave us overnight to decide. This led to one of the most remarkable of my trial experiences. Mr. Kiendl invited all of us to his sumptuous Bronxville home for dinner—Fletcher and his assistant and me and mine, as well as the rector of the Church of the Heavenly Rest, the principal beneficiary under the will. After generous drinks before dinner, good wine with dinner, and brandy at the end, so jovial was the atmosphere that before I knew what was happening, the rector was standing with one foot on his chair or the table calling for "Highland honors!" We all stood to drink a toast. I don't believe we all had to put our feet on the table, just on our chairs, but it was in this condition and this mood that we excused the rector and settled down to decide whether or not to call any witnesses to dispute the claim of undue influence.

The obvious witness would have been the rector. I had worked with him through the spring, cross-examining him again and again, and I was convinced that he had been discreet in his conduct toward the testatrix and that, lonely, she simply liked him very much in contrast to her inattentive relatives. She was also devoted to his church, which she attended and to which she had contributed a beautiful reredos. As Kiendl asked us each for our views, Fletcher opposed calling any witnesses. Confident that the surrogate would dismiss the objections, he did not want to risk the cross-examination of the rector. Speaking next, I favored calling the rector. I argued that if the surrogate did not dismiss and we lost with the jury, even though we might ultimately reverse the judgment on appeal, the reputation of the rector would be damaged. The case had had considerable press coverage. Although not our client, the rector's own lawyer had really depended entirely on us to protect his interests. The two other lawyers both supported Fletcher. Fletcher felt no obligation to the rector, our responsibility was to the testatrix—to probate her will. Kiendl agreed. He was concerned that Nickerson would cross-examine the rector with a series of suggestive, leading questions, which could affect the jury notwithstanding the rector's denials. So the next morning, we rested our case. As we expected, Surrogate Millard dismissed the objections and received the will for probate. The contestants did not appeal.

That summer, 1942, Maxine was in the last stages of pregnancy, so we did not go to Cape Cod but spent the summer at Shoreham, on the north shore of Long Island, 30 miles or so beyond Fletcher's home at St. James. Occasionally, I rode out with Fletcher on the Long Island Railroad steam train from Jamaica and had dinner at his home. To avoid the suburbanization of their estate country, the north shore residents never had sought electrification. The club car in which we rode when I was Fletcher's guest had its own air-conditioning equipment. In all of the others, with no air-conditioning, soft coal soot blew through the windows, which were opened for ventilation.

While on vacation, I read that 21 members of the German American Bund had been indicted for a conspiracy to violate the Selective Service Act, our country's first authorization of a peacetime draft, which had been enacted in September 1940. A New York federal judge had assigned defense counsel, picking partners from the leading New York firms to show that the bundsmen would get a fair trial, even in wartime. Without notice, he assigned Kiendl to defend three of the accused. Kiendl read about it in the newspaper. I telephoned him, told him of my familiarity with the bund, and offered to help. He asked me to be his principal assistant.[1] Our three assigned clients were the local bund leaders from Cleveland, Newark, and Bushwick, a former community absorbed as part of Brooklyn and Queens. The national officers of the bund were assigned to other lawyers. The general counsel for the bund insisted on retaining his own lawyer.

Through late summer and early fall, I interviewed our clients, who were held prisoner in the federal house of detention on West Street. Except for the national officers of the bund, the individual defendants had little to do with the events on which the charge was based. The national leader of the bund, Gerhard Wilhelm Kunze, had issued a national order that all members of the bund should refuse service in the armed forces as a protest because the act prohibited the hiring of members of the German American Bund to replace draftees. Except for the general counsel, who had drafted the order, and Kunze, who authorized it, the others had merely read the order at their local meetings. Some had also voted approval of the order at a national convention. Actually, nobody refused to serve.

The principal evidence for the government was Kunze's confession and the testimony of William Luedtke, the national treasurer of the bund, who testified for the government, reciting details of the various meetings leading up to issuance of the order. But he inadvertently transposed the sequence of two of the meetings. I recognized this immediately and told Kiendl. The other defendants apparently did not notice. Luedtke's testimony was unequivocal and impressive. As he finished in the middle of one afternoon, Kiendl immediately asked to start cross-examination but the lawyer for Wilbur Keegan, the bund's general counsel, objected and insisted that cross-examination proceed in the order in which the defendants were listed in the indictment even though he and the other counsel were not then ready to proceed. The court ruled with him and we lost a wonderful opportunity.

On the next day, Keegan's lawyer's cross-examination showed that he was not of the same caliber as those who had been assigned by the court

1. William H. Timbers, first in his class at Yale Law School, later counsel to the Securities Exchange Commission and then a judge of the Second Circuit Court of Appeals, was my young assistant.

for the other defendants. He was so ineffective that Luedtke became ever stronger as he impressed the jury with his answers. With this momentum, Luedtke brushed off the other defendants' counsel as they took their turns. On early Friday afternoon, Kiendl was given his chance. Within 10 minutes he demolished Luedtke, as Luedtke could not explain the obvious inconsistencies that flowed from his transposition of the dates of two meetings. Finally, as he gave up trying to work around the problem, he admitted that he had made a mistake, apologized, and acknowledged that much of his testimony was chronologically wrong. Kiendl left time in the afternoon for the government to commence its redirect examination, but the government pleaded for a postponement over the weekend, and the judge granted it. By Monday, the government had straightened out Luedtke's testimony, and although he had to concede that he had misstated the facts in his first testimony, he then gave a coherent statement of the facts in the proper order.

Kiendl also conducted a second brilliant cross-examination entirely on the basis of his own work, as he forced the FBI German interpreter to admit to ambiguities in the German text of the order, which, if given the interpretation most favorable to the defendants, was not peremptory. It was the equivalent of saying that "in a proper case," the bund member would refuse to serve. Kiendl's excellence, however, was of no avail in dealing with the trial judge and, under the judge's instructions, the jury returned a verdict of guilty for all except one defendant, who was deaf and did nothing in furtherance of the bund order.

While awaiting a verdict from the jury, I talked with our clients in the detention pen underneath the courtroom. The defendants, expecting conviction, were singing German songs. The shrewdest of those we represented advised me, "Don't hurry, let the appellate proceedings take their time, and hopefully the war will be over before the final appeal is heard." He was prescient. The court of appeals affirmed the conviction unanimously, but after the war had ended, the Supreme Court reversed the conviction on the basis of Kiendl's cross-examination of the interpreter and the illegal taking of Kunze's confession without proper warning.[2]

After the Bund trial, Kiendl showed his approval of my work by telling me that he would draw me into his best-liked area of litigation—defending personal injury suits for railroads. His skill, particularly in cross-examination, was developed for the Erie Railroad and had led other

---

2. I had left the office. Mr. Kiendl let Timbers argue the case, his first appellate argument.

railroads to retain him. He had me sit with him as he defended the New York, New Haven & Hartford Railroad against a claim for serious injury to a plaintiff who fell between two cars as she tried to reboard a moving train. After Kiendl's courteous but effective cross-examination, the case settled for a modest but fair amount. As a developing litigator, I was most surprised by the way Kiendl prepared the witnesses. I had learned not to question witnesses together because of their possible cross-examination about the preparation. Kiendl briefly spoke to the train crew as a group at the Grand Central Station on his way home. He talked to one or two individually but only briefly. I wanted to cross-examine them individually but he had me leave with him. "They will work it out," he said.

Married and living in a New York area with a high population of young, single males, my chance of being drafted was at first remote. Married men in the suburbs were reached more quickly, because there were fewer single males ahead of them. On Sunday, December 7, the day Pearl Harbor was bombed, Maxine and I had slept late. The morning papers had, of course, been published before the bombing. On the way to the office early that afternoon, I happened to meet Oren Root at the nearby Second Avenue elevated station. He was in full naval uniform. A grandson of Elihu Root and a former associate of Davis Polk, he had been active in local Republican politics and had made a name for himself by conducting a postcard write-in campaign for the nomination of Wendell Willkie. When I asked why he was in uniform, he told me about the Pearl Harbor bombing. As a member of the naval reserve, he had been ordered to report in uniform.

Throughout the next year, the Davis Polk staff was steadily depleted. A few partners were commissioned to important staff responsibilities. Others were recruited to work on the enormous program of government procurement. Still others with ROTC commissions or national guard commissions were called up for active service, while those who were young and single responded to the draft. I declined an offer of a lieutenant's commission in labor relations and enrolled in the newly created New York State Guard, which had replaced the National Guard after it had been nationalized for active service. While the state guard's immediate role was to deal with civil disorder, there was the more remote possibility that it might also supply a military unit. In any event, it offered elementary training for those of us who had had none. It required one evening a week and sometimes weekend assignments.

In the fall of 1942, the Navy announced a Deck Naval Reserve program to train civilians. The program included preparation for command of small vessels. After completion of the bund trial, I applied to enter the program but by then it had been temporarily filled. With encouragement from the recruiting officer, a former Davis Polk associate, I passed my preliminary medical examination with the expectation that the program would be reopened in the spring. Before then, however, there was a new development.

Two months after my attempt to enter the reserve program, while I was preparing for a valuation proceeding for a segment of the old Standard Oil pipeline from Chicago to Newark Charles Breitel, who had been appointed counsel to Governor Dewey following his election in 1942, invited me to become assistant counsel to the governor. The person then serving in that post was politically independent, did not fit into the tightly disciplined Dewey team, and seemed more interested in his second post as director of the New York State War Council. I had not been active in the governor's campaign except as an Election Day watcher in an unmanned election district in Harlem.

While moving to Albany would again subject me to the uncertainty of political office, I was ready to move. My instincts told me that, notwithstanding my satisfactory work, my competition for a Davis Polk partnership would be formidable. The firm was then slow in adding partners. At least one contemporary who had started five years before me had excelled in work for both Mr. Davis and Mr. Kiendl. While my annual raise was the normal wartime 10 percent, my contacts with partners other than Kiendl were limited. I had also decided that I would not stay at Davis Polk unless I became a partner. An associate's life, however pleasant and secure, was inevitably subordinate. Even though the birth of our daughter, Barbara, in September required Maxine to give up her work, I nevertheless told Breitel I was ready to move. He instructed me to wait and let him work the problem out.

A few weeks later, a somewhat perplexed Kiendl called me to his office to tell me that Governor Dewey would like me to become his assistant counsel. The previous day he had visited the governor to ask him to approve a tax exemption for the Metropolitan Opera Association, of which Allen Wardwell was the chairman. Dewey had asked him if he would release me to become assistant counsel. Kiendl spoke highly of me but agreed to talk with me. He told me that my future at Davis Polk was "wide open," that he did not want me to go, but that if I would like the post, he knew it would please the governor and I would be welcome to come back to Davis Polk when I was through. I thanked him and a few days later told him I would like to accept the governor's offer. The governor had asked that I be released almost immediately to assist Breitel during the 30-day bill period that followed the adjournment of the legislature, a period during which the governor had to approve or veto almost 1,000 bills left by the legislature. It was agreed that I would return to Davis Polk after the 30-day bill period to assist Kiendl in the Indiana pipeline valuation proceeding.

In the pipeline hearing, held after I returned in June, the valuation was satisfactory and there was no appeal. Two unimportant features were more memorable to me than the evidence itself. First, the hearing was held in the Huntington, Indiana, courthouse in the central atrium under a cast-iron dome during an extraordinarily hot spell of weather. Without air-conditioning, it was like an oven as we all worked in our shirtsleeves. Perhaps more amusing was the night trip from New York to Huntington on the Broadway Limited of the Pennsylvania Railroad. Kiendl, in fine spirits, quickly reviewed the testimony with our witnesses. By then, however, we were in Pennsylvania, and he complained because local blue laws prevented the railroad from selling alcoholic drinks. Then he and the witnesses started to play bridge. Kiendl, with his always strong instinct to excel, was a very demanding player. Our expert, a junior partner of Kuhn Loeb, later chairman and chief executive officer of U.S. Industries, apparently did not know the rules and, with too little support, raised Kiendl's opening bid. Kiendl immediately bid slam and went down five or six tricks. He was still talking about it to me the next day, shaking his head. How could a person be so smart as a pipeline valuation expert and such a hapless bridge player?

I left Davis Polk with the blessing of Mr. Davis as well as Mr. Kiendl, expecting to return in two years. Mr. Davis told me of the advice he had given Charles Poletti after the 1932 Democratic Convention. He advised Poletti to accept an appointment as counsel to Governor Lehman rather than a post in Washington. Although there was no discussion of it, we all assumed that Mr. Dewey would run for president in 1944. The expectation was that I would stay with him through the campaign and then return.

Mr. Davis personified graciousness. Never a reformer or prosecutor, he seemed free of the harshness that sometimes characterized them. Notwithstanding the intensity and volume of his practice, he tried to give every new associate a chance to work for him. I regretted having so brief an opportunity—the collection of authorities for a useful footnote in our New York Court of Appeals brief in the Russian Bond cases, a long-running litigation between the bond holders of the old Russian Empire and the Soviet Union. Overloaded with appellate work, sometimes arguing two cases before different courts on the same day, he had let the office trial work devolve upon Mr. Kiendl or, in non-jury cases, sometimes Ralph Carson. His last trial of a criminal case had been the 1933 defense of trial lawyer Isidor Kresel, who had been charged with perjury and conspiracy in the investigation of the failure of the Bank of United States. (While Kresel was convicted, one year later Davis secured a reversal by the appellate court.) After leaving the firm, I dropped in occasionally to visit Mr. Davis, always first checking with his secretary to be sure he was not working against an immediate deadline. With his door almost always open, he would have been too courteous to tell an outside visitor that he had no time to talk.

Chapter 8
GOVERNOR DEWEY

When I arrived in Albany at the end of March 1943, I had no guiding perspective. Tired from working nights to finish at Davis Polk, moving into the DeWitt Clinton Hotel without my family, surprised to find snow still on the ground in front of the state capitol, I felt like a child entering a strange lake to try to learn to swim. The legislature had just adjourned. The first wave of excitement and enthusiasm had drained from the new Dewey administration. Those in the governor's office who had been dealing with the legislature were even more exhausted than I was.

I introduced myself to Irene McKenna, the aging but attractive secretary to the counsel to the governor, who had held that post since 1917 when Charles Whitman was governor and who had served briefly as acting counsel to the governor under a good-humored appointment by Franklin D. Roosevelt after his election as president in 1932. Before Breitel brought me into his office, I noticed piles of unanswered mail on top of the file cabinets that lined the outer room. Still elated that the legislature had passed the governor's most controversial bill, which regained state control of waterways previously preempted by privately owned utilities, he explained that it was after this victory that he persuaded Governor Dewey to appoint me, notwithstanding the claims of the upstaters to a post on his staff.

Turning to work, Breitel introduced two temporary assistants employed for the 30-day bill period. Across the hall, he showed me the hundreds of bills still arriving from the legislature as they were engrossed by the printer, ranging from minor technical corrections to extensive recodifications, and from the Agriculture and Markets Law to the Workmen's Compensation Law. Others dealt with private claims, the boundaries of fire districts, or authorized some new patriotic observance.

Before we could start our own analysis, we had to request comments from government agencies, bar associations, municipal associations, and other groups expected to have expertise. To dispose of over 900 bills within the constitutional 30-day period, we would have to average 30 a day, but as comments had not yet been requested by my predecessor, the bills would bunch up near the end. Dividing the bills with the two assistants so as to leave Breitel free to review each bill with us, we worked seven days a week from nine in the morning until after midnight, usually having lunch and dinner together. When, after two weeks, Breitel and I told the governor that we were going to take a Saturday night off, he thought for minute and then, without any commendation, said, "Yes, that's a good idea. Take Saturday nights off."

Charles Breitel was the son of Austro-Hungarian immigrants. After his father died, his mother continued business as the proprietor of a small millinery store opposite R.H. Macy & Co. Under an innocent demeanor, Breitel derived from her an acute shrewdness as well as a deep-rooted sympathy for women in the workplace. As a University of Michigan undergraduate, he had hoped to become a professor of philosophy but, warned of academic barriers of anti-Semitism, he turned to law. After he married a third-year law student, they moved to New York to enable her to practice while he transferred to Columbia. Graduating in 1932, the worst year of the Depression, he had a long search for a job because he insisted on $10 a week. Hired by Leonard Boudin, a single practitioner who later championed left-wing causes, Breitel often appeared in court by day and dashed off memoranda of law at night. In another firm, his wife, almost as poorly paid, was relegated to matrimonial matters. Breitel's big break came when he was hired in the managing clerk's office of Engelhardt, Pollak, a leading Jewish law firm. After Murray Gurfein, an associate of that firm, joined Dewey in the rackets investigation, he recommended Breitel, who proved excellent in gaining the confidence of informers and accomplices. Politically Breitel was an independent, but ideologically probably a neosocialist. I was the only dyed-in-the-wool Republican in counsel's office.

Breitel and I had the same straitlaced view of public office and unwavering loyalty to the governor, but at first we occasionally collided on policy. An instinctive and frustrated teacher, Breitel patiently dealt with my early conservatism. He accused me of having "rivets in the neck." For example, bar association bills severely restricting derivative stockholder suits—suits by an individual stockholder purporting to act on behalf of the corporation against its management—had my full support. Sympathetic with corporations and corporate management, I regarded most of these suits as shakedowns to provide fees for lawyers. Breitel thought the restrictions unnecessarily severe. Although the governor leaned my way, he vetoed the bills for restudy and the following year more moderate restraints were approved. Breitel and I also strongly disagreed about a bill to professionalize opticians, a bill sought by ophthalmologists and opticians but opposed by optometrists. Biased against optometrists by my father, I was an easy subject for the bill's lobbyist, George R. Fearon of Syracuse, a leading upstate Republican and former minority leader of the Senate. His magnetism captured me but not Breitel, who argued that the bill would professionalize a nonprofessional group and was a cover for a restraint of competition because it "grandfathered" existing opticians while requiring new ones to complete a course of study and pass an examination. He and I actually debated the bill before Governor Dewey, who decided to veto it. A year later a much less pretentious bill was approved.

While Breitel took a short vacation after the 30-day bill period, I covered the office. After answering all of our accumulated mail, I started on that of the governor and other members of his staff. When I found a complaint about unprosecuted crime in Albany County, I acknowledged it and wrote the district attorney requesting a report. Because of the well-known, deep political animosity between the governor and the tough Albany political machine of Dan O'Connell, my letter drew headlines in the Albany newspapers, which speculated that Dewey was about to move against the O'Connell machine. The governor angrily telephoned Breitel and asked who was running the state, the governor or the assistant counsel to the governor. Although everybody finally agreed that I did the right thing, I obviously should have checked with the governor before I did it. Breitel resumed his long effort to teach me to avoid overgeneralization and oversimplification. While he welcomed my uprightness, he repeatedly cautioned me about being too ready to act on my own judgment. "Talk to someone first," he urged—"anybody."

After returning to Davis Polk for a month to help Mr. Kiendl try the pipeline valuation case, I moved my family to a small rented house in McKownville, just beyond the western outskirts of Albany. Receiving one of the few parking spaces on the steeply sloping capitol driveway, I replaced our old car and drove to work each day, leaving Maxine stranded almost a mile from the one general store. During the half-year when I could be home most evenings and Sundays, the isolation was mitigated, but from December first until May first, work related to the legislative session reduced dinners at home well below 50 percent. After September brought its gorgeous upstate autumn, December began a stretch of freezing weather that, except for a brief January thaw, lasted until the end of March. Tire chains were a necessity, at least during the first 24 hours after the frequent snowstorms. Leaving the office after midnight in sub-zero weather, when my car would not start, I would let it roll down the Capitol driveway and the State Street hill to start it by shifting into gear. Once, at the bottom of the hill I was saved by an all-night service station; a drop of water in the gasoline line had frozen and blocked the flow of gas. On some frigid winter mornings, a neighbor whom I often picked up talked so much that she would steam up the windshield. Having no heater or defroster, I insisted that she be silent. The few winter social affairs, such as the governor's reception for the legislature, requiring parking on the hilly, ice-cluttered sidestreets around the executive mansion, simply added to the tension.

The Capitol building seemed foreboding. It bespoke brass-knuckle politics. Its massiveness, its lack of grace, the inescapable gloominess of its immense, elaborately carved staircases contrasted with the straightforward efficiency of the Dewey tradition. Reputedly a Boss Tweed scandal as it was built, the very carvings circumstantiated the myth, ending abruptly in the middle of one corridor, the point at which, it was said, the carvers were fired for carving each others' heads. The lofty ceilings and thick, weight-bearing granite and sandstone walls suggested a fortress surrounding the beautifully elaborate Senate chamber and the less adorned but impressive Assembly chamber on the third floor. Even before I met them, I was in awe of the speaker of the Assembly, the chairman of the Ways and Means Committee, the majority leader of the Senate, and the chairman of the Senate Finance Committee. They personified the state government and, in those days, upstate control.

The handful of offices known as the Executive Chamber occupied one corner of the second floor. Arranged around the governor's large ceremonial hearing room at the very corner, the governor's personal office looked out across the city and the Hudson River, with the offices of his personal secretary and the secretary to the governor between his office and the hearing room. The rest of the offices were across the hearing room along the State Street side of the building: the governor's assistant secretary, his executive assistant, and beyond them, the offices of counsel to the governor. My first office was the room that connected the two groups. Notwithstanding its size and impressively high ceiling, it was also a thoroughfare through which staff members went back and forth. After the 30-day bill period, the governor had the offices renovated to reflect his demands for efficiency. Counsel's office was expanded. Breitel, whose office had also been the library, was moved to a large private office, and I was given a commodious office next to his.

We were a tight-knit group that reported directly to the governor, except that I usually reported through Breitel. Paul Lockwood, now the secretary to the governor, dealt with political relationships and campaign matters; Jim Hagerty, the governor's executive assistant, press relations; Ham Gaddis, assistant secretary to the governor, patronage. Except for fiscal matters handled by the budget director, Breitel and I were responsible for most problems arising from the 20 state departments, and also for dealing with members of the legislature regarding legislation. We disposed of clemency applications and recommended investigations of state, county, and local officers and other charges of misconduct. Intimate advisers outside the executive chamber were John Burton, director of the budget, whose office was immediately below ours, and, in New York City, Elliot Bell, superintendent of banks, the governor's economist, scholar, and major speech writer. In spite of trifling rivalries, we got along extraordinarily well. Our responsibilities were so demanding that we had little urge to try to expand them.

The governor seemed to me much the same as he was in the district attorney's office, not really tense but very aware of his load of work and jealous of his time. He almost always ate lunch at his desk, having it delivered from the Executive Mansion. Usually he ate alone but sometimes he dealt with business. When I happened to be present, I noticed his scientific selection: a lamb chop, green vegetable, and fresh fruit. His only training table deviation was coffee and cigarettes, which he dutifully smoked through a holder-filter. There were almost no idle conversations.

Breitel and I were, at first, largely excluded from political matters. Their nexus was the governor's suite in the Hotel Roosevelt in Manhattan. After spending Sunday night through Wednesday in Albany, Dewey would be in New York Thursday and Friday and at his farm in Pawling for the weekend. Often taking Lockwood to New York with him, he would meet with his principal independent political advisers and supporters: Herbert Brownell, New York City lawyer and leading member of the former Young Republican reform group, a former state assemblyman, frequently the governor's campaign chairman, and ultimately chairman of the Republican National Committee; J. Russell Sprague, the astute New York member of the Republican National Committee and powerful Nassau County Republican leader; and Edwin F. Jaeckle of Buffalo, Erie County leader and the Republican state chairman. During campaigns, the governor would often send Gaddis ahead as his advance man, leave Albany, and take Lockwood, Hagerty, Burton, and Bell with him. Breitel and I then became the Executive Chamber. The independently elected lieutenant governors, although friendly, were not intimates of the governor. Breitel or I made or cleared with Dewey the decisions necessary to run the state.

The state of New York was ideal for the study of government: large and wealthy and complicated enough to invite expert participation but small enough to be comprehended as a whole, remote enough to escape the personal intrusion of most complainants and single-issue advocates, yet close enough to its constituents to be responsive. The governor, in addition to directing the state departments, had the power to remove the mayor and police commissioner of the city of New York and all county sheriffs and district attorneys. He could, through the attorney general, supersede district attorneys and set extraordinary terms of court for investigations.

Each year, the governor and the legislature established special committees to solve important problems. In our first year, he appointed Breitel to a small, very high-level committee that included the speaker of the Assembly and the majority leader of the Senate. The committee was formed to modernize the politically sensitive formula for state aid to schools. He appointed me to an interdepartmental committee to deal with juvenile delinquency and I ultimately became its de facto chairman. It secured legislation providing greater flexibility in treating young offenders—permitting their transfer between the state departments of correction, social welfare, and mental hygiene—and creating a Youth Commission to promote and help finance municipal facilities for young people. I followed Breitel as the governor's member of another important and active committee that formulated measures for interstate cooperation.

The rhythm of the chamber changed after Thanksgiving as we prepared for the three-month legislative session that opened each year. Breitel and I solicited proposals for the governor's program, developed our own, and cleared them with the budget director. We drafted the governor's message to the legislature, which was then edited by Bell. We drew the bills to carry it out. December, including the Christmas holidays, was always a period of night work rather than jubilation. After the third year, I gave up trying to drive my family to Flushing to have Christmas with my mother and sister.

Unfailingly, emergencies arose almost once a year that required the governor to use his broad powers to prevent public harm. For example, in January 1945, when there was no thaw, the Hudson River froze; six to eight feet of accumulated snow drifted across highways, while ice-disabled switches in railroad freight yards endangered supplies of fuel oil, food, and animal feed. The governor created an ad hoc temporary emergency agency, under the direction of the superintendent of public works, to mobilize state power and deal with private organizations to prevent a disaster. In such cases in which the governor personally participated, Breitel and I would usually canvass the state officers and develop the original recommendations to the governor, and then draft his orders and proclamation. In shorter and simpler emergencies, Breitel or I would informally coordinate the appropriate state agencies for the governor.

During wartime, the state was largely in a backup position. As the country's seventh most important agricultural producer and second most important dairy state, it had to maximize production. It had to facilitate transportation, the hiring of farm labor, and, through the state school of agriculture at Cornell University, develop programs to assist individual farmers. As the country's most important seaport, it needed to prevent disruption on the piers. Similarly, it had to protect the nation's banking and commercial hub. The dislocations caused by the drafting of fathers, sons, and husbands increased the need for welfare assistance. The State Guard had replaced the National Guard as a backup in case of disorder or other calamity. In the first instance, many of those concerns were local, but through the State War Council, which linked most of the state's top officers and departments, these local efforts, particularly in smaller communities, were coordinated and kept updated.[1] One unusual occurrence grew out of these activities when Governor Dewey, on the recommendation of a naval unit, commuted the sentence of Charles "Lucky" Luciano, after he had served 10 years in prison, as a response to his assistance in keeping peace on the New York piers and encouraging the Mafia's aid to our armed forces in Sicily.

In his first two years, Dewey was enthused with his new responsibility and aggressively threw himself into state matters. His first concern was fiscal soundness. During World War II, when construction of state and civilian projects was impossible, he foresightedly deposited in a postwar reconstruction account the state funds that would have been used for construction. He preserved this fund until the end of the war, notwith-

---

1. For more complete discussion, *see* THE NEW YORK STATE WAR COUNCIL (K.D. Hartzell), THE EMPIRE STATE AT WAR, New York State Publication (1949).

standing bitter attacks by schoolteachers, state employees, and others who wanted him to dissipate it. He responded to an outbreak of amoebic dysentery at a state mental hospital as he would have investigated a racket. Bypassing the department, he appointed an investigatory commission headed by a former Young Republican Club reformer, Archie Dawson. He replaced the commissioner and all of the boards of visitors. A year later, addressing Dawson's broader recommendations, he led the country as he began the conversion of the state's mental institutions from custodial prisons to treatment facilities.

Similarly, irritated by the patchwork of welfare programs that required the poor to go from agency to agency, he and his outstanding commissioner of social welfare, Robert Lansdale, secured legislation for the effective utilization and expansion of state and federal programs. Workmen's compensation scandals led to another investigation and then reform and also liberalization of benefits for injured workers. A year later, he attacked arbitrary limitations on unemployment insurance coverage and then recommended a state minimum wage. The transition of Governor Dewey from a standoffish view of programs for the underprivileged seemed to originate less from charitable concerns than from his intolerance of crookedness, sloppiness, and inefficiency. Later, as he warmed and broadened, his concern for socially related government programs took on its own momentum.

The governor's preoccupation with state affairs was interrupted in the summer of 1943 when our first lieutenant governor unexpectedly died. As a forerunner of the 1944 presidential election, this required a statewide election to fill the vacancy, and it was essential that the Republican nominee win. Otherwise, if Governor Dewey should be elected president, he would be turning the state administration back to the Democrats. Fortunately, the senate Republican leader, Joe R. Hanley, won the election. Then in 1944, as Dewey swept one primary victory after another and Wendell Willkie withdrew, Dewey captured the Republican nomination for president, unanimously but for one delegate who voted for General Douglas MacArthur. At the request of the governor, Breitel, Burton, Hagerty, and I had been deferred by our draft boards until the end of this campaign. By then the lowering of the draft age eliminated us.

The 1944 legislative session was deliberately kept short and as noncontroversial as possible. The postwar reconstruction fund was held intact, but preliminary planning was started on the state thruway system, which would not only speed transport but also take a heavy load off the state's deteriorating highway system. One of the most sensitive issues in the 1944 session was how to provide for voting by persons in the armed services. Congress had authorized a ballot to vote only for president, U.S. senator, and congressman. At the recommendation of the governor, the legislature passed a bill to create a state war ballot commission to distribute to every New Yorker in the armed services a ballot for all state and local offices as well as all federal offices. Assisted by the commission, I drew the bill.

Working under pressure, while Breitel had other problems, I provided that the short form "bob-tail" federal ballot could be used to supplement the state ballot in cases where the state ballot could not be delivered in time. Just as the bill was sent to the legislature, which was nearing adjournment, Breitel realized that I had made an important political decision and that there was no time to consult the governor. He inserted language to create an ambiguity so that, we hoped, the law could be read as the governor should later decide. I recovered the bills from both houses and in the middle of the night from the printer and made Breitel's changes. Later, as voting by servicemen became a major issue, I argued that the ambiguity could and should be resolved to accept the supplemental bob-tail ballots. The governor referred the matter to John Foster Dulles, a leading New York City lawyer, for an independent legal interpretation. Over my strong protests, Dulles concluded that the supplemental ballots could not be used. A costly error. In the last few weeks of the campaign, their exclusion aroused widespread political criticism, not only in New York but in other states—damage that was not only self-inflicted but, if intended to reduce the soldier vote, in vain, because the procedures we had set up for the distribution of full ballots were so successful that our service votes doubled those of Pennsylvania, the next highest state.

In the 1944 campaign, Dewey had few issues available to him. The war effort was successful. While he believed that Roosevelt had prior notice of Pearl Harbor, he dropped the issue when General Marshall convinced him that the Japanese were still using the code that U.S. intelligence had broken. The issue of a third presidential term had been lost by Willkie. Roosevelt had concealed the evidence of his declining health. Dewey had to revert to his old prosecutorial line. He charged Secretary of the Treasury Henry Morganthau with arousing the last great German effort by his threats of postwar retaliation. He denounced Roosevelt's association with left-wing leaders. Unfortunately, the campaign became tinged with anti-Semitism, a charge Democrats were often quick to make, sometimes speciously, as during Dewey's 1938 campaign against Governor Lehman.

But in 1944, Republican insensitivity supplied a basis for it. When President Roosevelt replaced Henry Wallace as vice presidential candidate, he told his advisers to clear prospective substitutes with his strong labor supporter, Sidney Hillman, president of the Amalgamated Clothing Workers' Union and head of the left-leaning American Labor Party. "Clear it with Sidney," became a widely used Republican jibe. Some congressional candidates distributed anti-Hillman literature that unquestionably was anti-Semitic. In one of Governor Dewey's last campaign speeches, in Boston, he denounced as Roosevelt's Communist supporters Earl Browder, secretary-general of the Communist party, whose sentence for passport fraud had been commuted by Roosevelt, and Sidney Hillman. He followed this by citing David Dubinsky as a critic of Hillman and the American Labor Party, but the crowd booed Dubinsky's name before Dewey had expressed his full thoughts. Either because of fatigue or the structure of the speech itself, Dewey's reference to Dubinsky first sounded disparaging and hostile. Unknown to me, Breitel, after seeing the speech in advance, had warned Dewey of the danger that he would be misunderstood, but Dewey followed Bell and did not change it.

As the campaign closed, Breitel and I drove to New York to be with the governor's staff in defeat. Visiting a camera store that afternoon, the proprietor, whom we both knew, forecast the city's hostile reaction to the Boston speech. In contrast, on the same day as the speech, Roosevelt had lifted his supporters by driving through the city in an open car, enduring cold rain, to suggest his health and vigor.

Defeat in a presidential campaign, which I have witnessed on three occasions, dwarfs, in its enormity, any other political or professional setback. In spite of the odds, hopes began to rise not just for a good showing but for possible victory. Published polls suggested this possibility in 1944, but on election night the returns steadily worsened. After headquarters first suggested that later rural returns would offset the city returns, in the early morning, the governor conceded defeat and telegraphed congratulations to President Roosevelt. After his defeat, his enthusiasm for state government was never quite the same. Once focusing on national and international issues, it was hard for him to turn back. From 1944 until 1948, the prospect of a second presidential campaign was ever present.

The campaign had been bruising. Roosevelt had remained aloof, but cabinet officers like Harold Ickes received ample coverage for their attacks and even ridicule ("Dewey has thrown his diaper into the ring.").

Without television, Albany could not compete with Washington as a news outlet, and Dewey did not have supporting speakers of stature comparable to cabinet officers. It seemed to me that Dewey's physical appearance had changed slightly during the months he had been away. I thought it had softened. He was just a little less driving. He had a few minutes more to fill me in on matters outside my immediate responsibility. Later, I learned of the tense disputes among those responsible for the campaign. Ed Jaeckle, the New York State Republican leader, had broken with the governor over tactics. Herbert Brownell, the campaign chairman, had had differences with Elliott Bell, the principal speech writer. These incidents exposed the inevitable friction in a losing campaign.

With the governor and the political group exhausted, and with only one lawyer to help us, it fell to Breitel and me to recover momentum by developing an exciting program for the next legislative session. Public housing, as a stimulus for neighboring private investment, emergency housing for returning servicemen, a restudy of the state educational system (which as yet had no real state university), the reordering of welfare, improvement in the production and marketing of agricultural products, better working conditions for migrant laborers, a conservation program to restore forests and protect the waters of the state from pollution and expand the opportunities for outdoor recreation, and, finally, the vigorous implementation of recommendations to build an enormous hydroelectric power plant on the St. Lawrence River led to a productive legislative session. While awaiting the report of the commission against discrimination, the governor emphasized the importance of prompt and vigorous action in this field.

By then I had become, in many ways, an alter ego for Breitel. I had responsibility for reviewing the legislative programs of the state departments as well as proposals of individual legislators and outsiders so Breitel could concentrate on major programs, and I began to work on some of these. Clemency had always been my responsibility. This responsibility encompassed manning the death watch on the night of an execution to be sure no last-minute factor was missed. The executions all proceeded on schedule, except that of Louis "Lepke" Buchalter, the head of New York City's Murder, Inc., who at the last minute offered information. After the Hogan district attorney's office reported the information was not new, he was executed two days later. In one other case, the governor commuted the sentence of a young murderer on the basis of a joint recommendation by Breitel and me after we had interviewed him in the

Sing Sing Prison death house to verify his competence. We never repeated this procedure. An interview overshadowed by an imminent execution simply lacked the detachment necessary for an objective appraisal.

Because Breitel was only three or four years my senior, I did not hesitate to challenge him within the office but I appreciated more and more his role as teacher. An example was the antidiscrimination law. When we first talked about it in 1944, I doubted its effectiveness and I opposed its application to law partnerships, which, to me, had a family quality. I detested discrimination but I questioned a law that compelled its unwilling elimination, especially where intimacy was a requisite both within a firm and with personal clients. As we debated the issue in many luncheon conversations, I came around to Breitel's point of view and became a wholehearted advocate as we prepared to support a bill as part of the governor's 1945 program.

Breitel was then at his best. His New York City veneer and his superficial naïvete were gone. The upstate legislative leaders not only respected him, they liked him. On sensitive racial and religious matters, Breitel had begun to replace George Z. Medalie, the governor's original mentor, who had become a court of appeals judge and who died in 1945. Governor Dewey always opposed the concept of discrimination; his record of employment in the rackets investigation and the district attorney's office showed his determination to employ on the basis of merit, but even in the district attorney's office he had to give some consideration to avoiding an unevenly divided office. In dealing with juries and political realities, racial and religious prejudices of others could not always be ignored. At first, it was more a matter of dealing fairly with all groups but still recognizing the existence of racial and religious groups. In 1945, however, he went all out to try to destroy the concept.

Breitel, in one of his most adroit moves, drew to him, improbably, the most eloquent orator in the Assembly, a conservative itinerant minister from Broome County, Orlo Brees. With resistance still present among many upstate Republicans and even one or two from New York City, we needed every vote we could get. Brees swung not only enough to carry the measure, but to do it with a substantial block of Republicans as well as Democrats. Listening in the gallery as he spoke, Breitel and I, like everyone in the chamber, sat transfixed as Brees crystallized the issue by pointing to the backlit colors in the traceries of the Assembly Chamber's Tiffany windows and arguing that the bill would not blur but would preserve and refract the individuality of each group just as each color in the windows brought out the beauty of the others.

New York became the first state to outlaw racial or religious discrimination in employment. While Presidents Roosevelt and Truman had talked big, we believed theirs was a cynical performance because by refusing to moderate an extreme measure that could not pass, they had, in effect, supported the southerners in blocking any federal law. A few days later, Breitel gave me the honor of presenting the bill to the governor and drafting the governor's approval memorandum to accompany it. The governor particularly liked the paragraph: "Not only is this bill a reaffirmation of the great principles by which we live. It is an expression of confidence that government is not such a clumsy thing that it cannot solve delicate problems." The governor inserted the word "great."

Under tension, fortune's swings seem their most abrupt. As the session ended after midnight, Breitel took a weekend off to give me and our assistant time to assemble the first large batch of bills for presentation to the governor. The next morning, he telephoned me, distraught. His wife had just found their four-month-old daughter dead in her crib from a previously undiagnosed defect. Refusing manifestations of sympathy or ceremony, he was back only a day late. The governor invited me to present the accumulated bills, but he agreed with me that Breitel would probably appreciate it if we waited for him. Our assistant and I prepared 70 of the simplest bills for him to start.

As we moved into the fall it looked as though 1945 would be the best of all years, but we had to deal with the mayoralty campaign in New York City. Perhaps to erase the spectre of anti-Semitism in the 1944 campaign, the governor selected a Democrat, a general sessions judge, Jonah Goldstein, as the Republican nominee for mayor. Judge Goldstein was a decent but undistinguished lawyer who, after a successful practice, had been elected a judge by the Democrats and opposed by the Republicans. A lifelong East Sider, he had been active in the Grand Street Boys and similar local organizations, but he was unknown outside of Manhattan. Friendly and outgoing as he was, he had no qualification by training or experience to be mayor of the city of New York. Fiorello La Guardia, long jealous of and sometimes hostile to Governor Dewey, shrewdly realized that the governor had blundered. He organized an independent candidacy for Newbold Morris, the president of the City Council. The Democrats nominated William O'Dwyer, the district attorney of Kings County, who had successfully convicted Lepke as the head of Murder, Inc. O'Dwyer won easily. Goldstein ran a poor third. So, in December, Breitel and I were in the same position we had been in a year earlier, recovering from a political defeat. I dropped in to see Mr. Kiendl and

Mr. Davis to explain that although I had hoped to return to Davis Polk after two years in Albany, I hated to leave just as the governor had sustained a defeat. Mr. Davis agreed, sharing a West Virginia farmer's observation: "It's easier to get your fingers into the machinery than to get them out."

Breitel and I again developed a legislative program for the governor. This year, however, with the end of the war, it was the fiscal side of the government that was the showpiece. The accumulated surplus of the state was now ready to be applied to an extensive highway modernization program, to pay off debt, and to cut income taxes 50 percent. There also could now be substantial salary increases for state employees and funds could be set aside for future increases in state aid for education that would lift teachers' salaries. The governor obtained legislative approval for an all-out attack on tuberculosis, then a leading cause of death. He eliminated the "means test" as a condition for state hospital admission and sent a caravan with free chest X rays from city to city to detect the disease. The Commission on Municipal Revenues, headed by the highly respected state comptroller, Frank Moore, secured legislation to carry out basic local fiscal reforms. For the first time, the governor requested and received authority to study the feasibility of a true state university—a project exacting the utmost diplomacy in overcoming the doubts and concerns of New York's outstanding private institutions.

Because of our rigorous policy of vetoing bills that were imperfectly drawn, legislators began to consult with us during the session so that problems could be avoided. The time pressure was so intense that we had to reserve for legislators the days on which the legislature sat. After an early-morning session with Breitel and keeping abreast of the heavy flow of mail, I would start my interviews. A half hour was usually too short. If I allowed 45 minutes I could usually get rid of a problem with one meeting. Breitel handled the major programs and major headaches. I tried to take care of everything else. As the session reached its last month, just the list of telephone discussions and appointments would overflow the pages of my diary. We kept our rooms cold so visitors would leave more quickly.[2]

In the fall of 1946, Governor Dewey won reelection, defeating Senator

---

2. In 1945 we created the office of law assistant. The first three were John T.C. Low from Davis Polk; George M. Shapiro, a top Columbia law graduate; and Charles S. Whitman, Jr., son of Governor Whitman of New York and father-in-law of Governor Christine Todd Whitman of New Jersey.

James Mead, a popular Democrat, by over 600,000 votes. After the elimination of wartime gasoline rationing, Breitel and I began to travel to make speeches. During the summers of 1945 and 1946, the towns and counties of the large-scale maps on our office walls emerged as the unpretentious but overpowering beauty of upstate New York. At my first state bar association meeting at the Saranac Inn, Senator Fearon introduced me to upstate judges sitting along the broad veranda overlooking the lake and the mountains beyond it. To save gasoline, I had followed what seemed to be the shortest route on the map, but after 10 miles the pavement ended and I had no choice but to proceed through an Adirondack rutted logging road, fearful of what would happen if anything went wrong with the car, but emerging on a remote, beautifully unspoiled lake. Sent to Wellsville, in the "southern tier" of counties, to explain to municipal officials and schoolteachers why the governor's proposed program to expand local taxing power was better than an increase in state aid, I received compliments for my courage but few converts.

Travel on upstate two-lane roads had its hazards. Rounding a curve, I drove between two cows at 40 miles an hour, while the speechless farmer held back the others in the herd. On another occasion, descending a hill, I watched helplessly a deer cantering along the edge of a woods on a certain collision course with a car coming toward me. The deer could not see the car and its driver could not see the deer. As they met, the deer, without breaking stride, sailed over the hood of the car and went on his way. The poor driver pulled to the side of the road to recover. Speaking arrangements were often unusual. In an Adirondack county, I waited to be introduced by the local undertaker, who had been called out for an emergency. In Geneva I spoke from a float at the end of Lake Seneca, blinded by floodlights that made it impossible for me to see the audience on the shore. I rushed my first radio address so badly that its allotted time had to be filled by ad lib comments by the announcer.

In January 1947 Maxine presented our second daughter, Janet. Because both our children had been delivered by Caesarean section, we kept our New York City obstetrician. Not having mentioned this to the governor, I felt guilty as Lockwood, on the station platform, spotted us leaving for New York during the legislative session. After the delivery, I quickly returned to Albany and then went back to pick up Maxine and the baby when they left the hospital. Delayed in checking out of the hospital and by a novice taxi driver, we almost missed our train and my inexorable schedule. Maxine, still recovering from her operation, had to run for it. This was one of the times I thought of quitting. Tension overhung everything we did, even mowing the lawn or playing with the children. There was always a phone call from someone who hesitated to bother the governor or even Breitel but who wanted to share responsibility for a problem.

In contrast, the governor had become so confident of our work on legislative bills and other matters that Breitel began to feel slighted as his presentations were tucked into open spots in the governor's schedule, sometimes in the evening at the Executive Mansion. Mrs. Dewey, concerned by the growing independence of their two sons, firmly required the governor to leave the Capitol for dinner at 6:30 P.M. Breitel became most irked when he found out that the governor was sending for his car and his counsel at the same time.

Reelection somehow made us feel like old hands. The governor, in 1944, had begun to take golf seriously as an exercise. Typically, he did it well. He and Jim Hagerty, who also had improved, soon played together regularly. There was still the same amount of work to do, but the apprehension that originally accompanied exploration into strange fields and dealing with strangers was replaced by the confidence of teamwork in which all of the major players knew each other. Also, I had developed many friendships with upstate legislators and political leaders as well as with those in the state's career service. Even the foreboding Capitol building began to seem homelike. In his 1947 annual message the governor said, "Those who join us here for the first time may feel that this old Capitol is a cold and formidable mass of stone. But before long this old place will seem different—warmed by the glow of present associations, enriched by a deeper understanding of those who have gone before us."

Each year, the legislative correspondents of the state's newspapers lampooned the governor and other state officials at a dinner held in the Hotel TenEyck ballroom on the top floor of the hotel, a firetrap in which all of the top state officials and politicians could have been eliminated in one sad event. After reelection, the humor was less cruel but just as amusing. The governor's remarks at the end were more warmly received. This was symbolic of the improved relationship between the governor and the press and Jim Hagerty's patient work. The governor had gained the support of most state newspapers, including those of New York City. Even so, Albany was not a highly featured source of news. We felt lucky if we could get a column in *The New York Times*, even on an inside page.

Ben Feinberg of Plattsburgh, the Senate majority leader, had become particularly friendly with Breitel, with whom he worked on major state committees, and his friendship spilled over onto me. His father had been an upstate peddler and taught him unique methods of mathematical computation. He enjoyed surprising us as well as the governor and legislative leaders with his ability to out-compute the budget director and state controller by rapidly calculating in his head complex state formulas. Ossie Heck, the Assembly speaker, on the other hand, was more remote, even though friendly. As the second most powerful political leader in the state government, he was careful to avoid any diminution of his independence. The chairmen of the Senate Finance Committee and the Assembly Ways and Means Committee were the ultimate businessmen of the legislature. We never undertook to explore the financial undercurrent of legislation or the funding of legislative perquisites. Aware of soft spots, we sometimes took them into account in making our own recommendations to have the governor veto legislation. As Breitel more frequently permitted me to report to the governor, he continued to despair of my impetuousness, as when I volunteered that we would write a speech on ceramics for the governor to deliver to Alfred University's noted school of ceramics, even though we knew nothing about ceramics. It was useless to warn me against the governor, who recognized me as a soft mark.

In 1948 we moved back into high gear on the national stage. President Truman, having succeeded to office from the vice presidency, was in a weak position that was further damaged by scandals developing within his administration. Notwithstanding the governor's excellent 1944 run for the presidency, he faced serious competition for the Republican nomination. The Republicans had control of the 80th Congress. Robert Taft, the Senate majority leader, an ultraconservative, was an aggressive candidate for the presidential nomination with a tight hold on the delegates from southern states. Harold Stassen, the young governor of Minnesota, appealed to the Midwest. General Dwight D. Eisenhower, then president of Columbia University, had declined to run.

After the 30-day bill period, Breitel released me for work in the primary campaign. In 1948, few states had open primary elections. Stassen had beaten Dewey in the Wisconsin and Nebraska primaries. Dewey had won none. Oregon posed a critical test of survival. The governor told me that he thought he was going to lose but that he was going down on a good issue—that communism, hateful though it was, should not be outlawed but protected by the Constitution's guarantee of freedom of speech and assembly. I developed the legal material to support this proposition, drawing heavily on Louis Brandeis, Oliver Wendell Holmes, and Professor Zechariah Chafee.

During his whistlestop tour, the governor carried in his pocket 3 x 5 cards on which I had extracted the best language from my sources. He inserted two or three quotes in his extemporaneous talks from the rear of the train. Finally, the campaign culminated in his debate with Stassen, which was carried nationwide by radio. He soundly trounced Stassen and won the Oregon primary. With this new momentum he was on his way to the Republican National Convention in Philadelphia.

Sent to work in the New York office of Herbert Brownell's principal assistant, I gathered personal data on each convention delegate so that the governor would know how best to approach them. Working long hours, I happened to be present one night when Russ Sprague brought in the Republican state chairman of Pennsylvania to commit a large block of votes that would ultimately secure Dewey's nomination. I also was exposed to one of the handsome, do-nothing hangers-on that infest campaign headquarters. Unwilling or unable to work themselves, they expertly take credit for the work of others. I naïvely explained to one of these what I was doing, only to find out that he had afterwards secretly recorded in a notebook most of the information from my files and impressed the governor with his astute knowledge of the assembling delegates.

In a sweltering Philadelphia, still with limited air-conditioning, I ran the Dewey communication center on the convention floor, simply a telephone booth, assisted by two college volunteers, a son of Mr. Kiendl and a son of Whitney North Seymour. We were vigilant. The Taft booth was sometimes unmanned. I would answer his telephone too, always telling the senator who I was. He would laugh and have me call Governor John Bricker, his floor leader, to the phone. Stassen crumbled first and finally Taft was defeated as Governor Earl Warren threw California's support to Governor Dewey.

After the convention, I remained in Albany with Breitel. Except for our law assistants, we were alone in the executive chamber most of the time. Misled by highly favorable polls such as those of Roper and Gallup, which proved inaccurate, and underestimating the damage done by the Republican 80th Congress, which had, in a year of bumper crops, eliminated government support for grain storage, passed the Taft-Hartley Act to alienate labor, and tabled civil rights legislation, Governor Dewey conducted a high-level intellectual campaign, seeking to unify the country behind what he believed to be a strong Republican majority. In contrast, Truman criss-crossed the country vigorously denouncing the Republican "do nothing" Congress. On a Saturday night 10 days before the election, Breitel and I met with Dewey at the executive mansion to get some papers signed. He asked us whether we thought he could continue with his "unity" theme through the election. We opined that it was becoming dreary but we thought he could keep it up and that it was probably too late to change. When Truman attacked him personally and viciously the following week, virtually accusing Dewey of being a fascist, I hoped the governor would turn around and let go with his expert rhetorical attacks but he chose to play it on a higher level until the end.

The polls continued to show Dewey with a commanding lead. In 1948, before television, the pollsters believed that election campaigns changed few votes; they gave heavy weight to early polls. Still thinking that the governor would win, Breitel and I did not go to New York to be with him on election night. One of our law assistants invited the counsel office lawyers and their wives to a late pancake supper to listen to the returns.[3] His wife was the only one who was worried. Working as a secretary in an industrial plant between Albany and Hudson, New York, she had noticed that most of the plant workers, particularly those who were unionized, were going to vote for Truman. We discounted the early radio returns showing Truman leading, but as we listened together into the early morning, the trend continued, with only a few surges of Dewey support. We went home unbelieving. When we arrived at the office in the morning, the stenographers were crying because the governor had just held a press conference to concede defeat.

The admiration for the governor's 1944 campaign was absent in 1948. Whatever the reasons or excuses, we had bungled an extraordinary opportunity. The superb achievements of a lifetime were in danger of being washed away in the aftermath, including Dewey's party control, which lay exposed to the heavy-handed diehards on the far right. A death in the family would have been more easily surmounted. Friends and allies volunteering sympathy and support were, at first, more like mourners making condolence calls than a resurgent force. The governor seemed uncharacteristically embarrassed and physically shaken. But if a comeback is the true measure of a man, he had it and he led it.

So confident had we been that, during the fall, Breitel had made a superficial study of the federal government and anticipated the transition to Washington. He hoped that the increasing importance of the post of

3. After the war ended, we were able to expand our staff of law assistants. J.D. Crocker, who had received a Bronze Star, was joined by Robert Prince, who had served in the Rhineland, and Robert Moore, who had commanded a landing craft in the invasions of Sicily and Anzio.

counsel to the president would not prevent him from becoming attorney general. I don't think either of us fully appreciated the political nature of Senate-confirmed cabinet appointments and the limited personal prerogatives of the president. I was somewhat uneasy as he talked of leaving me in Albany to avoid abandonment of the governor's successor, Joe Hanley, the lieutenant governor. Although I had a good personal relationship with him, I thought he might want to select his own counsel, even though he might want me for a transitional year.

These discussions vanished as we turned back to our old assignment of surmounting a political defeat by developing a powerful legislative program to restore the momentum of the state administration. It was to be more difficult because of the expectation that the governor would not run for reelection in 1950. Not only had he been defeated, he might be a lame duck. For the first time, the governor's budget buckled under upstate tax resistance. Revolt simmered as the state university proposal barely withstood a serious legislative attack supported by religious and private institutions. On April 1, 1949, however, the state university trustees began to function as an administrative unit. They unified the 33 state-supported institutions of higher learning and established two medical centers, one absorbing the Long Island College of Medicine in New York City and the other the College of Medicine at Syracuse University. The trustees proceeded with a master plan of two-year and four-year colleges throughout the state.

As to other matters, the governor commenced a pioneering study to provide state-required insurance coverage of wage earners disabled by accidents unrelated to their work. He also obtained legislation that the commissioners of conservation and health and I developed, creating a water pollution control board and uniting the state department heads to classify the waters of the state and commence a state-aided program for their protection against the pollution of community sewage systems and industrial chemicals. With 36 percent of the state's highways old and worn out, it was two or three years after the war before busy contractors could be induced to undertake necessary work at reasonable cost. Confronted with a 41 percent increase in heavy truck traffic, the governor rushed the final planning for a New York State Thruway Authority and accelerated the preliminary work that had begun on stretches of its beautiful uninterrupted road from New York City to the state's western boundary.

Along with these more tangible concerns, the governor appointed me to a committee to explore the need for state assistance to libraries, saying in his message to the legislature, "I would like very much to see us help the libraries. I think the librarians, aside from the clergy, are the most underpaid people in America. Moreover, through no fault of the libraries, they are not keeping up with the times and if the communities won't or can't provide the money, I think the state ought to help." Ralph Beals, director of the New York Public Library, Harold Hacker, deputy director of the Erie County Public Library, James Allen, executive assistant to the Commissioner of Education, and I, along with other committee members, hammered out a formula for state support, helping large libraries but also designed to consolidate or federate on a county or multicounty basis the small local libraries and to subsidize balanced book selection that did not depend on "attic clearances" of local residents.

The governor also appointed me to a committee to consider the replacement of the Civil Service Commission by a unitary head of the department. It led to a compromise, strengthening the administrative powers of the commission chairman but preserving the commission to review possible abuses. To me it was important as an opportunity to work with John T. DeGraff, a leading Albany lawyer, counsel to the Civil Service Employees Association, and an exemplary draftsman. Like Breitel, he was an instinctive teacher and impressed on me the value of qualifying a statement not only to reduce the likelihood of challenge but because its manifest thoughtfulness would prove more persuasive than a flat or extreme assertion.

Left-wing groups were generally hostile to Governor Dewey. The governor would not treat *The Daily Worker* or *PM* ("the uptown Daily Worker") as newspapers, so they were turned over to me. I also met with the left-wing groups, which, from time to time, demonstrated at the Capitol. But there were two serious episodes. The first occurred when demonstrators seized the Senate chamber. To Breitel, this was shocking, and he would have expelled the demonstrators by force because he believed the legislature was the central feature of a democracy and that it was the elimination of the Reichstag that was the key to Hitler's dictatorship. The governor nevertheless followed others who advocated delay. After letting the demonstrators remain in the Senate but blocking access to them, the governor offered to meet with them in his ceremonial hearing room the following morning. Fortunately, they agreed. After he listened attentively to their complaints, they expressed appreciation and went home.

The second near disaster took place on a Sunday in September 1949, when the singer Paul Robeson persisted in conducting a scheduled pro-

Communist open-air concert and rally in a northern Westchester town that had but one constable. Robeson, now an acknowledged left-wing activist, was supported by busloads of furriers union "guards" armed with baseball bats and other weapons. I served as the intermediary between the state police, the local law enforcement agencies, and the spokesmen for radical groups, with Hagerty handling the press. Local American Legion groups and other anti-Communist groups threatened to break up the assembly. Some local law enforcement officers sympathized with the legionnaires. The governor, in a public statement, directed the county sheriff to protect the constitutional right of assembly and ordered the state police to support him. The sheriff also deputized a large number of police officers from Westchester municipalities. For the most part, the law enforcement agencies kept the groups apart. Robeson sang. Although there were some altercations and some injuries during the departure, prolonged by the persistence of Robeson's guards remaining on the field after their buses left, the stragglers were nevertheless loaded back on to commandeered public buses and sent home, while I received identical, extravagantly anguished phone calls from former Vice President Henry Wallace and Congressman Vito Marcantonio, who represented East Harlem, led the left-wing American Labor Party, and was all but an admitted Communist.

In 1949 one of the last bad outbreaks of poliomyelitis occurred. Tom Moore, who had been my partner in the district attorney's office, had been appointed counsel to the public works department. In May of that year, we both moved to adjoining summer homes at Thompson's Lake, in the Helderberg Mountains west of Albany. After a pleasant two months, both families were stricken with an odd illness and Moore's wife became gravely ill. Fortunately, a nearby nurse recognized polio and believed that was the illness with which we had all been infected. Breaking laws and speed records, I rushed Tom and Dorothy Moore to the hospital in time. She survived, but it took a long time for her to recover from early disabilities.

That fall, I moved my family to Altamont, a small community beneath the Helderberg escarpment about 45 minutes from Albany. Across the street from its few shops, we shared a converted two-family house with the family of a microbiologist, a member of the state health department's crack team that was then developing measures to control outbreaks of influenza. On weekends, he accepted me as a collaborator in his ongoing study of the "alpha formula," the ultimate blending of gin and vermouth. The Altamont railroad station was just across the street, but its usual quiet simply emphasized the community's remoteness. One day, however, there was an exception. As the train from Binghamton was approaching, a car stalled on the railroad crossing. The woman driver nimbly jumped out and joined the spectators. Then she shrieked, "Oh God, my husband is still asleep on the back seat!" Her prayer was heard. The already slowing train stopped. We pushed the car off the tracks without waking her husband.

At first not intending to run for a third term, in 1950 the governor began to place members of his staff in positions where they would have a few years' tenure. Lockwood was appointed to the Public Service Commission. When Ben Feinberg, the Senate majority leader, suffered a severe heart attack, he was appointed chairman of the commission. When Breitel began to explore possibilities in private practice, he found that the partners of most New York City law firms did not realize what the counsel to the governor did. Breitel had been the most important lawyer in the state government, but he received no attractive offers. For some time, my own hope had been for appointment as counsel to the Public Service Commission. This was one of the three top appointive law posts in the state government, with the same salary as counsel to the governor and the solicitor general. Its work was a well-understood specialty. For a would-be litigator, it seemed ideal, with a staff of about 17 lawyers who presented matters before the commission and its examiners, while the counsel himself advised the commission in its meetings and personally argued its appeals in the courts. The post had been kept vacant since its last incumbent was appointed a state supreme court justice. On August 1, the commission appointed me as its counsel.[4] At the end of the year, however, the governor appointed Breitel to the state supreme court and asked me to return as counsel to the governor. The commission then held open my job, expecting me to return after the legislative session and 30-day bill period.

One of the most important benefits of being counsel to the governor was my inclusion in the governor's meetings with the legislative leaders. This informal adaptation of the British cabinet system explained Governor Dewey's exceptional success with the legislature. He and the legislative leaders and the state-elected officers met every Sunday night during the legislative session and once or twice in advance of it. The group also included the budget director, secretary to the governor, counsel to the governor, and the governor's executive assistant (press relations officer). The governor only recommended measures that had unanimous agreement of the legislative leaders. The legislative leaders agreed that these

4. George Shapiro succeeded me as assistant counsel to the governor.

measures would pass without amendment. During the session the governor would add to his program, but each addition first received the same approvals. For 12 years, except for the budget fight in 1949, virtually every recommendation of the governor became law.

After I replaced Breitel, he would sometimes come back to join us, particularly if there were an extraordinarily difficult problem. Cocktails and dinner preceding the meetings relaxed and sometimes enlivened them, but as the informal executive secretary of the group, I did not drink much. (The governor would not let Ben Feinberg drink after his heart attack until he obtained a doctor's prescription, "two ounces spiritus fermenti.") In my first meeting, with the same outspokenness I had used with Breitel, I successfully attacked and ridiculed a proposal of one of the leaders to permit New York banks to "blue line" loans for Harlem businesses—a form of racial discrimination. The next morning the governor sent for me and in a friendly way explained that he liked brashness in young lawyers but that Breitel had gained the respect of the legislative leaders by limiting his early discussions to points of law. As they gained confidence in him, he said, the leaders began to invite his views on policy questions. He suggested that I follow that example. I realized, but sometimes forgot, what an appointed government official, no matter how important, must learn—that elected officials are "the government" and that they don't like to be preached to by someone who has never faced the challenge of running for office.

A shocking sex crime aroused a public demand led by the *New York Daily News* for mandatory life sentences for sex offenders. Fortunately, two years earlier the governor had authorized a pioneering study of sex offenders in Sing Sing Prison under the direction of the New York Psychiatric Institute, sponsored by the commissioners of Mental Hygiene and Corrections and the chairman of the Board of Parole. As assistant counsel, I had been the governor's liaison with the group. With this careful study about to be sent to the legislature, the emotional outcry actually resulted in a thoughtful and constructive overhaul of the laws dealing with sex crimes—not just the mindless imposition of mandatory sentences. While a life sentence became possible, it was simply the maximum available as part of a court's discretionary power. The new law, which my office wrote,[5] provided flexibility of sentence for the courts

5. Constance Eberhart of Ithaca, a new law assistant, the first woman lawyer appointed to the legal staff of the governor, was the principal draftsman. She was later elected state senator.

and authorized flexibility of treatment by the departments of Corrections, Mental Hygiene, and Parole. It incidentally eliminated such outmoded penal provisions as those classifying consensual sexual acts, except between adults and children, as felonies. The new law was approved by the press as well as by professional groups and bar associations.

The legislative session was short. Its controversy centered on ending commercial rent control and continuing residential rent control. On the late last night of the session, an attack of influenza, which I had ignored, developed into pneumonia, but a new antibiotic over a weekend had me ready to review bills at home and return to the office within a few days.

During the legislative session, notwithstanding Mrs. Dewey's wishes, the governor began to consider running for a third term. He had unsuccessfully urged General Eisenhower to run.[6] Instead, the general took a leave of absence from his post as president of Columbia University to become the European Commander of the North Atlantic Treaty Organization (NATO). Private polls showed that other Republicans lacked voter recognition; only Dewey offered the leadership for a successful ticket. With the approval of the Public Service Commission, I stayed as counsel to the governor for another year. In September, noting the emergency created three months earlier by the North Korean invasion of South Korea, the governor announced his decision to seek reelection. He had already telegraphed President Truman his full support for sending American assistance to South Korea. General Lucius Clay, who had organized the airlift to Berlin while he was the commander of the U.S. forces in Germany, accepted appointment as chairman of the New York State Civil Defense Commission. The legislature had already approved compacts with neighboring states for mutual aid and support in the event of nuclear attack.

The governor won reelection by a large plurality, slightly less than that in his first reelection. Breitel, running in New York County and the Bronx for election to a full term as a state supreme court justice, was defeated but ran 50,000 votes ahead of the other Republican judicial candidates. The governor reappointed him to another vacancy and at the next election, all parties nominated him for a full 14-year term.

During my first year as counsel, I had been working with a program that had been largely developed by Breitel. In 1951, I had the full responsibility and wrote the first draft of the governor's message to the

---

6. Richard Norton Smith, Thomas E. Dewey and His Times 553-65 (Simon and Shuster 1982).

legislature, which, although much shortened by Elliott Bell's sympathetic editing, was a coherent statement of the governor's achievements. A special message also addressed the drastic measures to be taken to prepare for a possible atomic attack on New York if Russia entered the Korean War. Because New York was believed to be a likely target, my most exacting job, assisted by the Civil Defense Commission, had been to prepare a model defense emergency act distributing the powers of state government in the event the legislature could not act. The bill's 13,000 words addressed the seizure of private property, conservation of banks and insurance companies, and even conscription for civil defense. It distributed the emergency powers among the governor, a defense emergency commission, and a broader-based bipartisan defense council.[7]

The governor's emergency message accompanying the bill acknowledged that "The bill . . . makes no effort to mask its repulsiveness." Its drastic provisions at first received harsh editorial criticism. Walter Winchell headed his column "Heil Dewey." The governor requested the legislature to withhold action for 30 days while he sent the bill to all of the state's mayors, boards of supervisors, local civil defense directors, and bar associations for scrutiny. Frank Moore, the new, strong lieutenant governor, convened the state's leading municipal officers and lawyers to review the bill. As its proponent, I presented the bill at a meeting of this group, suggested a few changes, responded to criticism, and received the solid commendation of the lieutenant governor and the other conferees. The bill, with few amendments, passed the legislature. It subsequently became a model for many states. After the shock subsided, most agreed that the bill's specificity was necessary as an educational measure as well as a sound legislative basis for the drastic authority it conferred.

Other measures of importance were somewhat overshadowed and shunted to weekends, but they nevertheless received full attention. No matter how complicated, if a measure required the governor's approval, it required his counsel's full-scale review. For example, highly technical changes in the required reserves for life insurance policies, the transfer of New York City's airports to the Port of New York Authority, and the resolution of basic leasing disputes between airlines and the authority had previously been handled by Breitel. I now had responsibility for analyzing the recommendations of a distinguished commission for the creation of an authority to take over the Long Island Railroad after two

7. Milton Alpert, a Columbia classmate, was lent by the state comptroller to be my principal assistant.

wrecks, with many people killed, made it obvious that the railroad's revenues were not enabling it to maintain safe service.

Of more immediate personal concern to the governor, I prepared his response to a dangerous threat of a hostile exposure of corruption within the state. In March, Senator Estes Kefauver, chairman of the U.S. Senate committee investigating organized crime in interstate commerce, invited the governor to testify before the committee at its New York City meeting. We knew the interrogation would center on gambling and corruption in Saratoga Springs, resulting from the long-standing indulgence of a few upstate political leaders and from the unique double boundary of that city. The city police took responsibility only for its inner boundary. The state police, a statewide force of only 600, by long-standing policy, policed only the highways and areas outside of cities. Between the two boundaries, gambling flourished so openly as to suggest corruption. No matter how the governor explained the problem, he would be subject to excruciatingly embarrassing cross-examination by Kefauver and a shrewish Senator Charles W. Tobey of New Hampshire, the ranking minority member of the committee. Yet if the governor refused to testify, he would be harshly criticized for refusing cooperation in exposing crime and perhaps for condoning it.

We solved the dilemma in three steps. First, at my suggestion, the governor explained that he could not leave Albany in the closing days of the legislative session. As an alternative, he invited the committee to Albany and offered to put them up as guests at the executive mansion. This, of course, did not fit in with the committee's schedule and would have deprived it of the more extensive publicity offered in the city of New York. The committee declined the invitation. A few editorials criticized the governor as stuffy but nothing worse.

Simultaneously, the governor, through the attorney general, superseded the district attorney of Saratoga County and appointed a special assistant attorney general to investigate possible criminal relationships between organized gambling and public officials. Then, most important, the governor established a New York state crime commission headed by former judge Joseph Proskauer, which, over two years, exposed organized crime in several areas, including particularly the New York City waterfront. Its counsel was first John Harlan, then, after his federal court appointment, Theodore Kiendl. In place of the governor, the superintendent of state police testified before the Kefauver committee and made a good-faith effort to explain the restraints upon the state police, but he was pilloried by Tobey, and to some extent by Kefauver. When Kefauver sent the superintendent's testimony to the governor, I reported on it and supported the superintendent. The governor sent my report on the testimony as well as these other actions to Senator Kefauver. Kefauver thanked the governor for it and commended the governor for his action.

Finally, after the completion of one of the most demanding single years of my work as a lawyer, the governor approved my return to the Public Service Commission. Breitel had served longer than anyone else as counsel to the governor—seven years. I had served longer than anyone else in the combined posts of counsel and assistant counsel.

Chapter 9
THE PUBLIC INTEREST

The Public Service Commission

Leaving the governor's office, I undertook two noncriminal law enforcement assignments in which I was responsible for protecting the public interest, first as counsel to the New York Public Service Commission, then as executive director of the Waterfront Commission of New York Harbor. Both were short term; both were rewarding; but both had to be left uncompleted. By making these moves, I lost touch with two of Governor Dewey's most important concluding achievements, the final organization of a true state university and his preservation, for a few more decades, of a moderate Republican Party by persuading General Eisenhower to seek the nomination for president and then leading the movement to ensure his success.

The initial successes of the Korean War had been offset by hostile Chinese intervention. The Soviet Union, however, remained ostensibly neutral, and the fear of nuclear attack never materialized. The war had turned into a bitter, casualty-heavy standoff along a line across the center of the Korean peninsula. It did not, however, evoke state and civilian activity comparable to World War II.

After Eisenhower accepted appointment as European Commander of the North Atlantic Treaty Organization, Dewey, as well as other leading Republicans, continued to press him to seek the nomination for president. While Senator Henry Cabot Lodge of Massachusetts loosely coordinated their efforts, Governor Dewey, General Lucius Clay, and Herbert Brownell personally tried to persuade him to run. Dewey also supported Richard Nixon as Eisenhower's running mate after being impressed by an eloquent extemporaneous after-dinner speech.[1] Finally, as the convention neared, Eisenhower permitted Brownell to take charge of his cam-

1. Richard Norton Smith, Thomas E. Dewey and His Times, *supra*, 584 et seq.

paign and challenge Robert Taft's large number of committed delegates. For the first time, television became an effective factor. As Brownell, assisted by Bill Rogers, skillfully challenged the Taft delegations from some southern states as illegally selected, television exposed the controversy, blow by blow, to the entire electorate. After the convention adopted rules permitting displacement of the autocratically selected delegations, public reaction to the scandal shook many convention delegates, even some leaning to Taft. In spite of bitter attacks on Dewey by Taft adherents, Eisenhower was nominated. He selected Nixon as his running mate.

After the convention, the New York Republican state chairman asked me to be state campaign chairman but Ben Feinberg, then chairman of the Public Service Commission, advised me against it. He was concerned that, in campaign-fund distribution, I might be drawn into questionable activities by local leaders. For my part, although I had dealt with many of the county leaders while in the governor's office, I was not anxious to get into full-time state campaign or party responsibilities. From past experience, while I liked street-level politics, I had a negative view of campaign headquarters work. For every hard worker there seemed to be a hanger-on, and many committed volunteers were unfamiliar with government. While I admired Brownell, now national campaign chairman, we were never close. He and Breitel kept their distance, as Brownell drew a sharp line between Dewey's political allies and his staff members. Having finally returned to the Public Service Commission, I regarded it as a sort of "halfway house" on the road back to private practice, perhaps upstate. I had no interest whatever in going to Washington. While I profoundly admired Eisenhower for his wartime accomplishments, I had no first-hand views of his Columbia presidency. I was not then an active Columbia alumnus. My interest in Eisenhower derived from my loyalty to Dewey.

Nevertheless, the governor, directly or through campaign officials, continued to give me assignments. During the campaign, I was asked to determine the legality of the fund that Nixon had accumulated from private contributions to cover some of his travel and miscellaneous office expenses. I concluded that if it was for personal rather than political purposes, it was illegal and sent a memorandum to that effect. I pointed out, however, that the Democratic presidential candidate, Adlai Stevenson, as governor of Illinois, also had a fund that was probably illegal. I suggested that the Republicans call for Governor Stevenson to appoint an independent counsel to investigate.

Instead, Nixon, assisted by Bill Rogers, who had been assigned to him after the Republican convention, executed a brilliant tour de force by facing the nation on television, acknowledging the fund but earnestly stating that neither the fund nor his intent were illegal. Instead, he claimed the fund was solely for legal political purposes, such as travel to assist other California candidates. He captured enormous public support as he dropped to the level of the average listener and pointed out that his wife did not have a mink coat and by vowing not to return Checkers, a cocker spaniel that had been given to his children. Eisenhower, who had remained aloof, welcomed him at their next meeting, putting his arm around him and calling him "my boy."

While being counsel to the New York Public Service Commission might seem an anticlimax, it was an enviable post because of its independence and the consistent importance of its work. With exclusive responsibility for the commission's litigation, and because the commission had such extensive power, it was particularly respected by upstate lawyers and by the upstate judges who regularly reviewed commission decisions. By 1943, when Governor Dewey first arrived in Albany, the Public Service Commission had become the ultimate consolidation of the regulatory commissions established in the early days of the century at the urging of Governor Charles Evans Hughes in response to his exposure of scandals growing out of the grants and abuse of monopoly franchises. While preceded by the Interstate Commerce Commission, these state commissions pioneered the establishment of standards for monopoly regulation. Their combined jurisdiction, consolidated in the Public Service Commission, was broader than any federal regulatory agency because it extended to all monopolies serving the public: railroads, electric and gas utilities, telephone companies, water companies, motor carriers, and intercommunity bus and transit systems. Charged to protect the public by requiring adequate service at reasonable rates, the standard was "the public interest."

While the commission responded to complaints, its major undertaking was the vigilant oversight of accounting and finance to ensure that the regulated companies received a reasonable return—but nothing more—on their private investment. This required a hard-boiled calculation of the private property dedicated to the public interest (the rate base) and an allowance of an appropriate financial return on this property (the rate of return). Under the former chairman, Milo Maltbie, the commission had helped to establish reasonable rate bases so that the commissioners appointed by Governor Dewey were in the enviable position of determining a rate of return for an already clean rate base.

This reduced, somewhat, the bitterness formerly present between the utility companies and the commission. The appeals from commission rate orders were fewer in number and more limited in scope. But while most of the utilities accepted the commission's determination that a rate base should be computed on the basis of its original cost less depreciation, New York Telephone Company and a few others were prepared to claim that, to escape unconstitutional confiscation, it was necessary to constantly recompute the rate base by determining its present value rather than its original cost. The commission consistently rejected this contention, arguing that by allowing a higher rate of return on original cost, it avoided confiscation and also avoided the wasteful hearings that would be necessary if it were to be dependent upon conflicting expert opinions of present value rather than a hard, established record of actual investment.

This fortunate state of affairs eased my entry into an otherwise strange field. Although a collision with the New York Telephone Company would be inevitable, and the day-to-day hearings before the commissioner who would make the original rate recommendation had started, it was being handled by a former member of the staff who had been specially retained. I broke in on more limited issues. But first I augmented my staff.

The staff already had an excellent reputation. The chief assistant, Sherman Ward, was a respected expert who had more than once served as acting counsel. Approaching retirement, he was glad to have me take over aggressive direction while he supplied, generously, the benefit of years of experience. The staff also included gifted brief writers, as well as those of established ability in conducting hearings and court matters. Nevertheless, having enjoyed the benefit of young law assistants in the governor's office, my first objective was to add to my staff three young lawyers with excellent law school records without requiring them to take a competitive civil service examination. With the approval of friends in the civil service department and the division of budget, I was permitted to hire, as an experiment, at salaries competitive with those then offered by leading law firms, three law assistants to be selected from the top of their classes for terms limited to three years. That year, I recruited two from Harvard and one from Columbia. They were so outstanding that the following year I was permitted to hire more young lawyers, and reach out to Yale (unsuccessfully) and Michigan and Columbia (very successfully). While these young lawyers tended to become my personal staff, they also assisted the older lawyers, who welcomed the infusion. Our office was both happy and effective. We rarely lost.

One of the second group of young lawyers was a top-ranking Stone scholar from Columbia University. She had missed the Law Review selection her first year but had risen near the top of her class thereafter. Strikingly good looking and enthusiastic, she was proudly welcomed by the lawyers and the experts in the regulatory divisions. The commissioners fell into line but, unexpectedly, Chairman Feinberg was at first hesitant. Concerned in a fatherly way both for her and for me, he sternly lectured me on my responsibility for bringing such an attractive young woman to Albany. If anything untoward happened to her, he warned, I would be responsible and, less directly, so would he. Having brought the first woman on to the governor's legal staff without dire consequences, I gave him my judgment that we could safely take the risk.

Relieved from the more nagging tension of the governor's office, I enjoyed the next two years as I did my last year in the district attorney's office. My relationship with my wife and children reached a new level of happiness. Along with the members of the commission, I was accepted into the Fort Orange Club, a congenial combination of state officials and local leaders. Because so many top state officials were really transients, their acceptance into the club by its permanent local members supplied a valuable sense of community. Many judges holding court in Albany lived out of town. The state judicial districts and departments that included Albany also included several other counties. The state's highest court, the court of appeals, sat in Albany but was composed largely of nonresidents. To some extent, the club dissolved the restraints between the judges and the commissioners subject to their review. Still accustomed to the impersonal attitudes of a big city, I was surprised when, on the eve of an appellate division argument, one of the five judges had jokingly disclosed to one of my commissioners the question with which one of the other judges intended to confront me. When, at the argument, I delivered a succinct and conclusive three-point answer to that question, the other four judges suppressed their grins.

During my first brief service with the commission before the governor recalled me to be his counsel, I had taken particular interest in a proceeding against the New York Central Railroad to stop broadcasting its Christmas jingles and commercials in the then-serene Grand Central terminal. Passengers waiting to enter the train platforms were forced to listen to the advertisements. In the hearing before one of the commissioners, we claimed that the right to be free of compelled listening was a counterpart of the constitutional right of free speech and that the railroad's franchise did not include the right to compel passengers to listen to material unrelated to transportation. The railroad depended upon a survey that purported to show that the majority of passengers enjoyed the broadcasts. On cross-examination, however, those who conducted the survey admitted that they had not questioned anyone who was reading. A Columbia University sociologist, Professor Paul Lazarsfeld, an expert in surveys, testified that such a survey was so distorted that it was valueless. Harold Ross, the editor of *The New Yorker*, one of the complainants, testified. When asked by railroad counsel whether *The New Yorker* was a comic book for adults, he parried the characterization as "to say the least, heavy-handed." After the hearing we convinced railroad counsel that the broadcasts desecrated the Grand Central terminal as it then was and the railroad voluntarily gave up the program. This was fortunate, because when a similar complaint about commercial jingles on the District of Columbia trolley cars reached the U.S. Supreme Court, it held that there was no constitutional right that protected the riders from this abuse. Justice Felix Frankfurter abstained because, he wrote, he was so deeply distressed by the programs.

In the fall of the year when I returned from the governor's office, I feasted on appellate litigation. Within a span of a month, I had two successful arguments before the appellate division of the state supreme court and one in the court of appeals (upholding the abolition of submetered electric rates, which had permitted building owners to buy power at large-volume rates and resell it to tenants at higher rates; a telephone rate increase; and jurisdiction over intrastate fares of an interstate carrier). Before the U.S. Supreme Court, however, I was not so lucky. The New Haven Railroad, by a motion to affirm, secured the dismissal of the commission's appeal from a lower-court opinion upholding Interstate Commerce Commission rates for intrastate passengers, permitting the New Haven to charge Westchester passengers the same rate per mile as Connecticut passengers, while giving the Westchester riders inferior service and crowding them three to a seat in slower and less comfortable trains. Justices Hugo Black and William O. Douglas dissented.

The following year, I successfully obtained a writ of prohibition against a state supreme court justice to keep him and the city of New York from interrupting a commission proceeding on a request to discontinue passenger service by the Staten Island Rapid Transit Railway Company, a subsidiary of the Baltimore & Ohio Railroad. After the appellate division unanimously denied my petition, the court of appeals unanimously reversed the appellate division, announcing its decision in three days, with opinion to follow. The commission and its staff were elated.

Some of our litigation was before and sometimes against federal agencies. The Federal Power Commission, created during the New Deal, was aggressive and well represented; we were concerned to protect our jurisdiction as New York became increasingly dependent on natural gas transported interstate in high-pressure lines. When interstate pipelines first came into the state, they created safety problems. Gas under high pressure burst directly into the distribution lines of a Rochester gas company, blew up a number of homes, and killed and injured residents. On another occasion, my commission had to block plans to lay a high-pressure pipeline under a schoolyard. It established general safety requirements. We settled most of our conflicts with the federal agency by negotiation.

The Interstate Commerce Commission, in contrast, was extremely protective of its railroads. When the Pennsylvania Railroad Company, as sole parent, requested that the ICC set aside the intrastate rates of the Long Island Railroad fixed by the Public Service Commission, I appeared in opposition, but Chairman Feinberg, who never quite overcame his instincts as a state senator, asked to make a brief introductory comment. One commissioner, well known as a railroad sympathizer, seized the opportunity to draw Feinberg into a series of questions that consumed our time but for which Feinberg was unprepared. I agonized until the commission finally let Feinberg sit down. In the time that was left, I abbreviated my argument, but the commission decided against us and authorized an increase in the Long Island Railroad rates to lift a "burden on interstate commerce."

I resorted to legislation by having a congressman from Nassau County introduce a bill to divest the Interstate Commerce Commission of jurisdiction over intrastate rates. In a rough-and-tumble hearing before the House Commerce Committee, we so impressed the general counsel of the Pennsylvania Railroad that he agreed that if we would not press the legislation, he would accept the rates fixed by the Public Service Commission. He and I became friends and we thereafter worked cooperatively together.

On yet another occasion, I turned to state legislation. The Allied Chemical Company owned a small illuminating gas company serving part of the City of Buffalo. This subsidiary contracted with another Allied subsidiary to buy all of the coke it used to manufacture illuminating gas. The price was excessive but, because the utility was entitled to recover its operating expenses plus a rate of return, the commission could not reduce its rates to the level being charged by a neighboring independent utility. Residents on one side of a street were paying gas rates substantially higher than residents on the other side. Allied and its subsidiary would not negotiate. I drafted a bill that was introduced by an assemblyman from Buffalo providing that a corporation controlling a utility, and its affiliates, were subject to the jurisdiction of the Public Service Commission as though they were utilities. This would include review of financial structure. Apparently Allied did not notice the bill as it passed on the last day of the legislative session after I had cleared it with my successor as counsel to the governor.

As the governor was about to sign the bill, Leighton Coleman, a Davis Polk partner and counsel for Morgan Stanley, telephoned me and asked whether I thought the bill would be approved. I told him I thought it would. Morgan Stanley was the lead investment banker for Allied in what was to be the largest private security offering up until that time. Subjecting Allied to commission regulation could have a serious effect upon the offering. When Allied's outside bond counsel, General Donald Swatland of the Cravath firm, and Allied's general counsel called on me, I explained the background of the bill and predicted that the commission would deregulate Allied if the prohibitive supply contract for coke were abrogated. The Allied general counsel wanted me to enter into an agreement to that effect. I refused to go beyond my prediction. I believed I knew what the commission would do and I promised to recommend it. General Swatland acquiesced and said, "These are the promises men live by." The coke contract was abrogated and the commission deregulated Allied. I believe Allied ultimately sold the gas company.

In 1953, after Eisenhower's election, U.S. Supreme Court Chief Justice Fred Vinson died. Governor Dewey called me to his office to join a group of his old advisers to consider whether he should accept appointment as Chief Justice. Our unanimous view was that he should not; that, having been a reform leader and powerful executive, judicial neutrality and the cumbersomeness of a nine-member court would frustrate him. He agreed. President Eisenhower appointed Governor Earl Warren of California, who later would amuse listeners as he described his initial dismay transferring from a powerful governorship to a personal staff that at first consisted of one messenger.

It is, of course, tempting to speculate on the course of the court if Dewey had been Chief Justice. Would he have had a relationship with Justice Douglas and Justice Brennan comparable to that of Warren? Probably not. Would he have attempted to intervene regarding Brennan's appointment? While firmly against vestiges of racial discrimination, would he have been equally supportive of antitrust enforcement or the expanding protections of the rights of defendants in criminal cases? Once he settled in, he would have been a powerful advocate for his positions and determined in his efforts to expose waste and unnecessary congestion in the court system.

The Waterfront Commission

As good things must come to an end, Governor Dewey called me to his office in September 1953 and invited me to leave the Public Service Commission and become the first executive director of the Waterfront Commission of New York Harbor, a bistate commission newly established by New York and New Jersey. He suggested that it had greater promise than my present job and that the two commissioners, both retired generals, needed someone who understood regulatory commissions and criminal investigation. I was not sure I wanted more government work. I had already begun to explore private practice and had talked with one prospective partner and with a few older lawyers, including Randall Le Boeuf, who had left government office to found a leading utility law firm. Nevertheless, I respected the governor's judgment and I agreed to talk with the new commissioners. By leaving the Public Service Commission, I would have to forego argument of the appeal of the basic regulatory issue in the developing New York Telephone Company rate case, whether a rate base could be calculated on original cost rather than present fair value. While I was completely self-assured in my relationship with the Public Service Commission and the state courts before which I appeared, should I forego this familiar turf to take on the racket-controlled International Longshoremen's Association entrenched in the city of New York and nearby New Jersey communities?

In 1953, before there were commercial jet aircraft and container ships, New York Harbor accommodated 12,000 deep-sea vessels a year, flying the flags of 170 steamship lines. Along its hundreds of miles of shoreline were 1,500 piers and wharves, 200 of which accommodated deep-sea shipping. Of the 150 million tons of freight that moved across its waters each year, 35 million represented foreign trade, one half of the dollar volume of the country's ocean-borne international commerce. More than 13 million people, almost one-tenth of the population of the United States, lived within 25 miles of the Statue of Liberty; one out of every 10 wage earners held a job related to the harbor.

New York's longshoremen were perhaps the most competent in the world, but criminal control of the local units of the International

Longshoremen's Association (ILA), their bargaining agent, had imposed such a tyrannical system of extortion and bribery that it was diverting traffic to other ports. Disdaining any pretense of democracy, union locals served as agencies for the enrichment of their officials and those who controlled them. Local leaders made deals and forced them on the longshoremen. Rebellious longshoremen called "quickie" strikes that left cargo stranded and, if it was perishable, rotting. Three stoppages in 1946, four in 1947, one in 1948, three in 1949, three in 1950, and five in 1951 cost hundreds of thousands of man-days.

The steamship lines subcontracted the loading and unloading of the vessels to stevedores, local corporations that served as go-betweens and made individual deals and payoffs. The New York Shipping Association, which represented steamship companies and stevedores in collective bargaining, had adapted itself to the realities. Ship owners, accustomed to getting their ships in and out of ports all over the world, were not particularly concerned with local immorality but, in New York, payments of accommodation did not ensure prompt discharge of cargo.

The corrupt elements, Irish gangsters on the Hudson River piers and the Mafia on those of the East River and Brooklyn, enforced their control through two strangleholds: the "shape up" and the "public loader." More than 40,000 longshoremen sought 20,000 jobs. No matter how long a vessel was at a pier, at 8:00 A.M. each day, there would be a shape up as applicants for work lined up before the pier hiring agent who selected those who would work that day. The hiring agent, supposedly acting for the employer, was in fact selected by the thugs who controlled the local union. Disregarding seniority or rotation, he picked those who paid bribes or those who were in debt to loan sharks who paid bribes. Some favorites only applied for work on days when there was overtime, displacing regulars previously hired.

Public loading was only slightly more sophisticated. The harbor's aging "finger" piers could not accommodate trucks. Cargo was unloaded and loaded piece by piece or on pallets at the mouth of the pier. In earlier days, truckers had hired persons whom they found at the mouth of the piers to help them, but corrupt union leaders formed corporations to monopolize this loading activity. At first they performed the service; later they simply extorted a fee and left each trucker to load or unload the truck himself. Unless the fee was paid, the cargo would not move.

Work stoppages were used indiscriminately to improve wages and working conditions and to protect the private interests of the individuals who controlled the union and the pier. Rebelliousness invited serious retaliation. Handling heavy items of cargo with baling hooks and swinging one-ton netloads of cargo over the heads of those working in the ship's hold constantly threatened injury. Particularly troublesome agitators were murdered gangland style.

When a two-year investigation by the New York State Crime Commission exposed the extent of these evils, the governors of New York and New Jersey convened extraordinary sessions of both state legislatures to authorize a bistate compact to address them. Approved by Congress and signed by President Eisenhower, the compact created a bistate commission to register or license those working on the piers, with power to exclude those with serious criminal records and those guilty of bribes, extortion, assaults, loan sharking, or similar activities. Public loading was forbidden and shape up was eliminated. Hiring for multiple piers was to be conducted under the scrutiny of the commission in information centers operated by the commission. Casuals, those who applied for work less than eight days a month, were to be eliminated. The commission, however, was not empowered to reform the union or to eliminate its thug control.

After requesting that the ILA clean itself and after granting it a hearing at the annual federation meeting, the American Federation of Labor (AFL) expelled the ILA and recognized seceding members as a new union, the International Longshoremen's Association–A F of L.[2] Five trustees, including George Meany, president of the AFL, and the heads of four other AFL unions oversaw the new union. Paul Hall, head of the Seafarers' Union, directed its organization drive. When, on September 30, 1953, the old ILA contract with the Shipping Association expired, the ILA struck all Atlantic ports from Maine to Virginia. Following a declaration of a national emergency under the Taft-Hartley Act, the U.S. District Court for the Southern District of New York enjoined the strike's continuance.

Governor Dewey appointed Lieutenant General George P. Hays as the New York waterfront commissioner. Hays had been awarded the Congressional Medal of Honor in World War I, was an army corps commander in World War II, served as deputy military governor and deputy high commissioner of postwar Germany, and filled the post of commanding general of the U.S. forces in Austria. Governor Alfred Driscoll

2. To avoid confusion, the two unions will be identified as "old ILA" and "AFL."

of New Jersey appointed Major General Edward C. Rose, who had been active in both business and the military. Awarded the distinguished service medal and the legion of merit, he had commanded a regiment and a brigade and served on the 44th division staff in the war. On September 25, I was appointed executive director of the commission—its chief executive officer and, at my request, general counsel.

Hays, while casual, was thoughtful, tough, and forthright. Rose was genial and shrewd. They obviously liked each other and I immediately liked them. They assured me they wanted me to assume leadership. While I recognized the danger of being out in front in a strange field, I was, by now, self-assured, except for a moment of suppressed tension when General Rose told me to open a bank account for the commission; I had never had to handle finances, other than personal matters.

Our most immediate problem was to get enough longshoremen registered to work the port after December 1, the effective date of the compact's substantive prohibitions. Claiming that the compact was unconstitutional, the ILA had instructed its members not to register. On the day I started work, it had struck to compel the employers to recognize it as the sole bargaining agent for pier personnel. Grasping this opportunity, I junked the elaborate registration application our investigators had developed and substituted a simple return postcard-type application—just the name, address, birthdate, and port security number of the applicant. I eliminated fingerprints and even notarization; with a little extra work, we could identify the criminal record of most applicants. We sent the postcards directly to the home of each longshoreman; the principal newspapers carried a facsimile, which we accepted as an alternative application form. Thousands returned their applications. Investigators worked day and night to match them to Coast Guard and FBI fingerprint files. When the ILA realized that nearly half of the longshoremen had registered, it reversed course and instructed its members to apply.

In 65 days we were ready to meet the operative date fixed by the compact. We had inherited a good staff of investigators and accountants from the Crime Commission. General Hays had brought two persons for the commission secretariat. General Rose had only one nominee, the head of the New Jersey department of insurance, whom I welcomed as the director of our information (employment) centers, the key administrative post in the day-to-day operations of the commission. From District Attorney Frank Hogan, I borrowed an outstanding assistant district attorney to head our prosecutorial arm, and I brought in three young lawyers from the Public Service Commission. As we expanded, I added other lawyers with prosecutorial experience.

To deal with the peculiarities of a bistate commission, Austin Tobin, the executive director of the Port of New York Authority, lent me one of the authority's top lawyers, Rosaleen C. Skehan, whom I had known in Albany when, just out of law school, she represented the authority on legislative matters. Tobin had offered her services without bothering to ask her, since she happened to be in Europe. Furious for having been traded without her consent, Skehan nevertheless agreed to stay for three months. (She also forgave Tobin and later married him.) Perhaps the most valuable member of the staff, she understood New Jersey. Through her we retained special counsel highly regarded by the New Jersey governor. She drafted our regulations for administration and hearings. She counterbalanced the investigative and prosecutorial group. She exploded speculation and she deflated all of us when we needed it.

We worked almost every evening. I had not moved my family. I commuted weekends back to Albany on Colonial Air Lines DC-3s. Hearings and meetings with outsiders consumed regular office hours. Once we found an old but secure office building that would accept our clientele, 15 Park Row, we usually had dinner together at Whyte's, a downtown landmark dining establishment just around the corner.

In federal court, the ILA challenged the constitutionality of the bistate compact. I argued the case before a three-judge court, two district judges and one court of appeals judge, which sustained its constitutionality. On direct appeal, the Supreme Court affirmed the decision without oral argument. In the next court showdown, on the eve of the December 1 operative date, a group of public loaders brought an action in the federal district court to suspend their abolition. By then I realized that I could not handle litigation and do my job as executive director. I retained, as special counsel, Whitman Knapp, an appellate expert with whom I had worked in the district attorney's office.[3] The district judge granted a brief stay until the loaders' application could be heard by a three-judge court. A few days later, the court upheld the compact and dismissed the action.

By December 1, we had leased, rebuilt, and staffed the commission's information centers (hiring centers). We had excluded 120 longshore-

3. Whitman Knapp later conducted a highly regarded investigation of the New York City Police Department. Still later he was appointed a U.S. judge for the Southern District of New York.

men with the worst records and had given only temporary registration to many of the others. A total of 787 hiring agents had applied for licenses; we denied 178 and issued temporary licenses to the others. Another 458 had applied for pier superintendent; we tentatively denied 101. During investigation, 241 applications for pier superintendent or hiring agent licenses were withdrawn. The largest stevedore, Jarka Corporation, withdrew its application and went out of business. Only 54 stevedores received permits, and they were temporary. Those expelled from the piers included Michael "Mickey" Bowers, his brother, Harold, and his associate, John Keefe, officers of the "Pistol Local," which controlled the North River "luxury piers" in the West 40s. Also expelled was Daniel St. John, a hiring agent in their area. All had records for felonies; St. John had twice been tried for murder but escaped because of jury disagreements. Also excluded was Albert Ackalitis, alias "Machinegun Kelly," a loft boss on a Canal Street pier and an enforcer for those controlling the Chelsea piers just south of the Bowers territory.

On November 30, the day before the operative date, tugboat captain William Bradley, the ILA national president, and Thomas Gleason, ILA national organizer and head of the checkers' local (those who weighed, measured, and counted each item of cargo), led a delegation to my office from the New York and New Jersey locals, including one of the Bowers brothers and "Tough Tony" Anastasia, the younger brother of the Cosa Nostra family leader, Albert Anastasia, who controlled the East River and Brooklyn piers. Bradley warned me that unless the commission deferred its rulings and permitted those excluded from the piers to work, the ILA would shut down the port. I explained that the commission could not defer the effective date of the statute and that it would not withhold its action. In a series of earlier conferences, I had already alerted law enforcement authorities and had been assured of their support. As my unsmiling visitors sat in a circle around my desk, I was glad that General Hays had ruled out drapes and other office frills. Our old building, with its uncarpeted floors, provided just the right atmosphere for this confrontation. While Bradley did most of the talking, I knew that Gleason and Bowers would make the decisions. They made no further threats. They left, grimly silent. I felt little personal fear because true professionals rarely attack honest public officials. (It was Dutch Schultz's threat to break this code and kill Dewey that led to Schultz's assassination on orders of Charles Luciano.)

On December 1, as the ILA president and organizer moved from pier to pier calling longshoremen off the job, the port was shut down. But the ILA was still under a Taft-Hartley injunction as a result of its earlier strike. The U.S. attorney was the same J. Edward Lumbard, Jr., who had given me my first job. Under his direction, U.S. marshals served every ILA picket with a copy of the Taft-Hartley injunction and a grand jury subpoena. One of his senior assistants started putting ILA representatives before the grand jury. The next day, after the ILA president and national organizer were subpoenaed, they called off the strike. As I faced my first strike, General Hays and General Rose showed their true class and gave me a most tremendous lift. Without any discussion, they simply put on their hats and told me that they were leaving for an inspection trip. They knew I could not reach them. They left me on my own in an ever-appreciated show of confidence.

On December 10, as soon as the court upheld the compact's prohibition of public loaders, we put them out of business in most parts of the port. Sixteen who persisted in continuing this activity were indicted. By February 1, they were all gone.

The AFL effort to displace the ILA local leaders had been following a parallel track. In October, the new AFL union petitioned the National Labor Relations Board (NLRB) to allow it to represent the pier workers, claiming that the old ILA was not a true labor organization but a corrupted servant of the employers. The old ILA intervened. Hurried by an ILA strike threat, the NLRB ordered an election on December 22 and 23, 1953. While the old ILA seemed to have won by a count of 9,060 to 7,568, 4,405 ballots were challenged and one-third of those eligible had not voted. Because the challenged ballots could affect the outcome, the NLRB withheld recognition until the challenges could be resolved. The old ILA threatened to strike unless it was accepted as bargaining agent before January 1. It backed away, however, as Governor Dewey, acting on reports from my commission, the chairman of the state Board of Mediation, and the New York City police commissioner, promised to "take every possible step to repudiate, expose, and prevent intimidation of government agencies by threats from any source." He retained Whitney North Seymour, a leading New York lawyer, to represent the state before the NLRB. We assisted Seymour and AFL counsel with facts.

After an eight-day hearing, the regional director of the NLRB recommended that the election be set aside. He found that leading representatives of the criminal element on the waterfront had acted on behalf of the old ILA, threatening waiting voters with economic reprisals as well as physical harm, and that supervisors who were also officials of the old ILA participated by making threats of economic reprisals. Uncontradicted evidence established stabbings and other assaults at polling places; the constant surveillance of voters by notorious criminal waterfront personalities; and the dispatch by the ILA of several busloads of these persons from Manhattan to Brooklyn, led by Albert Ackalitis and other persons excluded from the piers by the Waterfront Commission. Called before a Kings County grand jury, the president of the old ILA admitted that, at the request of Tony Anastasia, he had sent to Brooklyn up to 400 longshoremen "from uptown"—that is, Mickey Bowers's "pistol local." Bradley testified that while he thought the criminal element should get off the waterfront, he did not believe the ILA had to get them out; "organization-wise, it would not be right. . . I need everybody's help to carry my part out." The grand jury indicted Ackalitis and others, but Ackalitis fled and became a fugitive.

While the election controversy was proceeding to disposition, the organization drive of the AFL led to new tests of strength with the old ILA. The final showdown erupted from a dispute over the election of an AFL shop steward on Ackalitis's old pier, Pier 32, North River. After the ILA walked off the job, the employer fired an AFL shop steward to get them back. The AFL then picketed and members of AFL Teamster Local 807 refused to cross the picket line. The ILA longshoremen then refused to accept deliveries by Local 807 on other piers. At the request of the Shipping Association, the NLRB obtained a federal court injunction of the ILA boycott. The ILA president denounced the NLRB action as discriminatory, because the injunction did not also run against Local 807, which had voluntarily ceased its boycott. The "pistol local" led by Harold Bowers ignored the injunction. On February 26, the ILA announced its real objective—a contract with the Shipping Association—and struck all of its deep-water piers. The Waterfront Commission was expected to be neutral, but neutrality did not come easily. In one of our numerous meetings, Paul Hall, the Seafarer leader, angry because we had placed our employment centers handier to the old ILA local headquarters than those of the AFL, put it succinctly: "Don't be a fucking pussyfooter." Rationalizing that it was our obligation to keep the port open notwithstanding ILA illegal work stoppages, we coordinated closely with the AFL.

The strike continued for five weeks. The AFL longshore union, by now representing several thousand longshoremen, ignored the strike and worked its piers. The old ILA retaliated by having hundreds of pickets block their entry. They assaulted AFL longshoremen almost daily. Thugs threatened families of AFL longshoremen, overturned their automobiles, forced them off the road, stabbed and beat them. At Bush Terminal in

Brooklyn, 300 ILA pickets attempted to rush the gate but were driven back by the police. At other Brooklyn piers, ILA pickets stoned AFL longshoremen and stoned mounted policemen while throwing nails under the hooves of their horses. Elsewhere in Brooklyn, 500 ILA men attacked 100 AFL longshoremen, injuring four. In Hoboken, 250 ILA pickets blocked 100 AFL longshoremen attempting to enter a pier. At the Brooklyn Army Base there were many fistfights as several hundred ILA pickets stabbed AFL men and assaulted the police. ILA mass picketing of AFL piers was commonplace.

The ILA also picketed government institutions. In March, on successive days, there were 500 pickets outside the U.S. courthouse at Foley Square, 125 pickets outside the NLRB regional office at Pershing Square, and again 200 pickets in Foley Square. On East 45th Street, Manhattan, 200 ILA members picketed *The Daily Mirror*. As an extreme defiance, tugboat crews of ILA members cast off the lines of the S.S. *Queen Mary* as she entered the congested Hudson River, forcing her to dock unaided, even though the AFL was not working the Cunard pier. I provided a briefing during an emergency conference with Governor Dewey; U.S. Secretary of Labor James P. Mitchell (representing President Eisenhower); U.S. Deputy Attorney General William Rogers (my former district attorney's office associate); U.S. Assistant Attorney General Warren Burger, then in charge of the Civil Division; and U.S. Attorney Lumbard. It was agreed that Lumbard would coordinate all federal activity.

The commission expedited applications by new longshoremen, and we acted as an intermediary for employers who wanted to work their piers. Many refused, insisting on ILA members or protesting that the AFL produced inexperienced workers. But day by day, even though we could not promise security against ILA retaliation, the AFL gained members and jobs. Protected at times by Hall's husky seafarers, it captured the "breakwater" pier in the Erie terminal in Brooklyn, perhaps the largest single pier in the city, and the pride of Tony Anastasia. It then took Pier 84, a luxury-liner pier serving the American Export Line, from the Mickey Bowers gang. I supplied information to the AFL of hostile ILA movements. Over a tapped telephone at a bar and grill frequented by the Bowers gang, we learned that their hoodlums were bound for a Yonkers sugar refinery pier. As they rushed to Yonkers, the American Export Line agreed to take willing AFL longshoremen at Pier 84. The AFL entered the unguarded pier and then held it with the support of Paul Hall's seamen.

On April 1, the NLRB, acting on the recommendation of its trial examiner, set aside the December election and ordered a new one. It ordered the ILA to desist from thwarting the legal processes of the board under penalty of forfeiting its place on the ballot. By then my commission had suspended many pier workers for misconduct during the course of the strike. The ILA tried to turn the strike away from the NLRB and against my commission by conditioning the cessation of the strike upon the commission's rescinding its suspensions. Reading this in the evening edition of the morning newspapers, I woke up Whitman Knapp and had him come to my hotel room to plan an application for an injunction. After working the rest of the night, he obtained a court order restraining the ILA from striking against the commission. The ILA president, failing to vacate the order, ordered his men back to work. The strike was over. By then, one-third of the harbor's piers were using AFL longshoremen.

After we expelled 143 persons guilty of illegal acts during the strike from the piers, we assisted the NLRB and the U.S. attorneys as they prosecuted old ILA leaders for criminal contempt of the federal court injunction. Several were sentenced to the federal house of detention for six months and the old ILA was subjected to a substantial fine.

Some urged giving the commission power to remove union officers. We opposed these suggestions as a possible unconstitutional intrusion upon freedom of association. While the outcome of the AFL effort was uncertain, we were satisfied with our achievements: the identification and removal of most of the leaders of those who had actively coerced longshoremen and the public exposure of the self-centered indifference of the old ILA leaders and the unwillingness of certain large steamship lines to resist the mob. Regardless of the ultimate outcome of the election, the AFL had shown to the union members that the mob could be beaten. Its longshoremen had captured control of Port Newark, the great breakwater pier, and other important piers; 5,000 longshoremen had defied the waterfront thugs and passed through picket lines. Governor Dewey, Governor Robert Meyner (Driscoll's successor), Attorney General Brownell, and Secretary Mitchell had fused a successful team of government agencies to confront and defeat an arrogant and brutal group of thugs. Further upheavals were to be expected, because we had only begun to weed out the criminals. In speeches, I argued that the certainty of further upheavals was not a reason for discouragement; they would speed reform rather than delay it.

The second NLRB election was orderly. On August 27, 1954, the NLRB finally certified a chastened old ILA as bargaining agent. Of over 30,000 votes cast, it won by a mere 500. The closeness of the result promised that in the future, the rank and file would control the union. This proved to be true. Over the next 10 years, there were no quickie strikes or significant work stoppages.

When, in time, the Manhattan and Brooklyn piers were abandoned, it was not the fault of the longshore force. Instead, a North Carolina trucker named Malcom McLean had conceived of a container ship that would carry 35-foot prepacked containers loaded directly from truck trailers driven alongside the ships. His old rebuilt ships proved him right. Other steamship lines quickly followed him. Since the obsolete finger piers of Manhattan and Brooklyn could not accommodate the procession of trucks or the derricks to lift the containers, the ships moved to Port Elizabeth, New Jersey, for modern facilities and to escape the traffic congestion in New York City streets.

A few weeks after the port went back to work, Governor Dewey surprised me by offering me one of two newly created federal judgeships for the Southern District of New York, the most prestigious trial court in the country, the court in which Learned and Augustus Hand began their careers, followed by other greats such as Hough and Knox. Despite its tradition of excellence, the court was still relatively small, underpaid, and overworked. Its heavy workload and the low salary awarded to federal judges had protected it from idling politicians. As the governor and I talked, I made a rapid evaluation. I would have liked another six months to complete my work for the Waterfront Commission and to select my successor, but I realized that closure was rarely possible in political matters and an opportunity missed is often lost forever. Accordingly, I told the governor that I would accept the appointment.

The next morning I told General Hays and General Rose of my decision. General Hays was disappointed and urged me to reconsider. He felt that my future was too promising to rush to a judgeship. General Rose, on the other hand, was helpful. He said, "George, remember how you felt when you were given the first star." Hays laughed. They both shook hands with me and took me to lunch at India House, their favorite downtown club. I promised them that I would delay my swearing-in as long as I could.

As I thought more about it, I reassured myself. The commission was well established. No one had expected me to stay on after its work became routine. But a few months more would have been ideal, particularly to pick an outstanding successor. In doing this, I hurried and made a bad mistake. Having been impressed by a lawyer for a stevedore because he seemed bright, articulate, confident, familiar with the waterfront, and committed to reform—and because he had, with two other lawyers, opened a thriving law firm—I introduced him to the commissioners. They liked him, and on my recommendation and over the concerns of our chief accountant, who was still appalled by the false books of his stevedore client, they gave him my job. Later, he proved to have neither courage nor leadership and to be cozying up to waterfront clients. When, with my warning, Governor Dewey later convened a meeting of the commissioners with those responsible for the commission's creation, my successor made a fool of himself and embarrassed the commission as he naïvely argued an antireform line in a debate with me before the governor.

After I was confirmed, Chief Judge Knox let me delay my arrival at the court until July 25. Riding to work in the subway, I met Hiram Todd, for whom I had worked in the Drukman investigation. He congratulated me but almost severely told me that he did not want me to jump from the judgeship to any other job, emphasizing his respect for the court to which I had been appointed. I assured him I had no intention of leaving once I got there.

Chapter 10
UNITED STATES DISTRICT JUDGE

In late July 1954, in the brief, traditional ceremony of the U.S. Court for the Southern District of New York, I took my oath as a U.S. district judge. Without speeches, the robed judges of the court ascended the bench of the largest courtroom. The clerk read my commission as I stood in the well of the court. Acting Chief Judge Goddard, presiding because of Chief Judge Knox's ill health, administered the oath. A court attendant helped me on with my robe and led me to the most junior seat on the bench. Judge Goddard then adjourned court. I shook hands with my new colleagues. The staff of the Waterfront Commission had given me my judicial robe and almost all of them were present. Court of Appeals Judge John Harlan, who had formerly been counsel to the New York State Crime Commission and who was later appointed to the Supreme Court, sat among the spectators. My family and friends then met briefly in my borrowed chambers.

Built during the Depression, the elegant U.S. Courthouse was just beginning to be overcrowded. Its first six floors housed the U.S. attorney and the court clerk; the 20-story tower above held the handsome, high-ceilinged courtrooms, two to every other floor. Above the courtrooms were the individual chambers of the judges. I was the first judge who found the original chambers already full. Until one became vacant, I worked in a suite of offices on the 10th floor.

The other judges were friendly but we worked independently, rarely discussing cases with each other. Our informal daily meeting place was the 26th-floor cafeteria. There, while the U.S. attorney's staff had a large room, the district judges and court of appeals judges mingled in a smaller one. While active politics was not a part of court life, a group of elderly Republican judges welcomed the first of the Eisenhower infusion. Judge Goddard took me in hand and introduced me to his oldest colleagues, including former chief judges Learned Hand and Thomas Swan. Hand was indisputably the country's outstanding judge. Most believed he should have been on the U.S. Supreme Court, an appointment he narrowly missed during the Calvin Coolidge administration. In some ways his freedom to display his sagaciousness on a smaller court where he was revered may have been to his advantage and that of the country. His opinions were not easy reading—he wrote every word in longhand, without the intervention of law clerks. A protégé of reformer C.C. Burlingham and a losing candidate as Theodore Roosevelt's Bull Moose Party's nominee for the New York State Court of Appeals, he welcomed fresh political insights.

Among the more recent appointees, I soon became friendly with Harold Medina, who had taught me in law school and who had become well known as the district judge who presided over such major trials as the investment banking antitrust case and one of the first trials of Communist leaders. Also with Jerome Frank, a Yale Law School professor to whom I gravitated after his thoughtful dissent from the affirmance of my dismissal of a derivative stockholders' case. Among the district judges, I soon came to recognize Edward Weinfeld and Ned Dimock as models of judicial temperament. Archie Dawson, an important member of the Young Republican early reform group and a leading New York lawyer, appointed the same time I was, shared my interest in court administration.

Entitled to a personal staff of three, I brought my secretary from the Waterfront Commission and as my first law clerk, the young woman who had started with me in the Public Service Commission and followed me to the Waterfront Commission. As a bailiff, I appointed a second law clerk, another young woman just out of law school. I was the first judge to use the bailiff's position for a second law clerk, giving each bailiff the option of a second year as a law clerk. All of them chose to serve two years. Because a bailiff's salary was less than that of a law clerk, I had a recruiting handicap competing with other judges who used only one law clerk. As a result, I had several excellent female law clerks because in 1954 women were still at a professional disadvantage.

With a 10,000-case backlog and with some cases many years old, the court still had a central calendar system. Except for proceedings that were likely to be very extended and complex, such as corporate reorganizations and admiralty limitation of liability proceedings, an individual judge was not responsible for a case until it was assigned to him for trial. Under the rules of the court, a corporate reorganization or limitation proceeding was permanently assigned to the judge who heard the first motion. An unassigned case could lie dormant for years unless the lawyers moved it for trial or sought dismissal. Pretrial motions in unassigned cases were presented to whichever of the 19 judges happened to be sitting in the motion part. Several judges might rule on different motions related to the same case. There was no effective pretrial case management. While other federal courts were shifting to an individual calendar system in which each case was assigned to a judge when it was filed, most of the judges on my court were unconvinced of the value of pretrial control and resisted this advance. A few preferred a system that masked indifferent productivity. Still competitive, I was determined to be one of the most productive judges. The secret, I believed, was to avoid reserving decision. This meant that my law clerks and I would prepare ourselves in advance of every trial and every motion and I would try to decide each matter from the bench after hearing argument.

I was immediately thrown into the motion part. During the summer, before the introduction of efficient air-conditioning, courts in New York closed or reduced their activity. Once a week, one of the most junior judges handled accumulated motions. (A motion was simply a formal request for relief and could range from discovery motions, such as a request to set the date of a deposition, to a request to dismiss a case.) Over 100 motions would accumulate each week. My law clerks and I took the initiative. Calling every lawyer, we sifted out motions to be postponed and discovery motions that I could handle without extensive preparation. For more demanding motions, we requested extra copies of briefs and motion papers. By working through the previous weekend, I could finish a motion day with only a dozen undecided matters that required a written opinion.

One decision, however, for which I carefully wrote an opinion led to my first reversal. In a state court a principal recovered a judgment against a fraudulent agent who had defended himself by charging that the agreement with the principal was void and a violation of the antitrust laws. The trial court dismissed the defense and awarded judgement for the principal. The agent appealed to higher state courts and simultaneously commenced an antitrust suit in the federal court, renewing the same claim on which he had lost in the state court. I enjoined the prosecution of the federal case as duplicative of the state case then on appeal in the state courts. When the agent appealed from my decision, the court of appeals ordered me to vacate my injunction, holding that I had failed to give proper obeisance to a federal court's duty to protect the federal antitrust laws from state intrusion. Each of the three judges wrote a separate opinion. Learned Hand voted for a mandamus to direct me to reverse my action. Ned Dimock, sitting by assignment, held my decision appealable and voted to reverse it. Harold Medina dissented and voted to affirm my decision. Somewhat dismayed, I consoled myself that at least my first reversal had been by a great judge. I became especially grateful to Judge Medina, who frequently agreed with me and once claimed that I owed him an annual retainer for preventing me from being reversed more often than I was.

While I was working in chambers to complete my work on other motions, U.S. Attorney Lumbard dropped in to wish me well and then tell me that he wanted me to try an important criminal case—the 13 leaders of the Puerto Rican Nationalist Party who were charged with conspiring to prevent, by use of force, the continuing government of Puerto Rico by the United States. Three members of the group, firing weapons from the spectators gallery, had recently shot up the House of Representatives and wounded one congressman. They had also tried to kill President Truman and actually killed a guard protecting him while he was temporarily residing in Blair House during White House renovations. Recognizing the assignment of so important and difficult a first case as a compliment, and because of my long-standing respect for Lumbard, I agreed. As Lumbard started to leave, however, he almost casually said that he would arrange for police protection for me and for himself. The last judge to try a Puerto Rican Nationalist had been assassinated.

With no judicial trial experience, I quickly tried a short nonjury criminal case, but this was scant preparation for a several-week trial applying criminal law to a conspiratorial interplay of ideological and political issues and managing a trial of 13 defendants. As an additional problem, one defendant, Julio Pinto Gandia, a lawyer, the leader of the Puerto Rican Nationalist Party in the United States, insisted on defending himself. He was cooperative but had had little criminal experience, and he wanted to use the trial as an opportunity to publicize the cause of the Puerto Rican Nationalists and to outshine the rival Puerto Rican Communist party, which also advocated independence. From time to time, Gandia would approach the bench to inquire as to the propriety of certain tactics. Although these bench conferences concerned Lumbard and the prosecution team, they enabled me to complete the trial without inappropriate political or ideological outbreaks, while giving the defendants the benefit of their misplaced idealism. The case was completed in a little over a month. The jury returned a verdict within three hours, finding all of the defendants guilty. I imposed the maximum sentence of six years on each. The defendants seemed to agree that a lesser sentence would demean the public gesture they had made. (The three defendants who had assaulted Congress and killed the Blair House guard had already been convicted and subjected to much longer sentences in the District of Columbia. My sentence added to the ones they had received.)

The police protection had its humorous side. Having moved my family to New City in Rockland County, New York, I commuted to the courthouse on the 7:25 A.M. train from West Nyack to Weehawken, followed by a wonderful 25-minute ferry trip down the Hudson River past docked ocean liners to Liberty Street, Manhattan, then a 15-minute walk to the courthouse. During the trial, the New York City police picked me up at the ferry and escorted me back to it in the evening. The state police picked me up at the Nyack Station and followed me home. My neighbor, protesting that I had been blocking traffic by my slow driving, had previously persuaded me to ride with him to and from the station. As he noticed the state police following him evening after evening, he became convinced that he was a marked target for speeding.

Because this was my first trial, I had written out my charge to the jury and I started to read it, but halfway through, I found that I was losing the attention of some jurors. I then began to speak extemporaneously, following the outline of my written charge but watching the individual jurors and talking directly to them. After that, I always charged a jury extemporaneously. In all of my speeches and court arguments I had used this less formal, conversational method. I found that juries, courts, and other audiences would listen more closely as I at times had to grope for words. Judges Hand and Medina both complimented me on this. They told me that it was more important that the jury absorb the charge than that it be letter perfect.

Shortly after finishing the trial of the Puerto Rican Nationalists and again assigned to the motion part, I was requested to appoint a receiver for the Hudson & Manhattan Railroad, the Hudson tubes that ran between Newark, Hoboken, Jersey City, and New York. This was a first step toward corporate reorganization, and, under the rules of the court, it was assigned to me personally, an assignment that continued for my entire period on the bench. After I selected the trustee in reorganization and his counsel, lawyers for conflicting security interests would jockey for advantage in town meeting–like proceedings, frequently complaining about expenditures and other operational matters. I finally curtailed duplicative, extemporaneous presentations by ruling that no lawyer could speak unless he had previously submitted a brief. The reorganization proceeded efficiently but it took almost five years.

In that same motion period, I picked up another case that led to my second reversal by the court of appeals. A ship owner had sold tickets for a Mediterranean cruise to a group of schoolteachers. At the time, his ship was in dry dock for repairs, which he knew he could not afford. He was aware that his ship would not be available for the trip. When the disappointed schoolteachers sued, he disappeared. His lawyers claimed to be unable to find him. Unable to find property for attachment, I issued a body execution for his arrest and confinement, pending trial, and I continued the confinement even after he appeared. The court of appeals, responding to his petition for habeas corpus and, perceiving an analogy to imprisonment for debt, with no precedent since 1898 to support me, ordered his release. The defendant, however, had had enough; he settled with the schoolteachers.

Most of my activities ran more smoothly. Each year a judge spent three months trying criminal cases, three months trying jury civil cases, three months trying nonjury civil cases, then a month in motions. The easiest assignment was civil jury cases. While requiring some preparation, once the jury's verdict was in, the job was usually over. I never had a mistrial or a jury disagreement. Nor was I ever reversed after a civil jury trial.

Nonjury civil cases were more demanding because I had to make the ultimate factual decision, as well as decide the questions of law. Most judges would reserve decision at the end of the trial and then, after receiving briefs, write an opinion. This seemed wasteful. By getting the briefs before the trial started, and occasional supplemental briefs during trial, I kept on top of the developing issues. I reviewed my extensive notes as the case proceeded. With the testimony fresh in my mind, I dictated my opinion from the bench immediately after the last witness testified. I could watch the reaction of counsel and the parties as I explained my decision. I was only reversed once for a decision in a nonjury case. The court of appeals declined to follow a decision in another circuit on which I had relied.

Judges Hand and Medina urged me to continue this practice. Judge Hand put it this way: "It's better to get the case up to us. If you make a mistake we can take care of it." What the court of appeals judges did not want was procrastination in the district court when the ultimate decision on most questions of law was going to be theirs. One elderly district judge used to draft an opinion in favor of each side. He would then read and reread his opinions, trying to make up his mind how to decide the case. Because he was an old friend, the story went, Hand had once stormed into his chambers and said, "Bill, do you think 20 years from now anyone will care how you decided these cases?" The district judge, the only member of the court with a chauffeur, had always driven the Hands and other colleagues home each evening, but he thereafter expelled Hand from the group and made him take the subway.

The only nonjury case that I took back to chambers without reaching an immediate decision was a complicated civil case against the Reconstruction Finance Corporation (R.F.C.) concerning a shipload of rubber seized by the blockading Dutch during the Indonesian revolt against Dutch sovereignty after World War II. The new Indonesian government, the shipper, through its bank, claimed payment from the R.F.C., the banker for the United States agency, arguing that the consignee was indebted for the rubber after it was loaded for sea. Under the unusual circumstances of the transaction, the steamship line (Isbrandtsen), which had been selected by the Indonesians, made its own decision to try to run the blockade. I thought the United States was probably entitled to judgment, but the Justice Department lawyers would not deal with me candidly and help me narrow the issues. Unable to rely on them, my law clerks and I did our own research to support the view that I believed should prevail. As a result, the case became stale while I worked on other matters. I then had to review lengthy exhibits and work on the case during much of one summer. My ultimate decision in favor of the R.F.C. was affirmed on appeal.

While a trial judge's work in criminal jury cases, like civil jury cases, largely ends with the jury's verdict, there is still the responsibility for sentencing. I had no mistrials or jury disagreements. Except for one defendant in a four-defendant case, the court of appeals affirmed all of my judgments of conviction. I enjoyed working with jurors. As I worked longer with them, I concluded that the critical factor for a judge, like that for a lawyer, was that the jury believe that he was being fair. Clearly describing the defendant's rights and the jury's duty did not produce acquittals or disagreements. It reassured the jurors of my fairness and satisfied them that they could fairly convict if they so viewed the evidence.

In spite of a good probation department, however, sentencing was often an unsatisfactory intuitive activity. It did not become easier with experience. The longer I served, the less I liked it, particularly when a defendant pleaded guilty without trial. I frequently suspended sentence but I was probably on the high side when I did impose a prison sentence. Once or twice the court of appeals noted the severity of a sentence and suggested that I might want to reconsider during the permissible 60-day period after it had affirmed the judgment of conviction.

My most severe sentences, 15 years, were imposed on participants in organized crime who refused to expose higher-ups. I would offer in each case to consider a reduction in return for truthful cooperation with the government but this did not work out. In one unusual case, racket figures co-opted a jelly company to use as a front for black-market sugar operations during World War II and then failed to pay income taxes on their profits. The original owner of the jelly company, himself a black marketer, testified that they had forced him out of his own company by threats of racket retaliation. Notwithstanding severe cross-examination by one of New York's best defense attorneys, Lloyd Paul Stryker, he stood his ground credibly. I took note for the future of the young assistant U.S. attorney, Milton Wessel, who had matched Stryker blow for blow and so tellingly dealt with an organized crime syndicate.

The Southern District of New York, one of the financial and commercial centers of the world, drew consistently interesting cases. With most automobile accident cases going to the state courts, my court received a very high percentage of the country's complex civil cases, antitrust cases, and maritime cases. Somehow I seemed to get more than my share of maritime cases. I thought the admiralty bar liked to try cases before me and I also believe that I probably excelled in this work because of both my interest and my experience as a seaman.

During the last week of July 1956, as I finished my vacation on Cape Cod, the maritime world was stunned by a seemingly unexplainable accident. A few miles from the Nantucket Shoals lightship, the S.S. *Andrea Doria*, the pride of the Italian merchant marine, crossed the bow of the Swedish American Line motorship *Stockholm*. Rammed amidships, the *Andrea Doria* sank. As this beautiful ship slowly flooded, listed, and sank, the disaster was studded by intense personal tragedies. Half of her lifeboats, tilted inwards by her list, could not be launched. Panic hampered the rescue of passengers. Hysterical parents threw children into already launched lifeboats only to see them killed by the fall. Others jumped into the sea. One little girl, who was later rescued, lay helpless on the mangled bow of the *Stockholm* as it withdrew from the *Andrea Doria* after crushing her sister to death. Some members of the *Andrea Doria* crew sought only their own safety and rushed for the lifeboats. Others

Above—Port Maitland, Nova Scotia, in the 1920s. The Bay of Fundy is to the left.

Right—My father, grandfather and me, 1920.

Below—Grandfather Walsh's farm, Jordan Falls, Nova Scotia.

Academic high point . . . briefly coxswain of 1929 freshman crew. *The Columbian*, 1929

Law school graduate, 1935.

J. Edward Lumbard, Jr. overlooked my law school grades and employed me as a lawyer. Wm. B. Hubbell, New York, photographer, Courtesy U.S. Court of Appeals, Second Circuit

Below—United States Lines S.S. *President Harding*, on which I worked in 1930, is also the prototype of *President Jackson* and *Southern Cross,* on which I also worked in successive summers. The *President Monroe* was a smaller predecessor. Courtesy United States Lines

Above—Thomas E. Dewey and the first of three groups of lawyers to be appointed to the staff of the New York County District Attorney's Office, December 1937. Front row, l to r, Herman Stichman, Robert Thayer, Sewell Tyng, Joseph Brill, and Mr. Dewey. Back row, Whitman Knapp, James O'Malley, Aaron Benenson, Thomas Shaw Hale, Alfred Scotti, Fred Bryan, myself, Nathanial Kaplan, Francis Ellis Rivers, and Frank Severance.

Left—Assistant D.A. Herman J. McCarthy and me entering court for trial of Fritz Kuhn, national leader of the anti-semitic German-American Bund. Kuhn was convicted of grand larceny.

Below—Mr. Dewey's farewell dinner with his staff. Head table, l to r, Stichman, Fuld, Gurfein, Hogan, Mr. Dewey, Lockwood, Schilback, Rosenblum, Gelb, and Breitel. Rogers and I are a few places in front of Mr. Dewey. © Standard Flashlight Company, Inc., New York

Left—Governor Thomas E. Dewey and his personal staff, 1943-48. Seated l to r: Lillian Rosse Goodrich, personal secretary; Gov. Dewey; Paul E. Lockwood, secretary to governor; Charles D. Breitel, counsel to governor; standing, James C. Hagerty, executive assistant to governor; myself, assistant counsel to governor; and Hamilton Gaddis, assistant secretary to the governor. Gift of Frank Bauman, *LOOK* photographer, © Library of Congress, Prints & Photographs Division, *LOOK* magazine photograph collection

Hasty conference with Breitel on Boss Tweed's "million dollar" staircase. © Timepix

New York Governor Dewey, New Jersey Governor Driscoll, and Governor-Elect Meyner meet with Generals Hays and Rose and me as we organize the Waterfront Commission. © Waterfront Commission of New York Harbor

The collision between the M.S. *Stockholm* and the S.S. *Andrea Doria* was one of the most important matters I handled as a United States judge. The *Stockholm* survived. © Corbis

S.S. *Andrea Doria* listed severely and slowly sank. © Corbis

Senior Circuit Judge Learned Hand swears me in as the Deputy Attorney General of the United States.

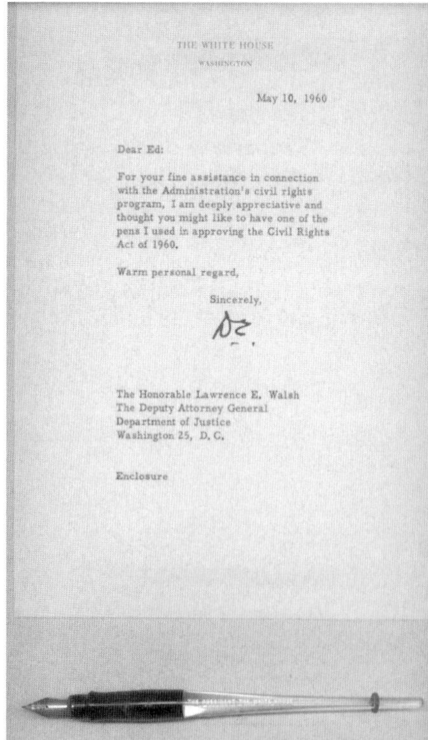

THE WHITE HOUSE

WASHINGTON

May 10, 1960

Dear Ed:

For your fine assistance in connection with the Administration's civil rights program, I am deeply appreciative and thought you might like to have one of the pens I used in approving the Civil Rights Act of 1960.

Warm personal regard,

Sincerely,

The Honorable Lawrence E. Walsh
The Deputy Attorney General
Department of Justice
Washington 25, D. C.

Enclosure

Above—My 1958 school desegregation task force briefs Attorney General Rogers on Little Rock. © Timepix

Left—Pen Certificate from President Eisenhower for Civil Rights Act of 1960.

Below—With Oklahoma judges, waiting to celebrate Chief Judge Alfred Murrah's twenty-five years as a federal judge. Judge Murrah is in center. © Meyers Photo Shop, Oklahoma City

Left—Mary and I preside at N.Y. State Bar summer meeting in Monticello, N.Y., 1966

. . . and then pick up son Dale from Mary's mother in Oklahoma City.

Daughters Sara and Elizabeth interrupt my work.

Ambassador Lodge and I meet with President Nixon before leaving for Paris, January, 1969. © UPI

U.S. delegation at first four-party meeting on Vietnam (Lodge, Vance, myself, Green. Future Ambassador Holbrook is behind Vance and me). © Corbis

With South Vietnamese President Thieu in Saigon.

After Judge Carswell was denied confirmation, the ABA Committee tightened its standards for Supreme Court appointments. The House of Delegates approved. © American Bar Association

Above—On Labor Day weekend, 1970, the Popular Front for the Liberation of Palestine hijacked four aircraft "to explode a revolution" in the Kingdom of Jordan. In litigation I represented the all-risk insurers against the war-risk insurers for a PanAm 747 aircraft hijacked as part of the plan but too big to land in Jordan. It was destroyed in Egypt. © Corbis

Left—Chief Justice Warren Burger opening the 1976 "Pound Conference," jointly sponsored by Burger, the State Chief Justices Association, and the American Bar Association, to expose needed improvements in the administration of justice. He opened the conference in the St. Paul, Minnesota, legislative chamber in which Dean Roscoe Pound had addressed the need for reform 70 years earlier. © American Bar Association/John Ryan, Minneapolis.

My ABA presidency coincided with our nation's bicentennial. The Board of Governors met in Independence Hall. © American Bar Association

Preparing for St. Philip's Cathedral service to celebrate our nation's bicentennial, Sunday, August 8, l to r, David Napley, president of the Law Society of England and Wales; Sir Peter Rawlinson (later Lord Rawlinson), chairman of the Bar Council; Chief Justice Burger; myself; U.S. Attorney General Edward H. Levi; and Her Majesty's Attorney General Samuel Silkin. © American Bar Association

Two months later, outside Westminster Abbey, Mary and I talk with Lord Chief Justice Widgery after the annual ceremony opening the English Courts. © London Daily Express

As Iran/Contra Independent Counsel, work in my hotel room was the rule. © David Burnett, Contact Press Images

U.S. Senior Circuit Judge George MacKinnon, presiding judge of independent counsel panel. Courtesy U.S. Court District of Columbia Circuit

Associate Independent Counsel Guy Miller Struve, legal analyst and my personal confidant. © Sara Krulwich, *New York Times*

With Associate Counsel Mike Bromwich and David Zornow, I explain the basic indictment of Poindexter, North, Secord and Hakim. © Karl Schumacker, *Newsweek*

National Security Advisor Robert McFarlane (left) pleaded guilty to withholding information from Congress.
© Timepix

McFarlane's successor, Rear Admiral John Poindexter (right). His conviction of five felonies was reversed because of immunity granted by Congress.
© Timepix

Right—National Security Council staff member, Lt. Colonel Oliver North. His conviction of three felonies was reversed because of immunity granted by Congress.
© Doug Mills, AP

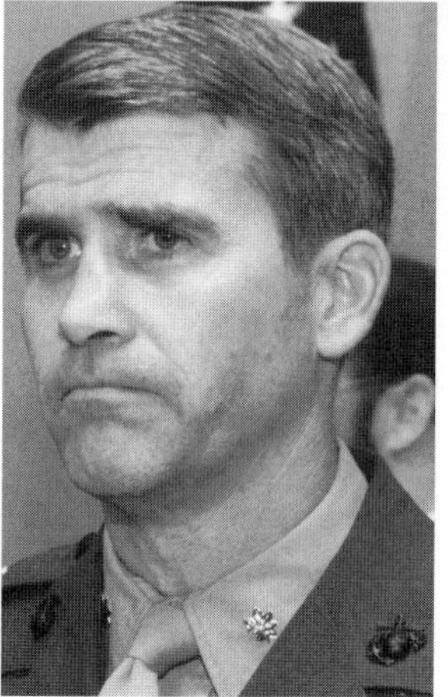

Below—Retired Lt. General Richard Secord organized Contra supply network to replace CIA. Pleaded guilty to a felony.
© Timepix

Lower right—Albert Hakim, Iranian financier and Secord's partner. Pleaded guilty to a misdemeanor. © Timepix

As directed by President Reagan but contrary to prohibition of Congress, this group kept the Contras together "body and soul." North, Secord, and Hakim also acted as intermediaries in sale of U.S. arms to Iran.

After exposure of illegal arms sales and the diversion of a part of U.S. proceeds to the Contras, President denies knowledge of diversion and Meese takes over press conference to announce a "runaway" NSC staff conspiracy, the resignation of Poindexter, and North's return to the Marine Corps. © Doug Mills, A.P.

Left—Warned of impending investigation, North shredded so many NSC documents that the shredder jammed. His loyal secretary, Fawn Hall, carried some past the FBI hidden in her boots. © Doug Mills, A.P.

Right—Donald Regan, President Reagan's Chief of Staff, joined Meese in claim of runaway conspiracy and at first withheld inconsistent records. © Corbis

Brendan Sullivan, Jr. (left) and Barry Simon, Oliver North's lawyers, won a significant tactical victory in forcing separate trials for North and his co-defendants. It made necessary a different prosecutorial team for each case because of possible exposure to the immunized testimony of the co-defendants not on trial. It also forced me to choose between trying a case and retaining supervisory control of the investigation. © *Legal Times*

I appear in court in unsuccessful opposition to their motion and in an effort to hold the cases together for a single trial. © Associated Press

Associate Independent Counsel John Keker, Zornow, and Bromwich meet reporters after North's felony convictions. © Stephen Crowley/*The Washington Times*

Associate Independent Counsel Dan Webb, Louise Radin, Howard Pearl, and Christian Mixter meet with reporters after felony convictions of Poindexter. © George Tames, NYT Pictures

Alan Fiers, chief of the CIA Central American task force, 1984-87, leaves federal court after pleading guilty to charges of unlawfully withholding information from Congress. He admitted that he had kept his superiors informed that North and Secord were buying arms for the contras with part of the proceeds from the sale of U.S. arms to Iran. © *New York Times*

Former Assistant Secretary of State Elliot Abrams makes statement after pleading guilty to withholding information from Congress. © *Washington Post*

CIA's third-ranking officer, Director of Operations Clair George, refused to "turn a spotlight on the White House." He stood trial and was convicted of lying to Congress. © Associated Press

Contrary to the Meese-Regan claim of a runaway conspiracy, North was closely supervised by a "restricted interagency group" known as the "RIG," and a smaller, more intimate group known as the "RIGLET," which included Fiers and Abrams and which reported to George.

Although he had 700 pages of notes exposing his opposition to the Iran arms sales and his warning to President Reagan of their illegality, Secretary of Defense Weinberger falsely denied that he had notes relating to Iran/Contra matters. His notes would have sped my investigation and that of Congress. He was indicted, but President Bush pardoned him on the eve of trial. © *Newsday*

After his conviction of Clair George, Deputy Independent Counsel Craig Gillen, accompanied by John Barrett and Tom Baker, explains the Weinberger indictment. © AP Wide World

President Bush also pardoned career government officers but, with one exception, only after they had pleaded guilty or stood trial. He explained his pardons as a response to the "criminalization of policy disputes." © Wally McNamee, *Newsweek*

We then turned to our final report, which was released by the court over opposition of President Reagan, Oliver North, former Attorney General Meese, and others. We reported that, confronted with the plight of Buckley and the Contras, President Reagan had drawn loyal associates into criminal conduct. © Wally McNamee, *Newsweek*

were broken by the tragedy. Because the *Stockholm* was at first concerned with sinking herself, she could not immediately contribute her own lifeboats. The French Line's *Ile de France* and three American ships turned back from their Atlantic crossings to launch their boats and save scores of passengers.

As I returned to court for my August assignment in the motion part, the Swedish American Line commenced a limitation of liability proceeding. Under maritime law, in the absence of owner misconduct, liability of a ship owner is limited to the value of its surviving vessel, in this case, the damaged *Stockholm*. In such a proceeding, the judge requires that all claims arising from the accident be brought before him so that no claim be paid until first determining that the limitation fund is adequate for all claims. If not, all claims would be prorated. Accordingly, I enjoined extraneous litigation. Under the rules of the court, I then became the judge responsible for all of the ensuing litigation growing out of the collision.

I took the initiative quickly. In a collision involving an American vessel there would have been immediate Coast Guard hearings to perpetuate the evidence. With two foreign ships, this procedure was not available, so I devised one of my own. The two steamship lines agreed to keep their crews in New York, available for immediate public depositions. I appointed four outstanding lawyers to preside, in turn, at these depositions to provide quick rulings subject to review by me if necessary. Two weeks after the collision, I set the deposition schedule to begin a month later. In the meantime, I ordered that all parties were to have an opportunity to inspect and photograph the *Stockholm* and the logs of both vessels, to the extent that they existed, as well as other relevant documents in the possession of both steamship lines. The two steamship lines supplied all claimants a list of officers, crew, and others performing functions related to the collision. Because the *Andrea Doria* had been lost, I ordered that the *Stockholm* officers be deposed first.

The Italian Line was represented by Eugene Underwood, a very hard-hitting cross-examiner who addressed the Swedish officers so vigorously that the *Stockholm*'s captain suffered a heart attack. But after the Swedish crew had been deposed, the Italian Line and its underwriters recognized the difficulty of their situation. In order to avoid a similar public exposure of their officers and engineering studies, they settled the case on the terms demanded by the Swedish Line. Each company bore its own loss. In other words, the Swedish Line did not contribute to the loss of the *Andrea Doria* but did bear the cost of the repairs to the *Stockholm*. Both lines agreed to cooperate and to share equally the claims of third parties who were injured by the collision. Their lawyers, I believe, dealt fairly with the third parties, the innocent victims of the tragedy.

This settlement was reached less than six months after the accident. While keeping all of my other court assignments, I completed hearings on the 50-odd unsettled third-party claims within a year. Unlike any previous disaster of this magnitude, the payments to claimants actually started going out in November 1957, 15 months after the accident, as it became certain that the limitation fund was adequate to pay the third-party claims. In the loss of the *Titanic*, the *Vestris,* and the *Morro Castle*, it had been 10 years before any claimant received payment.[1]

As I evaluated more trial witnesses each year than most lawyers hear in a lifetime, the variety of questions presented to me also exceeded the range of most lawyers. While self-consciousness briefly accompanied my actions in the courtroom, I gained confidence with each disposition. Meanwhile, personal problems, such as educating children and other family matters, were almost lost in my enthusiasm for my work. Our home was modest but adequate. The Rockland County judge let me use his library on weekends. (I entered the locked courthouse through the county jail.) In the federal courthouse cafeteria, I was welcomed as the latest entrant from the political world. While my brashness occasionally offended some of my colleagues, those I most respected began to show their confidence in me as one who understood and was not afraid to use the full power of my court.

Inequality of representation sometimes added extra strain and concerned me as it drew me toward an advocate's role. In a few complex civil cases, I had to use my law clerks to develop the position of a party represented by unskilled advocates against some of the best lawyers of New York. Department of Justice lawyers at times raised this problem. Whereas the lawyers from Lumbard's U.S. attorney's office were young, sparkling, respectful, and responsive, those from Washington, when questioned during argument, were at times unable or unwilling to be candid and were even disdainful, simply repeating positions to which they had apparently been committed by their superiors.

The most extreme example of the problem of lawyer imbalance, however, was private litigation brought by dissenting shareholders against

---

1. For the details of the collision, the events leading up to it, and the facts exposed during the depositions and in subsequent studies, see ALVIN MOSCOW, COLLISION COURSE (G.P. Putnam's Sons 1959).

Allan P. Kirby and Robert R. Young, who had exploited their control of Alleghany Corporation, an investment company, to obtain control of the New York Central Railroad system. With New York Central stock on the rise as a takeover was rumored, they bought large amounts of Central stock for themselves but little for Alleghany. Instead, they had Alleghany lend to their co-venturers, Texans Clint W. Murchison and Sid W. Richardson, $7.5 million without security and with a commitment to protect them from loss, to enable them to purchase 800,000 shares of Central stock. As a further accommodation, Young and Kirby had Alleghany exchange its voting stock control of Investors' Diversified Services, Inc., another investment-related company, for nonvoting stock held by Murchison and Richardson. Following close behind these transactions, after Young had just bought thousands of shares of preferred stock, they had Alleghany issue a new convertible preferred stock in exchange for previous nonconvertible stock, grossly overvaluing the old stock and, by the convertibility feature, greatly increasing its value.

To avoid scrutiny by the Securities and Exchange Commission, Young and Kirby claimed that Alleghany was subject to regulation by the Interstate Commerce Commission (ICC) as a "non-carrier controlling a carrier." It had indeed once controlled the Chesapeake & Ohio Railroad, but it had sold that railroad and held no other at the time of these transactions. If the ICC had approved the acquisition of the New York Central system "in the public interest," Alleghany would have again become a "non-carrier controlling a carrier." But the ICC was never asked to make such a determination. Instead, Alleghany and the ICC attempted an oblique approach in which, after Alleghany and its officers and associates won control of Central, the ICC, accepting as a fact their control, approved the merger of two Central subsidiaries.

Alleghany dissenting common stock holders, complaining of possible dilution of the common stock, commenced an action to enjoin the preferred stock issue. Appearing before me in the motion part, these stockholders were so inarticulately represented that I depended upon a non-lawyer stockholder to answer my questions. After piecing together their argument, I denied their motions for summary judgment on the jurisdictional issue and sent them back to the ICC to permit it to decide whether it had jurisdiction. The ICC refused a hearing or a ruling on jurisdiction. It left unchanged its approval of the exchange of preferred stock. This decision was then reviewed by a three-judge court—two district judges, Judge Dimock and me, and one court of appeals judge, Carroll Hincks. With Hincks dissenting, I concurred in Dimock's opinion granting a temporary injunction and holding that the Interstate Commerce Commission did not have jurisdiction at the time the stock was issued. This was awkward because Alleghany had already started issuing the stock; we nevertheless stopped the trading. On appeal to the U.S. Supreme Court, Justice Harlan permitted trading to resume, with Alleghany posting a bond to protect shareholders.

Alleghany then tried to frustrate the litigation by settling the case in the state court with a more compliant group of dissenting shareholders. I enjoined the use of the settlement in the federal court. The court of appeals, led by Judge Jerome Frank, dismissed the appeal from my order, holding it non-final and not appealable. With Court of Appeals Judge Frank replacing Hincks, who was fatally ill, the three-judge court, in a per curiam opinion, largely written by Frank with appendices by Dimock and me, granted a permanent injunction. Judge Frank unfortunately died. We lost the benefit of his incisive explanation of corporate maneuvers. Alleghany retained Whitney North Seymour to persuade the Supreme Court to lift the injunction. The plaintiffs kept their original advocate, a pleasant person and perhaps a good lawyer but a bumbler, neither incisive nor articulate. The Supreme Court reversed our decision and held that Alleghany was subject to the ICC and free of SEC supervision, because of its control of the multiple carriers in the New York Central system. It did not discuss the statutory requirement that the ICC find that the Central acquisition was "in the public interest." In a 5-3 decision, it remanded the case back to the three-judge court for reconsideration of the transaction's compliance with the Interstate Commerce Act. Justice Whitaker did not participate. Justice Douglas (a former chairman of the SEC) dissented, supported by Chief Justice Warren and Justice Black.

Court of Appeals Chief Judge Charles E. Clark replaced Judge Frank. The three-judge court, with an opinion by me, acknowledged the jurisdiction of the ICC, but remanded the matter to the ICC for a preliminary finding that the acquisition of the Central by Alleghany was "in the public interest." While appeal to the Supreme Court was pending, Young committed suicide. Seemingly stunned by this inexplicable event, the Supreme Court summarily reversed the three-judge court. Again Justice Whitaker did not sit. Justice Douglas dissented, supported by Chief Justice Warren and Justice Black, pointing out that our action was within the mandate of the court and complimenting my opinion.

Years later one of the most respected court of appeals judges told me that, in another matter, he had had to review this entire litigation. He thought that the Supreme Court majority misunderstood what had happened. If ever a true Supreme Court advocate was needed, it was in this case, but either for lack of funds or pride, the stockholders lost a case that a stronger advocate might have won. More than once, I wished that I could defend my own opinions in the appellate courts.

At one point, counsel for Alleghany requested that I disqualify myself for bias. I denied his motion but I later sought the advice of Judge Hand. He said that if the bias arose during the litigation, I should not disqualify myself. If it arose before the litigation, I should. As counsel to the Public Service Commission, I had had to deal with regulatory gaps caused by the ICC's narrow view of its responsibilities. Having been created during the roughhouse wars of the railroad financiers of the late nineteenth century, the ICC was, at most, secondarily concerned with stockholder mistreatment. Its concept of the public interest primarily focused on a healthy rail system. I did not regard my evaluation of the agency as a bias against any of the parties.

More than most judges of my court, I advocated improved court administration. I was its only member appointed to a committee of the Judicial Conference of the United States, the conference of the chief judges of the federal circuits, which oversaw the administration of the federal court system. Its specialized committees sometimes included district judges. After I appeared before its Committee on Supporting Personnel to request a raise and retitling for my "bailiff-law clerk," the committee approved my application and then invited me to become a member. The chairmen of the committees on administration and pretrial befriended me and I often sat in meetings of their committees. When a special committee was created to develop a manual for the trial of long and complex cases, Chief Justice Warren appointed me to it. My impression of the Chief Justice was that of a warm and fatherly person who missed the personal contacts of elective office and who enjoyed young people, particularly if he believed them to be hard workers who shared his concern for court administration.

In my own court, I advocated adoption of the individual calendar system, the early assignment of cases to individual judges to permit meaningful pretrial and accelerated disposition. While this view gained support, it also raised resistance and even antagonism. This exploded when the Judicial Conference was expanded to add one district judge from each circuit. At a meeting of the entire court, I nominated Judge Dimock, who favored reform. Unexpectedly, the most senior judge (other than the chief judge) denounced me personally for having "introduced politics into the court" and for trying to insert "Dewey-like" attitudes in a court that had been nonpolitical. I was startled but kept my peace. Judge Dimock was elected. I then had lunch with the critical judge, which was actually very productive. As we became candid with each other, we became friends, much to the relief of our colleagues. I had not realized that seniority might be so important or that he wanted to be a member of a group that would deal with administrative change.

Our court moved partway toward an individual calendar system. It created a committee to explore it and establish a true "ready calendar," which ignored dormant cases and started with new cases as they came in, and included old cases only when they were moved for trial. It also created a "calendar part," in which the judge assigned each month called in the lawyers for the cases on the ready calendar for settlement or immediate trial. This was onerous work, 10 or 20 conferences a day, some quite short but others protracted. Many cases settled when the alternative was immediate trial, but as the trial parts fell behind, the rate of settlements dropped. Because I was among the most successful in getting dispositions, the chief judge had me serve two successive months. After eight solid weeks of the these intensive, compressed negotiations, I vowed I would never do it again. A few years later, the court moved to an individual calendar system.

I enjoyed every aspect of my work. By my second year, my routine was both efficient and enjoyable. With a second family car and the narrowest courthouse parking space, I drove to work, no longer dependent on ferries that stopped running at 6 p.m. Getting to court early proved valueless, as I was constantly interrupted by phone calls that my law clerks could handle in my absence. So, although I continued to rise early, I worked at home each morning until 9:00 or 9:15. Then, after the peak rush hour, I could just get to court as it opened at 10:30. At one point, I explored scheduling trials from noon until 5:00 P.M., with a single recess, so lawyers and jurors could get to their offices in the morning. Everyone liked it as an experiment, but usually I followed the normal court schedule.

While always courteous, I wondered if I had attained an ideal judicial temperament. I worried that I was at times overly aggressive, coming to a view of the facts on trial too quickly and even developing a bias about certain types of cases and for or against some lawyers who appeared frequently before me. At other times I was irked by the poor prospect of promotion to the court of appeals. The Republican senators of New York, Connecticut, and Vermont had a strong voice in the selection. A judge in New York with four judicial districts including more than 30 district judges was at a great disadvantage compared to the two judges in Connecticut and one in Vermont. At the beginning of my second year, I grumbled when all of the district judges in the circuit were passed over in favor of Sterry Waterman, a lawyer unknown to me, from St. Johnsbury, Vermont. That year, however, the circuit upgraded its circuit judicial conference, an annual meeting of all judges and twice as many lawyer-guests. At lunch, Learned Hand invited me to sit with him as Waterman spoke. His impressive speech shamed my earlier feelings. Hand told me that he had the simplicity and modesty of a great judge—an observation that proved correct.

At that conference, also, Sir Patrick Devlin, a noted barrister, later appointed to the English high court, eloquently struck a responsive chord. He emphasized the importance of the trial judge in the course of justice, making the point that mistakes of law can be corrected but that the fairness and capability of a trial judge, his spontaneous treatment of lawyers, witnesses, and jurors, was not really subject to effective review except by his own conscience. I came away almost completely reconciled to being forever a district judge, hopefully one of the best.

In the fall of 1957, while I was so enjoying my work, Bill Rogers, now deputy attorney general under Attorney General Herbert Brownell, asked me to come to Washington. The next morning on the plane, I read that Brownell had resigned and that President Eisenhower had appointed Rogers in his place. Noticing that, as I entered, I was impressed by his imposing office, Rogers asked, "How do you like the splendor?" A few minutes later he asked me to take his job as deputy attorney general. Surprised, intrigued, but dubious, I listened. While he talked, Vice President Nixon telephoned to congratulate him and to invite him to lunch. Bill asked to bring me along.

Nixon and Rogers had remained close friends since the first Eisenhower campaign when Bill had cemented Nixon's close friendship by guiding him through the campaign charges of an illegal expense fund. The vice president took us to lunch at La Salle du Bois, just off Connecticut Avenue. As we drank before lunch, he impressed me. Almost carefree, he seemed to enjoy people, even to be gregarious as he joked about some aspects of the deputy attorney general's job and Rogers. I thought I saw in him the drive, ability, and intelligence of Governor Dewey but the political advantage of a more earthy attitude. We did not talk politics.

There was no suggestion then or in my dealings with him thereafter of any dark traits. He obviously enjoyed his work. He showed no impatience with his number two position. After five years in office, he seemed to be a very relaxed and happy man. As we talked, I of course realized that the relationship between Nixon and Rogers would be valuable to Rogers's deputy.

Rogers urged me not to make a hasty decision. During the tormented weeks that followed, I went from one adviser to another. They divided almost evenly. Twice I called Rogers to tell him I would not do it, that I was going to stay on the court. Each time he said, "Take a little more time and think it over." Finally, I went in to see Learned Hand and asked for his judgment. After we talked a little he said, "I think you should take it. If you return to the court, you will be a better judge. If you don't, you will land on your feet anyway." The next day I called Rogers and told him I would join him at the end of the year.

That night, at a dinner meeting of the trustees of the William Nelson Cromwell Foundation, a group of leading New York lawyers to which I had been added as the youngest member, I sat next to Judge Joseph Proskauer. When he heard my intention to leave the court, as he had done many years before, he spent the next hour in an intense effort to persuade me not to do so. I deeply valued his friendship and I recognized his sagacity. He had been a key adviser for Governor Alfred E. Smith and a trusted counsel to important clients and other public officials. His position shook me, but I decided to stay my course and to leave the court with uncertainty and regret at the end of the year.

Chapter 11
REMOTE CONTROL

At first I missed the deference shown to judges, and I felt some shame in leaving the bench so soon. While a judge occasionally leaves the bench for a high government post, traditionally an appointive judge is expected to serve for life. Never having worked outside of New York, I was also apprehensive of Washington. And, of course, we were reluctant to give up our home, the first we had owned. For a few weeks, I stayed in the hotel suite of the Republican leader of the District of Columbia. Then the head of the Civil Rights Division and I shared a furnished apartment until we could move our families. I drove back and forth weekends, leaving home at 4:00 A.M. Mondays and leaving Washington late afternoon on Fridays.

This was also the first time I had entered near the top of a large, proud ongoing organization. Brownell and Rogers had uplifted the department after its demoralization by scandal during the Truman administration. Attorney General Howard McGrath had been fired and the assistant attorney general in charge of the Tax Division, Lamar Caudle, convicted of a felony. Some of Brownell's best-known assistant attorneys general had just become appellate judges and their successors were well in place before my appointment. The office of deputy attorney general itself was somewhat of an upstart, newly created by a reform attorney general who served briefly at the end of the Truman administration. Rogers had been the first incumbent to lift it to the second highest office in the Department of Justice, over the old and professionally respected post of solicitor general.

"I want you to run the department so that I can handle my responsibilities as a member of the cabinet," Bill told me. He meant to keep the advisory work and of course the Opinions of the Attorney General. He then took back supervision of the always-controversial antitrust division but there was plenty left to do. Relying on me to alert him to problems, Rogers really turned over to me oversight of the department's litigation, the Bureau of Prisons, the Immigration and Naturalization Service, and the Alien Property Custodian, as well as the development of recommendations for federal judicial appointments, U.S. attorneys, and Justice Department personnel.

For the 15 years since I left the district attorney's office, we had seen very little of each other. Rogers had served in the Navy during World War II. He had returned to the district attorney's office but then shifted to Washington, where he had served as counsel to Senate investigatory committees and formed a friendship with Richard Nixon. He became a partner in one of the two offshoots of the firm of Charles Evans Hughes. In 1952, he volunteered for the Eisenhower campaign and soon became an important assistant to Herbert Brownell. When Brownell was appointed attorney general, he picked Rogers as his deputy.

Bill seemed to have hardened with Washington experience. He had also broadened. He was no longer a litigator, he was an executive. His five years as deputy attorney general could not have been easy. Brownell, however admirable, had never impressed me as an administrator. He was frequently under hostile press scrutiny as a political leader appointed to a law enforcement position. From time to time individual decisions were subject to criticism. The major divisions of the department were headed by appointees who had established themselves in the 1952 campaign. Bill's two natural competitors included, as the head of the office of legal counsel, one of Brownell's old Nebraska friends and, as the attorney general's executive assistant, first, a young Republican who had been New York State campaign chairman and then John Lindsay, future congressman and mayor of New York City.

Eisenhower's first term had also been a time of difficult relationships with Congress, particularly Senator Robert Taft, the Republican leader. Eisenhower then frequently depended on Brownell for political guidance in a strange area. Individual senators had created threatening problems as they clutched at the patronage and judicial appointments of the first Republican government in 20 years. Then there was Senator Joseph McCarthy, who had to be brought under control. Rogers's earlier Washington experience had been valuable. While I recognized the increased distance between us, and that Bill was playing "hardball," I was confident that we both had a common understanding that our personal, selfish interests were best served by excelling in our jobs. A client who had once starred in professional football explained the difference between a good college player and a professional: just one step—one step faster on each play. Bill had passed that test. Could I?

I quickly filled my personal staff. To deal with Congress, I chose a partner in a small admiralty firm, John R. Sheneman, a gregarious, instinctive diplomat and a graduate of the Naval Academy. To follow the Justice Department litigation and to be my own lawyer, I selected the assistant chief of the civil division of Lumbard's U.S. attorney's office, Leon Silverman, who brought with him three outstanding young lawyers: Miriam Goldman Cedarbaum, later U.S. district judge, Southern District of New York; David Klingsberg, later managing partner of an important New York law firm; and Victor R. Friedman, later a partner in Silverman's firm. Silverman had been an editor of the *Yale Law Journal.* Trained first by litigation perfectionist George Spiegelberg, then by Lumbard, he retained his challenging aggressiveness albeit tempered by a sparkling sense of humor. While Sheneman had arrived first and taken the office of Rogers's one assistant, Silverman received an office roughly equal in size but slightly less convenient. When his title was put on the door, he measured the size of the lettering to make sure it was at least as large as Sheneman's. In return, Sheneman regularly smoked Silverman's cigars, even though Silverman protested that "Christians can buy them too." Sadly, Sheneman, after leaving the department, later became ill and died young. Silverman became one of my closest friends. In addition to becoming managing partner of his firm, he has served as president of the New York Legal Aid Society, the American College of Trial Lawyers, and the Supreme Court Historical Society.

I started a weekly meeting of the assistant attorneys general. Four of them had been important U.S. attorneys. Friendly as most were, I soon recognized the difference between my control of my own appointees and those independently appointed by the president. The attorney general's own monthly meeting with division heads was larger and more stiff and formal. It included the heads of nonlitigating divisions. His best interchange with us was at our staff lunches three days a week in his private dining room.

Unaccustomed to my remoteness from the department's thousands of cases and lawyers, it took me a while to emulate Rogers's skilled and more detached oversight of the department. Essentially, his policy was to keep the department out of trouble and watch for a few big breaks. When I was learning to sail a boat, a Cape Cod skipper warned me, "Don't be eager." He meant let the boat do the sailing without being overintrusive. The larger the boat, the more valid the advice. With a backlog of thousands of cases and several thousand lawyers, half in Washington and half in the United States attorneys' offices, the department was the largest law office in the world. And, like the State Department, it was an agency of professionals, in which each of its individual lawyers had been appointed with the expectation that he or she would develop his or her own judgment as a lawyer, even though subject to overall policies of the department.

The division heads resisted radical change. When I explained the deficiencies I, as a judge, had noticed in department lawyers and recommended the regular rotation of lawyers from the antitrust division into the criminal division and vice versa so that the litigating skills of the criminal division could permeate the antitrust division and the antitrust division's imaginativeness could be useful in the criminal division, I hit a stone wall. While the head of the criminal division was dubiously willing, the head of the antitrust division, which included some of the worst offenders, was adamantly against it. Rogers saw no advantage to it. I soon realized that none of the top officers of the department had had anything like my trial court exposure, except perhaps one or two who had been "hands-on" U.S. attorneys.

An early visitor was Milton Wessel, the assistant U.S. attorney who had so impressed me in his trial against Lloyd Paul Stryker. He urged the creation of a special unit to concentrate on organized crime and assemble all of the scattered government information regarding each suspected racketeer. With Rogers's approval, I appointed a small group under Wessel and used my weekly meetings with the division heads to support it. The unit collected useful information but the FBI refused to cooperate, claiming that it could not share its confidential files with transients who might soon leave government service. Rogers was firm on one policy: Don't antagonize J. Edgar Hoover. He did not want any recurrence of previous running controversies between Hoover and former division heads. Wessel's program nevertheless received impetus when the leaders of the Mafia national crime families assembled at Appalachin, New York. A state trooper, curious about the convergence of limousines in so tiny a rural community, called for an investigation of the meeting. As the police moved in, over 60 guests fled into the woods or tried to get away. When apprehended, they gave false, inconsistent, and unbelievable explanations for their presence. Wessel convicted about one-third of them in federal court on a charge of an illegal conspiracy to obstruct justice, but the reversal of the conviction the following year for insufficient evidence gave Rogers an excuse to terminate the Wessel group. Subsequent investigations by Senator Estes Kefauver, Senator McClellan, and his counsel,

Robert Kennedy, exposed this meeting as a conference of the Mafia dons, family heads, to iron out differences and agree on certain underlying policies to minimize the danger of exposure. A successor group to investigate organized crime was later revived and formalized by Robert Kennedy after he became attorney general.

A month or two after my arrival, tension increased when President Eisenhower told Rogers that he intended to withdraw military support for the desegregation of schools in Little Rock, Arkansas. There, the local federal court, following holdings of the U.S. Supreme Court, had ordered desegregation of a high school. Governor Orval Faubus supported a movement to undermine the Court's order and encouraged mob intimidation of the entering black children. Eisenhower sent in a detachment of paratroopers who quickly and effectively dealt with the would-be troublemakers. The black children safely attended school. The National Guard later relieved the paratroopers and continued the protection for a full school year. For the following year, the president expected the Department of Justice to enforce the Court's order.

With only a few months before the fall school term, Rogers turned the job over to me. My weekly meetings with the division heads and my own staff generated a series of options as we collected all government information on Faubus and other Arkansas state and local officials. I called in the Little Rock U.S. attorney, who was upright but reluctant to litigate against his community. It was the United States marshal who provided the most helpful solution. He explained that he had many cousins in the Ozarks, where desegregation was not as bitter an issue as in other parts of the state. He suggested that if his relatives and friends could be deputized as marshals, permitted to carry weapons, and wear a badge, he believed he could control potential violence in Little Rock.

I had never thought of the U.S. marshals as a true peacekeeping force, their primary responsibility being to protect the safety of the Court and those who appeared before it. Rogers and I concluded that this was the best plan available to us. I authorized the marshal to recruit and train his new deputies for the fall. I then extended the concept to other parts of the country. Luckily, the marshal in the District of Columbia was an outstanding officer. He agreed to train 50 picked deputy marshals to be available wherever needed, to see that the desegregation orders of a court were not impeded by local violence.

Virginia's legislature had adopted "massive resistance" legislation to block desegregation. As the school term was about to start, violence was forecast for Charlottesville and for Hampton Roads, which had a large and tough blue-collar population that worked in nearby shipyards. At the same time, in Monroe, Louisiana, 40 miles south of Arkansas, a grand jury threatened to indict our assistant attorney general in charge of the Civil Rights Division, who had not been in either state. Knowing him well, I realized that he did not relish a personal showdown in Little Rock or any other hostile community. In contrast, the head of the Office of Legal Counsel, Malcolm Wilkey, a former outstanding U.S. attorney in south Texas, welcomed the chance to get back into the courtroom. I picked him to go to Little Rock.

While we had several possible legal options against Governor Faubus, Rogers, in one of his best political judgments, told me that he did not want to prosecute Faubus, he did not want to try affirmatively to force anyone to do anything. He wanted to keep the public schools closed until they complied with the court's order. The strategy was flawless. Wilkey obtained a new court order forbidding anyone on the school staff to participate in the operation of a segregated school. The Supreme Court affirmed it. Overnight, the new deputy marshals served every employee of the school system, from principal to janitor. The next morning the schools were closed. No one was willing to violate the order. For the rest of the school term the Little Rock Public Schools remained closed. When newly created, publicly aided, segregated private schools attempted to replace the public schools, the injunction was extended to them. At the end of the school term, the community itself asked to have the schools reopened on a desegregated basis.

In Virginia, Governor John Battle, in an extraordinary feat of statesmanship, defused the "massive resistance" problem by submitting the state legislation to the courts of his own state. The Virginia Supreme Court held the statutes unconstitutional. The governor then protected the desegregation of the schools from violence.

But this constructive event did not occur in time to prevent my most embarrassing confrontation with the FBI. Hoover and the agency were not sympathetic to school desegregation. It threatened the agency's cherished relationship with local law enforcement officials throughout the South. Before Governor Battle acted, I had called in the U.S. attorney and the U.S. marshal from Charlottesville to brief me about trouble spots and community resources. Unknown to me, the U.S. attorney had requested information from the head of the local FBI, who immediately informed FBI headquarters in Washington. Hoover responded with a harsh memorandum to the attorney general, saying that inasmuch as the deputy attorney general had undertaken enforcement of the civil rights laws, the FBI had withdrawn from activity in that field. Rogers and I looked at each other and laughed. I spent the next week trying to reach Hoover, who was on vacation in California along with his deputy, Clyde Tolson. The agent left in charge would only take a message and give me no response.

When Hoover returned, I called on him. He became jovial. We talked for over an hour as I explained what I was doing. He then rescinded his memorandum and we began a long friendship during which he helped me in many ways. I always recognized that we were dealing with a powerful, dedicated, and able individual who, at times egocentric, had for over 40 years protected his agency and himself against powerful political figures, Congress, cabinet officers, and presidents. I felt no need to challenge his protectiveness of the FBI. I became a regular commencement speaker for graduating classes of FBI-trained local law enforcement officials. He had me throw out the ball for a game of the Washington Senators. He tried to teach me: "Never promise what you are going to do. Always talk about what you have done."

Some of his autocratic excesses provoked FBI amusement as well as pride, as when the FBI laboratory worked through the night duplicating his favorite coffee cup before he knew it had been broken, and the tension of the local FBI agents as they routed him around traffic congestion in his regular last-minute dash to the Bowie race track. Hoover simply did not fit into the groove of ordinary persons. By a lifetime of commitment, he had achieved virtual autocratic freedom of action in a very powerful post. Any challenge would have been very costly. In the absence of some immediate need, once we acknowledged Hoover's sphere of freedom, he was a gracious and valuable associate.

Rogers and I both argued our first Supreme Court cases. Even those who specialize in appellate litigation rarely enjoy the ultimate thrill of their profession—an argument before the United States Supreme Court. Because the Court has almost complete control to select the cases it will hear, it restricts them to the number it can handle well. Its selection depends less upon the amount at stake or even justice between the parties than the value of the Court's decision to the country's jurisprudence. A large percentage of its cases are government cases handled on one side by the Office of the Solicitor General. Other cases are often argued by a small number of lawyers who specialize in Supreme Court work. Those who litigate more broadly may work a lifetime without a Supreme Court appearance.

Having nine members, the Court is larger than other courts. Because it has a tradition of reading the briefs and preparing in advance of argument, a lawyer may be subjected to constant interrogation by justices having conflicting preliminary views. In addition to the thrill of the argument itself, the atmosphere of the Court and its courtroom suggests an inviolability found rarely in secular places. Dominated by the long nine-place bench and framed by walls and floors of purest marble, the courtroom itself evokes respect and even awe. The formal dress of the court staff and the quill pens on counsel table remind the advocates of the ancient profession they briefly represent.

Traditionally, the Court does not interrupt or question the attorney general, but it had no forbearance for his deputy. I represented the Civil Rights Commission in an appeal from a lower-court decision that due process required the commission in its hearings in southern states to permit lawyers for those mentioned in testimony to cross-examine the witness who testified against them. As counsel for the commission, I argued that the commission had no power to take action against individuals; it had a fact-finding responsibility but only for use in the formulation of policy and generalized recommendations. In hearings set in segregated communities, the commission invited truthful testimony about community conditions and local officials from persons vulnerable to community ill will. Aggressive cross-examination would intimidate them. My opponent was the attorney general of Louisiana. Justices Hugo Black and William O. Douglas had written opinions in earlier cases generally supportive of the need for such cross-examination. They questioned me vigorously but I was well prepared, having been briefed by two deputy solicitors general and having spent every morning for two weeks reading opinions and talking my argument out loud in the attic and to my wife. The Court reversed the lower court with only Justices Black and Douglas dissenting. Justice Tom Clark had thoughtfully telephoned the morning of the decision to suggest that my wife and I might like to be in court at noon.

While control of litigation was perhaps my most important responsibility, my control was imperfect. U.S. attorneys throughout the country did report to me and I did advise them on specific problems. They were, however, independent presidential appointees confirmed by the Senate. One U.S. attorney misused the power of his office to harass a state agency that was condemning part of his farm. As he was supported by a powerful Senate leader, I could not ask the president to replace him without drawing the president into confrontation with the senator. Notwithstanding my warnings and in spite of my request that he not do so, a U.S. attorney permitted an assistant, a protege of right-wing advocate

Roy Cohn, to proceed with an indictment of Congressman Adam Clayton Powell of New York for an income tax violation. Powell was one of the few black congressmen and a flamboyant, well-liked Harlem minister. The department suffered an embarrassing acquittal. When that U.S. attorney resigned, I recommended that the president appoint a replacement from outside the office, Hazard Gillespie, a litigation partner of Davis Polk, who was recommended by Judge Bruce Bromley of the Cravath firm and Judge David Peck of Sullivan & Cromwell.

Our division heads in Washington were more accommodating. The head of the civil rights division regularly sought my views. I blocked a weak criminal antitrust case against James Hoffa, national head of the Teamsters Union. Instead, I approved an investigation by the criminal division and brought George MacKinnon, the U.S. attorney of Minnesota, to Washington as a special counsel to direct it. He developed the case that was later tried during the Kennedy administration. It resulted in a jury disagreement but led to Hoffa's conviction for jury tampering.

A few of the career lawyers in the antitrust division who had been held over from previous administrations were doctrinaire. Working on long cases and trying very few, they had poor judgment as to trial judges and juries and relied on the ultimate support of the Supreme Court. In one case, when told to proceed by civil suit, which required proof only by a preponderance of the evidence, they disobeyed and obtained a highly publicized criminal indictment against the officers of leading oil companies, which required proof beyond a reasonable doubt and which was dismissed at the close of the government's case. They claimed the grand jury had "run away." At other times, I consistently supported the antitrust division in its disputes with the State Department regarding international anticompetitive activities. Similarly, I also backed the Immigration and Naturalization Service in its controversies with State.

Occasionally I dealt with an individual case. Robert Frost, the poet, urged us to dismiss an indictment against Ezra Pound, who, during World War II, had become a propagandist for our enemies. Deemed mentally incompetent and unable to stand trial, Pound had been committed to the criminal section of St. Elizabeth's Hospital in Washington. Frost explained that Pound, in earlier years, had been an important benefactor to young American poets. He urged that Pound not be required to die in criminal custody. Rogers and I suggested that he have a lawyer move to dismiss the indictment and agreed that we would not oppose it. He, or those for whom he was acting, retained Thurman Arnold, former head of the antitrust division under Roosevelt and Truman, to make the motion. After the indictment was dismissed, Arnold and Frost invited Rogers and me to the Jefferson Hotel for lunch. Trying to keep up as one martini followed the other, I was fascinated by the interchange. Sadly, my only specific recollection was Frost's definition of poetry—"Joe DiMaggio in action."

Also amusing but less profound was the postmaster general's concern about the sexual candor in D.H. Lawrence's novel, *Lady Chatterley's Lover*. He tried to block its transmission through the mails. After a district judge ruled against him with an eloquent opinion, he wanted to appeal. At one point, I had to appear before President Eisenhower and explain to him why we were unwilling to pursue the matter. The postmaster general had given him a copy of the book in which he had underlined its explicit sexual passages. As I discussed the matter with the president, he finally laughed, put the book aside, and thanked me for my views. He consistently supported us on legal matters.

While I saw the president in cabinet meetings and defense council meetings when I occasionally substituted for Rogers, this was one of very few meetings I had with him alone. In spite of two heart attacks, he somehow most reminded me of an athlete. He had the ease and assurance of the crew captain I had so admired long ago when I was a college freshman. He never seemed talkative. He was, instead, an intent listener. He appreciated brevity but gave the feeling that every word had been absorbed and without discussion converted to a decision. For years, I had read uncomplimentary press comments suggesting that he was inarticulate. I found, to the contrary, that he chose his words well. He simply was not glib. He had been trained to be responsible for the lives of thousands and millions. He focused intensely on the correctness of his answer, not a rationalization for it. President Nixon wrote of President Eisenhower's "warm smile and icy blue eyes."[1] I saw this combination only once as I passed through a receiving line at Columbia, after he had left office, and, having just seen his portrait in dress uniform, absentmindedly addressed him as "general."

In addition to supervising litigation, the deputy attorney general was responsible for the department's relations with Congress. Rogers had shrewd instincts, developed when he had been counsel to a Senate committee and during the period when he was Brownell's deputy. He actually did not welcome appearing before congressional committees. He would usually appear once to support the department's budget and maybe

---

1. The Memoirs of Richard Nixon 376 (Grosset & Dunlap 1978).

on one other occasion during the year. When he did, he would read a statement so long that there would be little time for questions. Most other appearances were left to me. While these were primarily negotiations with respect to the confirmation of judicial nominees, they also included opposition or support for legislation.

My principal congressional contact was Senator James Eastland, chairman of the Senate Judiciary Committee. A Sunflower County plantation owner in the Delta country of Mississippi, he was also a shrewd and upright lawyer with deep loyalties to the South and to the Senate. As desegregation slowly followed the precedent-breaking rulings of the Supreme Court, he had joined the handful of able southern senators, led by Senator Richard Russell of Georgia, twice the southern candidate for the Democratic presidential nomination, who, while recognizing its inevitability, effectively used his influence with Senate committees and leaders and the threat of filibuster to delay the enactment of readily enforceable civil rights legislation during the 1940s and into the 1950s. With ample power to block confirmation of the president's judicial nominees, they never did. They would vote against confirmation, but they would let the nomination come to the floor of the Senate and be approved.

Routinely the judiciary committee extended courtesy to other senators. When another senator, claiming personal courtesy, asked the committee to hold up a nomination, Eastland would ultimately tell me who was responsible so that I could try to persuade that senator to withdraw his opposition. During the three years that we worked together, I angered Eastland once only, when I failed to let him know in advance that the Justice Department was going to desegregate the beach at Biloxi, Mississippi.

Responsible for recommending judicial nominations, I invited suggestions from the local Republican senator, if there was one. If not, I would ask the chairman of the Republican National Committee. I would then get a quick informal evaluation by the American Bar Association's standing committee on the federal judiciary, composed of a leading lawyer from each federal circuit. If it was favorable, I would request a more extensive formal report of the nominee's reputation for integrity, ability, and temperament. I would also ask the FBI for a thorough community background check. The ABA committee would grade the prospective nominee as "exceptionally well qualified," "well qualified," "qualified," or "not qualified." I never submitted a "not qualified" name to the president, and most of those I recommended were "well qualified" or "exceptionally well qualified." I believe that during my three years, President

Eisenhower's nominees more frequently received these higher classifications than those of any other president.

Almost all nominees were confirmed, but some drew hard-fought controversy. One state had no federal judge for two years because the Republican senator first insisted the president nominate his brother-in-law, who had gone into the real estate business, and then his college roommate, who had had no trial experience. One unfortunate Texas nominee unknowingly caused a tie-up of over 30 nominations. Senator Lyndon Johnson, the Democratic Senate leader, had approved the nomination but then privately decided to favor another lawyer. After the nomination had been sent to the Senate, the judiciary committee held no hearings on any nomination for several weeks. Senator Eastland told me that I had to see Johnson to break the logjam. Reaching Johnson with unusual difficulty, he finally told me, "Sure, I told you that you could send the nomination up, but I didn't tell you it would be confirmed." His preferred lawyer had once been cited for contempt of court, but Rogers and I decided we had to acquiesce; the unfilled vacancies were tying up litigation in many parts of the country. With extreme embarrassment, I asked our nominee to withdraw, even though he had started to shut down his practice. The ABA committee strained to find Johnson's favorite to be qualified. The Senate confirmed his appointment overnight; most of the other pending nominations were then confirmed within a few days. I had few other direct dealings with Johnson. Usually Eastland would clear a problem with him. He was big, good-natured, and essentially friendly. When he gave lack of military experience as his reason for not approving our original nominee, he so exaggerated his concern that we both had trouble keeping straight faces.

But still the nomination of Henry Friendly to the Court of Appeals for the Second Circuit (New York, Connecticut, and Vermont) did not move. Friendly, a most highly regarded New York lawyer, had been recommended by the Association of the Bar of the City of New York. The ABA committee had reported him" exceptionally well qualified." Learned Hand had strongly impressed President Eisenhower with a supportive letter. But an ambitious and able district judge, a favorite of the president of the Schenley Distillery Company, also coveted the position. The company lobbyist persuaded Senator Styles Bridges of New Hampshire, the leader of the conservative Republicans and ranking minority member of the powerful Senate Finance Committee, to block Friendly's nomination. New York's Republican senator supported Bridges, arguing that the elevation of a district judge would leave a second district judgeship to fill, and thus resolve a conflict between the state Republican organization and the "Citizens for Eisenhower" as to my own successor. Rogers and I would not yield. Notwithstanding the senator's personal request, the president backed us and refused to withdraw Friendly's nomination. Finally, after a second court of appeals vacancy permitted the accompanying appointment of the district judge, Friendly's nomination was confirmed.

About a year after I went to Washington, Supreme Court Justice Harold Burton retired. I recommended Potter Stewart of Cincinnati, a court of appeals judge on the Sixth Circuit. To my surprise, Rogers told me that he regretted that he could not recommend me because he needed me on civil rights problems and other matters. I had never thought that I could be in the running for the Supreme Court after such a short period in Washington. I shepherded Stewart's nomination through the judiciary committee. The southern senators voted against him because they feared embarrassment from his future decisions, but Senator Eastland did not delay the nomination. Senator Sam Ervin of North Carolina took the lead in a lengthy series of questions designed to commit Stewart to observe the Tenth Amendment and other provisions of the Constitution most protective of state's rights. Stewart gave essentially noncommittal answers that he would of course consider those provisions along with all of the other provisions of the Constitution. He was favorably voted out of committee and easily confirmed.

I had met Stewart, a top Yale Law School graduate and former member of the Cincinnati city council, as one of the first group of Eisenhower judicial appointees. A few years younger than I, he then became the youngest federal judge. As a Supreme Court Justice, he frequently joined Justice John M. Harlan as the pair of moderates who eased the split between the "liberal" and "conservative" wings of the court. His opinions over the years were consistently temperate, scholarly, and excellent.

During the time of most intense bitterness over desegregation, particularly school busing, the Supreme Court also aroused antagonism by significantly stiffening the procedures for getting criminal convictions, putting new burdens on arresting officers and prosecutors. Chief Justice Earl Warren frequently seemed a reformer at heart. Justices William O. Douglas, Hugo Black, and William J. Brennan, Jr., supplied the necessary rationalizations. Concern for the neglect of black defendants' rights in some southern courts invited correction but sometimes also led to generalizations tightening procedures in all states, including expanded protections against search and seizure. Some congressmen took advantage of the growing criticism of the Court's concern for rights of defendants as a cover for their hostility to the Court's stand on desegregation.

I was the spokesman for the Eisenhower administration in opposing legislation to curb the courts. I had already become friendly with some of the Justices. When I first arrived in Washington, Justice Tom Clark invited me to his chambers to meet the other members of the Court. Justice Harlan and Mrs. Harlan had my wife and me to dinner at their home with Justice and Mrs. Brennan. Chief Justice Warren had become friendly because of my interest in court administration. He appointed me to the Court's advisory committee on the federal rules of criminal procedure.

Because the Department of Justice was the court system's most frequent litigant, I continued my efforts in favor of pretrial and the individual calendar system. I spoke to bar associations. I also organized a large two-day Justice Department conference on court congestion. Justices Clark and Brennan attended, as did leading lawyers and judges from all parts of the country. It supported the need for more federal judgeships and higher judicial salaries to attract leading lawyers in mid-career so that they could give many years of service.

As my friendship with Eastland deepened, it added a few moments of pleasant relaxation to a constructive working relationship. Washington was a convivial city. Senator Eastland agreed to have lunch with Sheneman and me. He insisted that a layer of lemon juice on top of a martini would prevent it from being intoxicating. We thoroughly tested and, I believe, exploded this hypothesis. From time to time, in the late afternoon, he would take me to a room behind the office of the secretary of the Senate where he and a few other senators would enjoy a highball. We rarely discussed desegregation. We recognized each other's position and were absolutely candid with each other. We solved many problems.

Perhaps, as our culminating achievement, we reached agreement on a bill to add 25 critically needed new federal judgeships during the last year of the Eisenhower administration. Politically, this was unheard of. Ordinarily, the Democrats who controlled Congress would postpone new judgeships, hoping for a Democratic president to fill them. I convinced Eastland of the need. I also told him that while I could make no commitment as to who would be nominated, I would consult with him and the Democratic senators from each state just as I talked with Republican senators in the ordinary course of judicial appointments. He convinced Lyndon Johnson. The bill started to move to a vote but Rogers, afraid that I had made a possibly embarrassing deal with Eastland, sent him a harsh letter, which he relayed to Senator Johnson, underlining the fact that there had been no commitment as to future appointments. There had in fact been none, but Eastland and I were counting on our trust in each other to do the fair thing. The letter offended Eastland and outraged Lyndon Johnson, who called the bill off the Senate floor. Rogers, always watching out for the larger questions, was glad not to have new political controversies about judicial nominations thrust on us during a presidential campaign when political sponsors of dubious appointees would be strongest, just to reduce the everlasting overload of the courts.

Other congressional contacts were frequent but less significant. Often they consisted of minor patronage problems, important to a senator's constituents but not to the country. Almost unbelievably, Senator John Sherman Cooper of Kentucky, a former ambassador to India, pursued with diplomatic tenacity, in visit after visit, an effort to have us appoint as deputy marshal a loyal constituent's son who had been convicted of murder. He claimed that in eastern Kentucky this was not a disqualification.

The department's legislation did not become heavy until I drafted a new civil rights bill to supplement the one that had been achieved by Eisenhower in 1957, the first civil rights legislation since Reconstruction.[2] Our bill provided for fact finding by court-appointed special masters and civil rights remedies by injunction to eliminate the need for reliance on criminal law enforcement and jury trials. It also created an equal job opportunity commission. By executive order, Eisenhower had already created a committee on government contracts to persuade and require government contractors to desegregate their plants and work force. Vice President Nixon was chairman of the committee, which included civil rights leaders such as James Nabrit, later president of Howard University. As deputy attorney general I was its ex-officio counsel. The bill we drafted would have formalized the committee and would have given it subpoena power, but this provision was sacrificed to get the bill passed. It was Senator Johnson who permitted the bill to pass, but it was Senator Jacob Javits who handled the negotiations with him. This provision for the commission was later restored in the next civil rights act drafted by Robert Kennedy and passed during the Johnson administration after President John Kennedy's death.

As the 1960 presidential election approached, I occasionally represented Rogers in the president's legislative meetings with the Republican con-

2. John D. Calhoun, a Cravath partner on leave who had succeeded Leon Silverman, assisted me.

gressional leaders, Senator Everett Dirksen of Illinois and Congressman Charles Halleck of Indiana. Dirksen had been a Taft supporter and had harshly attacked Dewey during the Republican Convention. He was amiable and popular as a legislative leader but essentially "don't rock the boat." Halleck was an out-and-out reactionary, anti-civil rights and anti-court. Dirksen was a colorful personality. Halleck was colorless. Asked to comment on their dull program of minor legislation, which ignored civil rights, I told the meeting that, speaking for my home community of 10 million, I had not heard anything that would get a vote for Nixon. When Dirksen mocked me, "Larry, I've never heard you so serious," I countered, "Everett, you always bring out the best in me." Everyone laughed, particularly the president. Labor Secretary James Mitchell and Health, Education and Welfare Secretary Arthur Fleming backed me up. Nixon was sympathetic and one of the best members of the administration in support of civil rights. The Justice Department's civil rights bill became part of the program.

Forever unforgettable to me was my "debate" with then-Senator John F. Kennedy on civil rights, before the leaders of the combined civil rights organizations at their annual dinner in Washington. The senator, then a presidential candidate, was, as always, witty, charming, and eloquent after I, as a last-minute selection, stiffly outlined the program of the Eisenhower administration. Senator Kennedy, while generous to me, contrasted unmet needs with our progress. The audience politely applauded my talk but gave Kennedy a standing ovation. When I told Rogers the next morning how things had gone, he said, "Well, you can't expect to beat a presidential candidate." But I had a deeper concern. Rogers and I had never regarded Kennedy as a heavyweight, but Kennedy was a formidably ingratiating speaker. A few weeks later he subjected Rogers to a similar experience when they each spoke for their respective political parties at the Gridiron Dinner. Then, a few months later, I listened with dismay to the first of his debates with presidential candidate Nixon. Skillfully and with grace, he turned the tide of the 1960 election. I met Kennedy only once after his election when, in the White House, he addressed the first members of a new organization, Lawyers Committee for Civil Rights Under Law. While Lyndon Johnson was cordial and effusive, Kennedy seemed distant and preoccupied.

I met Martin Luther King. Joe Rogers had me talk briefly to him about our civil rights program. On my way to the White House, I dropped him off at a nearby office. The few minutes with him impressed me with his grace, strength, and charm, even though we had little opportunity to talk about tactics or strategy. He was friendly but noncommittal about the details of our program. When, during the 1960 presidential campaign, he was arrested and imprisoned in Georgia for driving an automobile without his driver's license, I instantly drafted a letter for President Eisenhower to telegraph the governor of Georgia stating that the federal government was prepared to react strongly against this effort to misuse a trifling offense as an excuse to imprison King. I dictated the letter to my old friend Jim Hagerty, the president's press officer, but the president did not want to be drawn into the controversy. He was strict in separating the presidency from what he might regard as partisan politics. I also tried to reach Rogers, who was on Nixon's campaign train, to ask that Nixon intercede, but as he came to the phone, the connection broke and the train pulled out of the station. It was hours before I could reach him again. By then Robert Kennedy was on his way by private plane to Georgia to intercede for Martin Luther King.

Socially, Washington was a trying period for my family and me. I had taken a slight cut in salary when leaving the court. Our children were in public school. Never truly at ease socially, we usually had meager household help. Nor did we have much money for entertainment. We declined diplomatic receptions. Once a year the president included us as guests for his annual dinner in honor of the Supreme Court. After having been limited to short vacations at nearby Delaware beaches, in my third year I accepted an invitation to an international conference on antitrust laws in Frankfurt, Germany, one of the preliminaries to the formation of the European Union.

I found the slowest transatlantic crossing, the Cunard Liner *Parthia*, making an 11-day trip to Greenock, the port for Glasgow. She was small and not quite up to date but I enjoyed every minute, even the salt-water showers reminiscent of my days as a seaman. Seated at the captain's table with the president of Cypress Mines and an officer of Rolls-Royce, a war-time air commodore, both still smarting from the cruel treatment of the Highlanders after their defeat at Culloden in 1745, I was assured that my Scottish ancestors were on the right side. A day after skirting the green, resplendent coast of Donegal, we listened to the ship's master, a proud Scot, use the ship's announcement system to identify the fabled isles as we entered the Firth of Clyde, one of the world's most beautiful waterways. No passenger went below until we docked.

With only a weekend in Scotland, my friends routed me from Edinburgh to Stirling and Killin and then through the Trossachs to Oban on the Atlantic Coast and, somewhat reluctantly, back through lovely Inverarry and Argyle, the Campbell stronghold. Attending an admiralty conference in London, I witnessed at Lloyd's my first formal English dinner, with the heads of its syndicates in full dress, wearing their military decorations and the insignia of their orders. The following night in Paris was an unpleasant contrast because the embassy had booked my reservations for a day earlier. Professing outrage, the hotel management assigned me a tiny room just above the service entrance. Nevertheless, my first jet flight to Frankfurt, in the impressive new French Caravelle, restored my spirits.

While the conference itself impressed me and I enjoyed meeting the American and European lawyers, my language deficiency was a handicap. The person translating from German to English was not a lawyer and she missed distinctions made by the speakers, using the same English words for different concepts. Some listeners switched to the German-French interpreter but my French was not adequate. After three days, I returned home by air, my first transatlantic flight.

The Justice Department tried to stay out of politics. During Nixon's campaign to succeed President Eisenhower, I was inactive, although I did write a civil rights speech for the president, which was never delivered. It emphasized the waste of a national asset, the underuse of 19 percent of the population, because of racial bias. The campaign was close. Nixon suffered some bad breaks, primarily due to overscheduling and painfully injuring his leg just before his first debate with Kennedy. Kennedy's victory turned on narrow margins in Illinois and Texas. Late votes, produced by Chicago Mayor Richard J. Daley's machine, with rumors of gangster support, gave him Illinois. Inconsistent rulings by election officials discriminating between Republican and Democratic districts helped him win Texas. I started legal research and wanted to investigate election violations in those two states, but Nixon quickly decided not to put the country through a period of uncertainty. He accepted defeat.

Robert Kennedy, amidst controversy, was appointed attorney general by his brother. As he and Byron White, the new deputy attorney general, prepared to take office, Rogers and I assisted them. Kennedy, as counsel for Senator McClellan's Senate committee investigating organized crime, had impressed me more by his energy and zeal than by his legal analysis. He would call me requesting prosecution of witnesses who gave conflicting testimony. I would have to explain that conflict was not enough, even though one must have lied. It was necessary to prove beyond a reasonable doubt who the liar was. Kennedy had checked with Eastland about me and very generously offered to have his brother reappoint me as a judge in my former court. Deeply grateful as I was for his generosity, I had already committed myself to become a partner in my old firm, Davis Polk Wardwell Sunderland & Kiendl. Although I had really loved the court, I would not have felt comfortable moving out and moving back. The Davis Polk opportunity had been something I had hoped for since law school. Perhaps, at last, financial security would be achieved.

Rogers and I left the Department of Justice at one of its highest points. Its honors program was attracting top law students. Its commitment to quality was reflected in the caliber of the judges appointed by President Eisenhower. The department was ready for Attorney General Kennedy's more dramatic civil rights activities. President Eisenhower had listed Rogers as one of 10 Republicans he thought worthy to be president. He had recommended me to Vice President Nixon as a possible successor to Rogers.

Chapter 12
TRIAL

"Can we close or not?" James Ling asked as I sat in his windowless office in the plant of Ling-Temco Electronics, Inc., an aircraft subcontractor in Garland, Texas. He and his associates had just obtained tenders of thousands of shares of stock of a much larger Dallas aircraft company, Chance Vought Corporation. As a financial entrepreneur, Ling had made a fortune purchasing small companies, invigorating them, and then acquiring larger ones. Leaving the Navy at the end of World War II as an electrician, he had first prospered as an upstart electrical contractor and then moved to the manufacture and installation of sound systems for theaters and similar organizations. Through this electronic sound company, he had obtained a controlling interest of the Temco Aircraft Company, owned by a group of former employees of North American Aviation who bought the plant at the end of World War II. Under Ling, Temco, which had been subcontracting parts for aircraft and repairing them, was converted to Ling-Temco Electronics and hoped to reach out to provide complete aircraft systems, but to take the giant step it envisioned, it had to acquire a much larger and more sophisticated company.

Chance Vought had established an enviable reputation during World War II as the provider of fighter aircraft for naval carriers. After the war it continued as a supplier for the Navy and tried to enter the field of missiles and spacecraft. Both Ling-Temco and Chance Vought were almost totally dependent on government work, which had been steadily declining. Although some of Chance Vought's officers and directors had favored the merger, its president retained Covington & Burling, a prominent Washington law firm, to block it and alert the Justice Department's antitrust division. As Ling confronted me, I was waiting to go to court to defend him and Ling-Temco from a Chance Vought motion for a preliminary injunction.

I had never handled an antitrust case. When I arrived at Davis Polk a few weeks earlier, I had started work for my first client, referred to me by Warren E. Burger, eventually to succeed Warren as Chief Justice of the United States but then a recently appointed judge of the District of Columbia Circuit. Burger had asked me to help a group of university professors, the trustees of a charitable foundation that had been given control of a valuable fleet of American oil tankers when the civil division of the Department of Justice under Burger had divested control from a group of Chinese entrepreneurs. Burger had shrewdly concluded that the professors and the foundation were being victimized by the fleet managers who had been installed by the original Chinese owners.

I had just immersed myself in these facts when I was called into Kiendl's office to meet Ling-Temco's Dallas counsel and a delegation of officers and supporting venturers seeking a larger firm to respond to Covington & Burling's claim that the union of the two companies constituted an unlawful restraint of trade detrimental to their principal customer, the United States government. While they waited for our answer, Kiendl and Ralph Carson, our next senior litigation partner, an expert in antitrust law, discussed our response. Kiendl wanted me to take on the case and handle it. Carson, not selfishly but out of concern for me, suggested that he and I do it jointly or that perhaps he might exercise a sort of oversight until I became more familiar with antitrust law. Kiendl persisted. It was agreed that I would take the case and seek help if I needed it.

Though I knew little about antitrust law, I knew the shortcomings of the antitrust division—it was understaffed, plagued by delays, too reliant on the sympathy of the Supreme Court, and suffered due to an indifferent regard for district court judges. I also suspected Covington & Burling would play for time to hold off the union. Conversely, most federal trial judges would expect forthrightness, particularly from a former judge. So I quickly decided that we would move as aggressively as possible. Happily, I was assigned the most promising litigation associate in the office, Henry King, who would soon become a partner and, many years later, the managing partner of the firm. From Tag Whipple, another partner who specialized in antitrust advice, I obtained a compendium of all of the court and Federal Trade Commission decisions interpreting section 7 of the Clayton Act, the law relating to our problem. Because none of these earlier cases had arisen in Dallas, I realized that our judge might share my lack of antitrust familiarity. Accordingly, we compiled a small printed volume of nonargumentative summaries of all of these opinions to give the judge and my opponents at our first meeting. With King and two younger associates, I virtually moved to Dallas, working long hours with Ling-Temco personnel to learn about the aerospace industry in order to surpass the knowledge of our opponents and to gain the confidence of the judge.

When Ling asked me his critical question, whether to purchase the tendered stock before the judge heard the motion for a preliminary injunction, I told him that there was no restraining order that prevented it but that the judge might feel that we had precipitated the deal and deprived him of an opportunity to preserve the status quo. The question was how critical the danger if he delayed the purchase. Ling convinced me that delay did present a danger and that he was not sure he could continue to hold the financial arrangements with the other venturers. I advised him to go ahead. The deal went through. I hoped that I would be able to satisfy the judge if the question was raised before him a few hours later. Fortunately, it was not raised. The judge denied a preliminary injunction.

Our good fortune abounded. Our judge was Joe Estes of Dallas. He and I were among the first group of judges nominated by President Eisenhower. We had met when the president greeted us at the White House. Although we had little contact after that, we respected each other as members of this early group of Eisenhower appointees. More important, Judge Estes knew the background of Ling-Temco and Chance Vought. Dallas was then a thriving, growing city but not so large that a well-informed judge would not know the fundamental facts as to Chance Vought and even the smaller Ling-Temco. As I argued for an early trial, Judge Estes agreed. He wanted to grasp the case quickly. I pressed my adversaries to accelerate their presentations. Within a few weeks, the Chance Vought officers favoring merger prevailed, and Covington & Burling consented to a dismissal of its case. On March 31, Chance Vought agreed to be merged into Ling-Temco.

But by then the Department of Justice antitrust division had been aroused. While we held up the transaction and supplied the government lawyers with all requested information, they hesitated. Finally, on August 16, the merger was consummated. On that day, the government filed its complaint in Judge Estes's court requesting that the execution of merger be enjoined. Judge Estes pushed the case along rapidly. At each session I noticed our compendium of cases on the corner of his desk. We freely provided additional information to our opponents.

The trial began the Monday before Thanksgiving. We finished in two days. The government offered primarily a documentary case. We had consented to the introduction of documents to avoid live witnesses. Our defense completed the documentation. King examined a company witness and our two industry experts. I examined a highly decorated combat commander and former chief of the Navy Bureau of Aeronautics and then our expert in market analysis, who had also conducted the basic study of naval procurement for the Hoover Commission on the Organization of the Executive Branch of Government. They persuasively demonstrated the separateness of the markets of the two companies and the lack of restraint of competition that would result from their merger. Moreover, they showed that the merger would increase the competition with other government suppliers. As court adjourned, Chance Vought's former Dallas lawyer (later president of the American Bar Association) told me he had never heard a more convincing expert witness examination. Unable to respond, the government asked for a postponement to try to get a rebuttal witness and to prepare a closing argument. The judge allowed them only until the day after Thanksgiving.

After closing arguments, the judge gave an immediate decision. Although I believe we had convinced him that the government's legal interpretation was extreme and unacceptable, I nevertheless urged him to accept it because the facts were so strong in our favor and I hoped to minimize the likelihood of an appeal. He did this. Accepting the government's position as the law of the case, without leaving the bench, he dismissed the government's action. Later Byron White congratulated me on the outcome and the nonappealability of the judge's decision. The merged company, later named LTV, became a Davis Polk client for major litigation until, after Ling had been disabled by illness, the company failed, overloaded by later acquisitions.

Before this litigation had ended I was asked to defend an important international case for Esso Research, a subsidiary of the Standard Oil Company (New Jersey) and a client of our firm. In a complex transaction, Esso had designed the reconstruction of two oil refineries of the Italian hydrocarbon monopoly, one of which had been destroyed during World War II. The Italian owners complained that the reconstructed refineries did not produce gasoline with a high enough octane to satisfy the Italian market. Although Standard Oil was also named as a defendant and represented by another firm, I was given the primary responsibility for the litigation and reported jointly to the general counsel of both defendants. After several weeks of preparation, including a hard-working week in Italy, we were about to commence the discovery process when the general counsel of Standard Oil told us to discontinue, that the Standard Oil directors, looking beyond the details of our case, had disposed of it in a "global" settlement of several controversies with the Italian government. I valued the experience for the relationship with the general counsel of Standard Oil and Esso Research but also for the glimpse of the still sovereign-like qualities of the old Standard Oil Company, whose full-time directors made worldwide decisions from their lofty floor at Rockefeller Center.

Working for Davis Polk's long-standing clients did not get me into court as often as I would have liked. Well managed, they were an infrequent source of trials. Occasionally a disappointing corporate acquisition raised a question of possible fraud or breach of contract, or antitrust concerns required investigation, or private antitrust complaints could lead to preliminary litigation. But while these matters might be important and demanding and produce a deposition or two, almost all ended in settlement for less than the cost of litigation.

One antitrust matter, however, revealed the stature of Morgan Stanley, the investment banking successor of J.P. Morgan & Company. It had underwritten the securities of an agricultural equipment manufacturing company, which, after a period of success, was confronted with declining fortunes. When it had an opportunity to sell out to an important competitor, I persuaded the Department of Justice that it was a failing corporation and therefore not subject to the ordinary restraints of the antitrust laws. After I had done this, however, Morgan Stanley's officers and directors rejected the opportunity and decided to throw their weight behind the corporation they had underwritten. Putting some of Morgan Stanley's own directors on the failing company's board, they turned the company around and restored it to its prior prosperity.

Another case, a stockholder's derivative action complaining of the interrelationship between the Western Electric Company and its parent, the American Telephone & Telegraph Company (before the breakup of the old Bell System), permitted me to regain former litigation clients of the firm and to develop friendships with the general counsel of those companies, which became one of my most important sources of work for 20 years. Executing a "retreat into Siberia" defense, I exhausted our very sophisticated opponents with discovery information demonstrating overwhelmingly the careful arm's-length nature of the intercompany relationship. They accepted a token settlement.

While I relished these glimpses of the top management of Davis Polk's traditional clients, I missed the courtroom. Reaching for cases that might lead to trials, I began to urge the acceptance of new clients who came to us. This drew me into the "trading stamp wars." One company, Sperry & Hutchinson (S&H Green Stamps), had originated the concept of selling to merchants, for distribution to their customers, trading stamps redeemable for prizes given by the trading stamp company. After many years, a group of smaller companies entered the field, competing with Sperry & Hutchinson and with each other.

A newly organized trading stamp company, MacDonald's Plaid Stamps started an expensive campaign to enter the New York City market. Late in the afternoon before Good Friday, the company had been served with a restraining order by a rival company and a motion returnable the day after Easter for a temporary injunction preventing MacDonald from soliciting the rival company's customers except after a 105-day contractual waiting period. Although I knew I could have had an adjournment as long as the restraining order stayed in effect, I decided to be ready the morning after Easter by working a group of young lawyers through Easter weekend. While my office popularity plunged, on Monday morning I persuaded the judge that the contractual waiting period to which our opponent's customers had agreed was a form of penalty and an unlawful restraint on competition. My opponent, a partner in a large firm, had assumed I would ask for more time and was unprepared. He had to turn the argument over to a young associate. The court vacated the restraining order and denied the injunction. Our client successfully completed its campaign of solicitation, although an intermediate appellate court several weeks later reversed the first judge's decision. While awaiting appeal to the New York Court of Appeals, the state's highest court, we then settled the matter by an agreement that, in the future, our client would observe the waiting period. Our client had already secured its customers and no longer intended to raid those of its competitors.

Thereafter, in two short cases, I represented my client in its assertion of the industry position by defending gasoline dealers and the trading stamp company from attacks by a gasoline dealers' trade association and by the city of New York, which claimed that the trading stamps constituted a price reduction inconsistent with the posted prices required by city ordinance.

The expense of litigation, however, was more telling on small corporations and on individuals than on our larger clients. Contesting a will for an individual referred by another lawyer produced a satisfactory settlement but still a disappointed client. Tempted by another challenge, I agreed to Kiendl's request that I accept the case of the daughter of the original proprietor of a large and successful Memphis family business who was being squeezed out by her father's partner with the support of the Memphis banking community and its larger law firms. After defeating a motion for summary judgment and conducting several successful depositions, we received what I thought was a very satisfactory offer of settlement. To my surprise, the client and her husband rejected it. The lawsuit had become a preoccupation. After the client and I had reached an impasse, Robert Fiske, who had been helping me, continued the case with a well-known trial lawyer from another firm. Notwithstanding their excellent work, our client lost the case.

This somewhat artificial effort to return to the courtroom came to an abrupt end when I was called in to represent Richardson-Merrell, Inc., the renamed Vick's Vapo-Rub Company, in its defense of two tragic experiences as it expanded its business, through a newly acquired subsidiary, from over-the-counter drugs to complex prescription drugs. In one early venture, it became the United States licensee for Thalidomide, a sedative drug of great promise that had been developed in Germany. Unfortunately, it was belatedly discovered that it caused terrible birth defects if taken by pregnant women. Fortunately, it was never marketed in the United States because a vigilant Food and Drug Administration scientist had withheld approval, but there were a few cases in the United States that grew out of its use during prelicensing clinical studies. Fiske ultimately took these cases from me, settling them and leaving me to deal with the problem of a second disaster, a widely sold cholesterol-reducing drug, MER-29.

This drug had shown remarkable success and had been widely prescribed for lifetime use, but in some cases its extended use caused cataracts. The clinical trials before licensing had been too short to expose this danger, even though they met the standards of the time. The animal studies that did expose the danger because of the heavy dosages to which animals were subjected were misinterpreted and misreported. One test on beagle dogs showed a marked association with cataracts, but the scientist carrying out the study believed that the strain of dogs was atypical and naturally prone to cataracts. After he had repeated the study with another group of beagle dogs without adverse side effects, he discarded the first test and failed to report it. This was contrary to the requirements of the Food and Drug Administration and resulted in a false report to that agency.

The company had been a client of a small law firm. Confronted with both criminal and civil litigation, it needed help. At first I took responsibility for possible criminal liability. Later, with the approval of the company's casualty insurer, I took over the basic investigation and planning of the civil litigation. Having negotiated a nolo contendere plea for the scientist who had failed to report all of the animal studies and for his two immediate supervisors, I convinced the Justice Department lawyers that the executives of the parent company were unaware of these mistakes. This preserved the line between management and subordinate employees that would become critical in avoiding punitive damages in civil actions. Having established a constructive relationship with the company's officers, they elected me to the parent company's board of directors as its first "outside" member.

Ultimately, I tried two test cases against the most formidable plaintiffs' counsel. A few MER-29 civil cases had been tried in scattered parts of the country and had ended successfully for the company, but as hundreds of cases were filed, a leading personal injury lawyer, joined by a younger lawyer who was expert in pharmacological matters, became the company's most dangerous opponent. My first case was a disappointment. It was a trial in my old court. Somehow, I always disliked appearing there, either because I felt exceptional responsibility to be candid and deferential or just because I was self-conscious about my old association. It seemed to me that I never did as well in that court as I did in others. In that case, I was joined as co-counsel by the lawyers who regularly represented the casualty insurance carrier. Since I had never defended a personal injury case, they were immensely helpful, taking over the cross-examination of the plaintiff's treating physicians while I cross-examined his scientific experts. In my opening address, I conceded the negligence of my client in failing to report the adverse animal test. The only issues left were whether the drug caused the plaintiff's cataracts and whether the management of the company had been reckless or grossly negligent and thus subject to punitive damages.

Like most of those who had used the drug, the plaintiff was elderly, at an age when cataracts develop naturally. Our experts testified that drug-related injuries occurred in three steps: (1) heavy dermatitis, (2) abnormal hair loss, and (3) cataracts. I invited generous compensatory damages for whatever injuries the jury concluded were caused by the drug. We convinced the jury that the cataracts were not drug related and it limited the verdict to dermatitis, only $1,900, but the jury also added a verdict for punitive damages of $100,000. This was a serious setback because the hundreds of pending cases could not be settled as long as there was a likelihood of recovering punitive damages. I appealed to the Court of Appeals. It reversed the judgment for punitive damages and, by its opinion, supplied us with a valuable legal interpretation narrowing our exposure to punitive damages in future cases.

In the meantime, however, the company counsel decided that the next scheduled case should be defended, as he said, by a "real trial lawyer," meaning someone who tried personal injury cases regularly. The result was worse—a $1 million punitive damage verdict. The company then returned to me. The final showdown came in a third trial in Binghamton, in upstate New York. During a 17-week trial in the state supreme court, assisted by only one associate and for the first few weeks by a young partner, I again used the local counsel representing the casualty insurer to cross-examine the treating physicians while I cross-examined the academic experts. But in this case, I used the cross-examination of the plaintiff's first witness, our executive vice president, more effectively than in the first trial. With an easygoing judge, I kept the witness on the stand for several days as I had him explain in detail the scientific aspects of each test and the subsequent review of the drug by outside experts, even after it had been licensed. In this way, I gained the initiative with the jury, a good upstate jury with which I had an excellent rapport, even though seven jurors were employed by IBM—the same company as the plaintiff.

The jurors carefully absorbed the scientific data and seemed to enjoy the exhibits, which we developed for them to explain the various scientific studies. In the end, they restricted their verdict to $19,000 (by coincidence the same amount as the first trial) for the plaintiff's dermatitis, and returned a defense verdict on punitive damages. It was a perfect outcome. The judge had been very fair to the plaintiffs and there had been relatively little controversy about the law. No appeal was taken. The jurors so enjoyed the experience that for several years they had annual reunions. After this, my opponent and other plaintiffs' counsel settled rapidly. There were no more trials.

I liked out-of-town cases because I could work effectively and without interruptions 12 or more hours a day. Ling-Temco's Dallas law firm referred one of its important clients to me for a case in Sioux Falls, South Dakota, brought by a midwestern insurance company controlled by Lloyd Bentsen, the future senator from Texas, claiming that my client had guaranteed the loan of a defaulting borrower. After several motions it settled for less than the cost of litigation. My South Dakota opponent became friendly and subsequently referred another case to me for an appeal to the Supreme Court.

Extracurricular activities slowly intruded. They started innocently enough. Living in an East River apartment remote from the subway necessitated commutation by taxi down the East River Drive to our downtown office. Rush-hour taxis being hard to find, Cloyd Laporte, a semiretired partner in the Dewey, Ballantine firm, organized a taxi pool, five passengers at $5 a week, leaving a nearby streetcorner at 9:00 A.M. Among the passengers was Bruce Bromley, the Cravath firm's leading litigation partner. Laporte was a dedicated bar association leader, regularly elected as the state delegate to the American Bar Association, one of the 50 state delegates who selected ABA officers. As a past president of the New York State Bar Association, he was also a life member of its executive committee and influential in its selection of officers. At his suggestion, I was elected to the state bar association executive committee, then, in two years, as vice president for Manhattan and the Bronx. Two years later, I was elected president of the association. Laporte also arranged for me to be selected as a delegate to the American Bar Association House of Delegates, representing the New York County Lawyers Association.

Judge Breitel, completing his service as president of the Columbia University Law School Alumni Association, invited me to succeed him. With the approval of the dean, I was elected and then later elected president of the alumni federation of the entire university. I was also elected to the American College of Trial Lawyers and then to the Council of the American Law Institute, the organization of judges, lawyers, and law school professors that continues the restatement of the common law in order to harmonize the holdings of the courts and that had also begun to draft model codes.

In 1963, Governor Nelson Rockefeller, who had been embarrassed by his appointment of a corrupt chairman of the State Liquor Authority, appointed me chairman of a state commission to investigate the administration of the Alcoholic Beverage Control Law. With my two fellow commissioners, Dean William Warren of the Columbia University Law School and Manley Fleischmann, a law partner of Congressman John Lindsay, we conducted hearings and ultimately reported to the governor, criticizing the crime-inviting, hypertechnical aspects of the statute, remnants of Prohibition distrust, and especially its price-fixing and other restraints on competition, which cost New Yorkers an extra dollar for each bottle of liquor. With a staff headed by Miriam Cedarbaum, who had assisted me when I was deputy attorney general, we completed our report recommending elimination of these restraints. The recommendations were carried out by appropriate legislation. During the course of our work, Dean Warren asked me to consider a teaching position at Columbia. I could not accept, but at last I felt that I had lived down my law school record.

As we were holding a public hearing in the Education Building in Albany, we received word of President Kennedy's assassination. Dumbfounded, we first suspended the hearing and then, with the consent and approval of the witnesses who had traveled from upstate communities, we terminated the hearing. No one had the heart to go on. I expressed the grief of my colleagues and all others present. We talked a little about the president among ourselves and then just went home to be with our families. We admired the grace of President Kennedy, his family, and his cabinet. While I had never felt the confidence in his handling of foreign affairs that I had in Eisenhower, I welcomed his stand against racial segregation and his brother's dramatization of his position. Finally, however, it was Mrs. Kennedy's quiet leadership of the nation as it mourned, her example and that of her children, that forever lifted the Kennedy administration to the heights of national respect and affection.

Adjusting to a partnership was not easy. For a time, I felt the tension, insecurity if you will, of a partner inserted in the middle of the firm hierarchy without previously established firm relationships. Half of the partners had not known me as an associate 19 years earlier. None of the associates had. For 25 years I had worked in offices where the line of command was simple and clear, but Davis Polk was more democratically organized than many large firms. While almost immediately responsible for lawsuits involving millions, I had no law clerk or other assistant reporting exclusively to me. There were no permanent "teams" to which associates and younger partners were assigned to serve under older partners. Associates worked for an individual partner on case-by-case assignments. Organizing a team for a new case was usually a voluntary agreement between the associate and partner and between one partner and another who might also be using the associate. Civility became important. While I could never cultivate the more gracious, paternal attitude of those who had been trained by Mr. Davis, we always worked out our problems in spite of occasional controversy.

As the partner most likely to take a jury case or a case threatening a client's survival, I seemed excessive to some and to others insecure. Drilled under Lumbard and Dewey and Breitel, I undoubtedly was excessive in my preparation. An opponent once observed sarcastically that I left nothing to chance. Clients, nevertheless, approved. Notwithstanding occasional partner conflicts and unfavorable comparison to Mr. Davis's legendary incisiveness, this sort of preparation usually ensured a smooth-running trial in which I could seize the initiative early without fear of an unexpected boobytrap.

Certain partners were so highly regarded that their views would usually prevail. They were not dogmatic; they were admired. They were expert in developing a consensus. As the firm grew larger, these leaders were given the title of managing partner. Under their leadership, the familylike firm was institutionalized. Near the end of my first year, two important partners returned from government service, one as U.S. attorney and one as counsel to the Treasury Department. A larger than usual group of outstanding associates were elected partners, an election known throughout the firm as the "gaol delivery." Outdated fraternal restrictions on firm membership, such as race, religion, and sex, were unambiguously eliminated. The firm name of Davis Polk & Wardwell was to be kept unchanged. More reluctantly, a little later, we adopted a policy of compulsory retirement of partners at age 70. I was chairman of the committee making the recommendation, although I personally favored age 75.

During my period in the firm, none of the managing partners were litigation partners. There were three of us of equal seniority. On most matters we would agree, but there were rare disagreements about who should become a partner, usually over "lateral entry"—my occasional effort to bring in a senior associate with trial experience outside the firm. While I advocated that we reach out to the U.S. attorney's office where young lawyers received early trial work, others defended their view that partnerships should be limited to those who had earned them through their past contribution to the firm. Over the years, our partnership selections seemed to complement each other as the new partners brought their varying capabilities to the firm.

At first it seemed that my family life would become easier and more assured. With an income five times my government earnings, I thought we might even be prosperous but the cruel tax pattern of the sixties mocked my expectations. The federal income tax included a 70 percent bracket. Our New York state income tax added an additional 17 percent (credited against income for federal tax purposes). The combined taxes produced a tax between 70 and 80 percent on my highest level of income. Nevertheless, in 1962, we bought our first house in Wellfleet on Cape Cod. Our new home was everything we had wanted. With a beautiful view of Cape Cod Bay, it was located in Cape Cod National Park and its future privacy protected.

That winter, however, an X ray showed an alarming white spot on Maxine's right lung. Various tests failed to bring reassurance, and at the end of January most of her right lung was removed. Unfortunately, the cancer had already spread to her chest lining. Notwithstanding a brief period of radiation, the surgeon told me her prospects of survival were, at best, one in three. Taking an optimistic view, we resumed our life as though the shadow did not overhang us. But at the end of the summer, while on Cape Cod, her chest cavity began to fill with fluid. Gravely ill, she had to return to her New York hospital. The diagnosis showed that her cancer had spread to her brain. At first, a new drug seemed to bring a remission, but after two or three months, the drug dosage itself became intolerable. When the dose was reduced, the cancer resumed its course. In May 1964, she died. The months intervening between the forecast of impending death and its occurrence actually proved a treasured part of our relationship, notwithstanding the increasingly severe symptoms and the dread under which we lived.

While the firm generously overlooked my distraction, the quality of my work suffered. Perhaps my worst experience was arguing an appeal from a temporary injunction before the Sixth Circuit Court of Appeals in Cincinnati for a client of my friend Leon Silverman. After acquiring control of a company in Grand Rapids, Michigan, it had been harshly enjoined by the federal district court from exercising its stockholder rights in the acquired company. Although the court of appeals modified the lower court's injunction, it did not vacate it. I felt all the worse because I had mishandled my preparation, letting myself be preoccupied with details of the merits of the case rather than the need for release from the immediate hardship of a preliminary injunction.

For many years, I had taken pride in my independence and self-reliance. Now, really for the first time, I felt the depth and strength and even tenderness of the firm's support. On the night of Maxine's death, after the nurse had left my daughter Janet and me alone, it was my partner, Andy Rogers, who unexpectedly dropped in after midnight to sit with us while the undertakers arrived and left. With no church membership of my own, he introduced me to the Brick Presbyterian Church, whose minister, Dr. Paul Austin Wolfe, embraced us all in the simple eloquence of his low-key, moving funeral service.

Chapter 13
REVITALIZATION

One morning in the spring of 1965, as I was appearing before an Interstate Commerce Commission examiner, representing the County of Westchester in opposition to the closing of New Haven Railroad's Mount Vernon station, U.S. Senator Jacob Javits dropped in. During a recess, he asked me whether I would accept the Republican nomination for mayor of New York City if Congressman John Lindsay should decline it. He said I could not win but the party needed a creditable candidate. We both hoped that Lindsay would accept. After talking with Davis Polk's then managing partner, Fritz Schwarz, I thanked Javits but told him that for professional reasons, I could not accept. In fact, however, for personal reasons I did not want political exposure. I was in full pursuit of a wife. Fortunately, a day or two later, Lindsay accepted.

Six months earlier, returning to New York on the Sunday morning shuttle from Washington, I had happily put aside a Law Review article when a well-dressed, beautiful woman sat down next to me. The prospects of a dreary weekend dissipated as, noticing what I was reading, she told me that she needed a lawyer because she was about to sue the Oklahoma City bank of which her father had been a respected director. Its trust department had refused her request to invest part of her trust in gold-mining stock. In a patronizing letter, a vice president had explained that gold stocks were not a fit trust investment. Unfortunately, the stock had increased ninefold in value, and the woman was actually a shrewd investor who had been trained by her father. Finding out that I intended to vote for President Lyndon Johnson, whom I had come to know while deputy attorney general, she made a brief effort to convince me to vote for Senator Barry Goldwater, notwithstanding my concern that, decent as he was, he was also a reactionary who would undo the Dewey-Eisenhower moderation of the Republican Party and the progress made in civil rights under Eisenhower, Kennedy, and Johnson. We shared a taxi and I dropped her off at her hotel. We met for dinner, then a movie, for which she had to pay because I had forgotten to bring enough money. Of course, I took her case. Fortunately, we avoided legal action and accepted the bank's apology through its president, who agreed that her future views would be respectfully considered.

By the end of 1964, her marriage had disintegrated. With as much civility as possible, during the next few months, she and her husband worked out the necessary property disposition and completed the divorce proceedings. Shortly after the decree was entered, Mary and I were married in the chapel of Southern Methodist University with Ling-Temco's Dallas lawyer and his wife as witnesses. The speed of events surprised even me. When I stopped in Dallas, I was actually on my way to San Francisco to seek a modification of an adverse decision against Richardson-Merrell in an early MER-29 case tried by another lawyer. The marriage did not interrupt the schedule. After the court reduced the punitive damages, we flew to the island of Maui, where we spent the next month at the beautifully simple Royal Lahaina Hotel. Laporte made my excuses to the annual meeting of the New York State Bar Association without damaging my prospects for election as president the following year. We returned in time for the annual meeting of the American Bar Association in Miami. Mary was quickly liked by wives of other members of the House of Delegates, and she was particularly welcomed by those from the West and Southwest. On the way to the meeting, we visited Maxine's parents in Tampa.

My two children had already left home—Barbara, the older one, to teach in South Carolina and Janet to marry a Harvard senior whom she had met during the previous summer. With the adoption of Mary's two children, Sara and Dale, not only was my household reestablished, it was electrified. Returning to New York, we bought a new apartment and slowly furnished it while members of the firm and their wives helped place the two children in excellent schools. At first Mary traveled with me while the children amazingly adapted themselves to New York City. After I was elected president of the state bar association, we ran the summer meeting in the Catskills and then the winter annual meeting in New York. This was followed immediately by my first MER-29 trial and then, a year later, by the 17-week trial in Binghamton. Mary stayed with me in Binghamton while her mother took care of the children until their illness required Mary's return.

Mary also accompanied me to Greensboro, North Carolina, for a short antitrust trial. The government had charged the large paper companies with price-fixing container board. As is often the case in industrywide litigation, there were significant variations in the vulnerability of the companies. The better-advised, more conservative, and better-established companies avoided flagrant misconduct and did not expose themselves to explicit participation in any conspiracy. At most, the government could show some parallelism in pricing, which arguably could be explained by natural competitive factors. On the other hand, sales managers for more reckless companies not only engaged in vulnerable conversations but proudly wrote reports of these conversations to their chief executives and preserved their records. In conflict with my co-counsel, I urged that we emphasize these differences among the companies not only in fairness to the better-behaved companies but also to convince the judge that there was no uniform industrywide illegal activity. At the trial, before an early Eisenhower appointee, Chief Judge Edwin Stanley, our acknowledged chief counsel, Whitney North Seymour of New York, urged me to participate on certain issues. In doing so, I was candid and argued that the differences among the companies showed a lack of concerted action. While we impressed the judge, who decided in our favor, I was unforgiven by some vociferous corporate counsel.

Under the antitrust laws, the government took an immediate appeal to the Supreme Court. While Seymour was to be the industry advocate, I urged, with his approval, that the companies with the cleanest records also retain Archibald Cox, the former Kennedy administration solicitor general, then back at the Harvard Law School, for a supplemental presentation showing lack of industry uniformity. Cox agreed to do this, believing that it would be helpful for all parties. The most exposed companies protested. Finally, to avoid strife within the industry, we declined Cox's representation. As a result, Seymour argued the case for the undivided industry and, as we feared, the Supreme Court reversed the lower court's judgment and decided in favor of the government.

During this period, I began to do more appellate work. The general counsel of the New York Telephone Company asked me to represent the company against the New York Public Service Commission in a crucial rate case—important not only because of the millions of dollars involved but also because of the precedent it would set if not reversed. Appearing against my old commission for the first time, I convinced an upstate judge that the commission was guilty of confiscation, and I sustained this position on appeal to the highest state courts. This was one of the first cases in which I was assisted by Guy Miller Struve, who was to work with me until my retirement and even after that in other professional activities.

Earlier, having been retained by the Insurance Company of North America (INA) to reargue an adverse decision in the New York Court of Appeals, I had needed scholarly help. I was literally waiting at the office front door as Struve first arrived after completing his work as law clerk for Chief Judge J. Edward Lumbard, Jr., my old boss. First in his class at Yale, third in his class at the Harvard Law School, and an editor of the *Harvard Law Review*, he drafted a compelling brief. The court of appeals had held that a nonresident insured by a New York casualty company could be sued in New York by another nonresident injured in an accident occurring elsewhere, leaving open the possibility that the judgment could exceed the value of the New York insurance policy. New York insurance companies were concerned that this holding would impose a disadvantage to their insureds. After receiving our brief, the court of appeals denied reargument but explicated its opinion to specify that the exposure to liability was no greater than the value of the New York policy. Thereafter, INA continued to be a firm client.

The New York Telephone Company used us steadily to handle its appeals from regulatory decisions, not only by the Public Service Commission but also by federal agencies. Sometimes we joined with the agency against other appealing parties, sometimes we opposed the agency. We were exceptionally successful. In an early conference with that company's general counsel and other executives, I placed Struve in the middle of the table because he had a hearing problem. I was at first delighted but then somewhat taken aback, as he not only heard well but took over the discussion and impressed our new clients. In future conferences I showed him no deference; he did not need it. Volkswagen and the Ford Motor Company also came to us to appeal from lower-court decisions attacking the crash vulnerability of their automobiles. Here we were less successful, winning the former in the intermediate appellate court and losing the latter when a divided appellate court upheld a judgment for the injured plaintiff. In another matter, the appellate division of the state supreme court itself retained us to defend in federal court the constitutionality of its regulation of the practice of law by nonlawyer organizations. We were successful. An organization of newspaper reporters had us submit a brief to the U.S. Supreme Court, amicus curiae, on First Amendment issues.

This flow of new clients was accompanied by extracurricular requests and assignments. John Lindsay, after his 1965 election as mayor of New York City, appointed me chairman of his post-election Committee on

Crime and Law Enforcement to produce a program for him when he took office. One controversial question was alleged police brutality against blacks. My task force recommended a civilian review board for complaints against police officers, consisting of four civilians and three senior police officials. We argued that if the police officer could not get one out of four civilians to support his position, he probably was in the wrong. The police department opposed the recommendation and it was later modified, but Lindsay was impressed. He asked me to accept his appointment as police commissioner. He explained that while he would welcome me as the city's corporation counsel, there were others available for that post and he particularly needed me as police commissioner. Again, after a serious discussion with Fritz Schwarz, I declined. Grateful though I was for the honor, I simply was not in a position to leave the firm to take the post. For once, I bowed to security.

Two years later, in 1968, after I had declined Governor Rockefeller's request to serve on a commission to investigate the New York City administration, the incoming president of the American Bar Association, also general counsel to the Ford Motor Company, asked me to become chairman of the ABA Standing Committee on the Federal Judiciary, one of the most important and demanding appointive positions in the association. The committee, consisting of one member from each federal circuit and a chairman, was then the most influential lawyers' group reporting on the fitness of prospective nominees for federal judicial appointment. It reported both to the deputy attorney general of the United States and to the Senate Judiciary Committee. The deputy attorney general supplied the committee with names of persons under consideration before their nomination was announced. Sometimes, preliminary to a full committee report, he requested a quick informal review of one or more persons by just the chairman and circuit member to minimize the public embarrassment of a negative report. The time demands of the committee were enormous. It did not use a staff; the committee members did all of the investigative work. Each year we reviewed dozens of prospective nominations as elderly judges died or took senior status to make room for a new appointment.

1968 had already been a tumultuous year. Civil disorder tore at the country after the United States had been drawn into a TV-portrayed, brutal, hemorrhaging war in Southeast Asia. For a dozen years after the French had been expelled from Indochina, Vietnam had been divided between a militant Communist North and a more easygoing anti-Communist South. Fearing the spread of communism into Southeast Asia and

Indonesia, the United States had tried to bolster a succession of unpopular South Vietnamese governments against Communist guerilla insurgents and North Vietnamese infiltration. Financial aid and military supplies and advisers had been followed by military and counterinsurgency support and finally by the bombing of North Vietnam and the commitment of an American military force of hundreds of thousands. An extraordinary resurgence of the Communist forces in February 1968 revealed that Americans had been misled in any expectation of early victory. President Johnson forwent reelection. Antagonism to the war, particularly the one-sided bombing, the casualties, and the draft, erupted on many university campuses.[1]

In the middle of an alarming student strike at Columbia, I had been elected to fill a vacancy as alumni trustee. Trustees, meeting in a midtown club because the president's office and the trustees' room were occupied by strikers, supported a firm line in dealing with them. The original protest against the construction of a university gymnasium on the edge of Morningside Park had been superseded by distorted charges of racial discrimination—separate but equal—because a community recreation facility was planned beneath the Columbia gymnasium, which was to be on the upper floors at the level of Morningside Heights. Other grievances concerning the unavailability of faculty members distracted by private consulting work widened support, but underlying the student anger was the hated insecurity caused by the Vietnam War. Hardened antiwar revolutionaries from outside the university gained control of the strike. Ironically, on the day the strike started, the university president, Grayson Kirk, speaking in Virginia, had publicly urged that the war be ended at any cost.

The strike ended in a bloody confrontation after the police, with a minimum of injuries, had cleared the university buildings of the strikers. As they were leaving, the police were threatened by a large gathering, which actually included many spectators. The police attacked. This confrontation produced injuries, arrests, and public revulsion. To overcome the lasting bitterness, the university president sacrificially resigned. Fortunately, his acting successor, a master diplomat, through a series of exhausting meetings, drew from the true student leaders and thoughtful faculty members a negotiated settlement. The university senate was upgraded to supply an effective consultative body of students, faculty, and administrators. The tradition of aging life trustees was abandoned in fa-

---

1. For a succinct and well-documented account of this history, see BARBARA W. TUCHMAN, THE MARCH OF FOLLY 232-377 (Alfred A. Knopf 1984).

vor of limited service for two six-year terms. The hard-line student lawbreakers were expelled.

As president of the alumni federation, I provided a written report on the strike to the alumni, while others reported to the trustees. While noting problems within the university, my main concern was the hostility between the university and the surrounding community. With Harlem offering the ultimate in municipal problems, welfare problems, health problems, and economic problems, it seemed an ideal area for study and improvement and emancipation by the university's distinguished faculty and eager students. The obvious possibility of mutual advantage invited cooperation, not hostility. *The New York Times* gave the report a lead editorial, a column on page one, and singled it out for the "quote of the day." This community relationship has much improved. For example, Columbia's medical school now helps staff Harlem Hospital.

These activities became secondary when Mary told me that she was pregnant. Long a heavy smoker with other medical problems, this raised a challenge to her health, as she had reached her 40s. A well-intended physician, whom she had been seeing for other reasons, recommended termination of the pregnancy. While we respected him, we both rejected the thought. If we were to be entrusted with another child, we would gratefully accept the risks and responsibility.

As the new year began with this momentous expectation, a new extracurricular activity enfolded both Mary and me. President-elect Richard Nixon had selected William Rogers as his secretary of state. The most absorbing and contentious issue in our foreign policy was the Vietnam War. In the last half year of the Johnson administration, a United States delegation in Paris had begun meetings with delegations from North Vietnam, South Vietnam, and the South Vietnamese insurgents, the Viet Cong. Headed by former New York governor Averell Harriman and President Johnson's former deputy secretary of defense, Cyrus Vance, the United States delegation and the North Vietnamese, after several months of negotiation, had finally agreed on procedures. Rogers invited me to replace Vance in a delegation to be headed by President Nixon's 1960 running mate, former U.S. senator Henry Cabot Lodge. Lodge and I would both be personal representatives of the president and we would both have the rank of ambassador. I was to be in Paris on January 22, 1969, when the Nixon administration took office.

Chapter 14
FRINGE OF TRAGEDY

When *New York Times* reporter Anthony Lewis told me of President Nixon's surprise appointment of Bill Rogers as secretary of state, I recovered quickly enough to commend it as a fortuitous decision. What the State Department needed, I said, was a person qualified as a congressional advocate, an area in which Rogers excelled. I believed the policy of the United States in going to war to block Communist expansion into Southeast Asia and possibly Indonesia was sound and that our principal problem was the political undercutting of our military effort. I thought Rogers would skillfully address this problem in Congress. Rogers's calling on me, wholly untrained in foreign affairs, to replace Vance was even more surprising than his own appointment—except that he knew he could count on my personal loyalty and that I would not let self-concern keep me from challenging experts in strange fields. "I want to know what's going on, push into things if you have to," Rogers instructed me as I reported to President-elect Nixon's temporary headquarters in New York's Hotel Pierre.

Rogers exaggerated the comparability of my background to that of Vance. We had both been the second-ranking officer of an important government department and I could use the title "judge," an out-of-the-ordinary title for a diplomat. But Vance had had a long association with the problems of Vietnam, first as general counsel to the Department of Defense, then as secretary of the army under President Kennedy, then as deputy secretary of defense under President Johnson. Just before his Paris assignment, Vance, as a special representative of President Johnson, had successfully mediated negotiations between Turkey and Greece regarding Cyprus. Admired by President Johnson, he had stature with career diplomats and military leaders. While I said nothing, I recognized the overreach of my assignment to replace Vance.

After talking briefly with President Nixon, I was interviewed by Henry Kissinger, the president's prospective national security adviser. Rogers had spoken of this as though I were doing it as a courtesy, not as though it were a necessary approval. Under Eisenhower, I had not been impressed by my very few contacts with the National Security Council or its staff. I usually regarded the NSC meetings at which I substituted for Rogers as a waste of time as we listened to Allen Dulles, a friend from my old assembly district, tell us what we had already read in the morning paper. Kissinger, however, strongly impressed me. He was pleasant, articulate, and shrewd. He warned me that I would be in danger of being squeezed out because of Lodge's former close relationship with Philip Habib, the senior career officer on the delegation's staff, who had served as Lodge's political officer five years earlier when Lodge was ambassador to South Vietnam. Kissinger himself had also worked with them as a consultant.

We did not mention, let alone discuss, the far more important problem, the relationship of Nixon, Kissinger, and Rogers. Even though Rogers had no foreign policy experience, I expected that, as in the Department of Justice, the delegation would report to Rogers and receive its guidance from him, not directly from the president or from Kissinger. Actually, the president intended to formulate policy with Kissinger and count on Rogers to keep the State Department professionals in line. In *White House Years*, Kissinger has since written:

> Nixon considered Rogers's unfamiliarity with the subject an asset because it guaranteed that policy direction would remain in the White House. At the same time, Nixon said Rogers was one of the toughest, most cold-eyed, self-centered, and ambitious men he had ever met. As a negotiator, he would give the Soviets fits. And "the little boys in the State Department" had better be careful, because Rogers would brook no nonsense.[1]

I also assumed that Nixon and Rogers had maintained their old friendship when in fact, according to Kissinger, it had cooled. During the eight years Nixon was out of office, they had competed for clients. I knew Rogers was a formidable competitor. While I was in Dallas handling the Ling-Temco case, he had gained one of the investment banking clients of an overloaded Davis Polk partner. Rogers, as former attorney general, could outdraw a political figure, even a former presidential candidate. His firm was well established, while Nixon's was a combination of lesser firms.

---

1. Henry Kissinger, White House Years 26 (Little, Brown & Co. 1979).

A few hours after my meetings at the Pierre Hotel, Richard Holbrooke, one of Habib's young assistants, dropped in to my Davis Polk office and began briefing me on extensive background facts and candidly evaluating the strengths and weaknesses of our military and civilian agencies in Vietnam. His sparkling recital foretold the promise of a bright future.[2]

Logistically, the defense of Vietnam was challenging to the extreme. The southern third of South Vietnam consisted of low-lying accretions of the Mekong River, its delta, and the alluvial plain adjoining it. Here over half the population had its historic home and produced the country's basic agricultural crops. But much of the delta was barely 10 feet above sea level, and its small meandering streams were easy routes for guerilla harassment by the Viet Cong. Saigon, a seaport that was the South's largest city and its capital, was on the northern edge of the delta. The adjoining plain offered easy excavation for a bewildering network of underground tunnels, supply centers, hospitals, and other support facilities for the successful guerrilla warfare of the Viet Cong. Farther north, the fertile seaboard narrowed sharply, sometimes with less than 40 miles between the Laotian boundary and the sea. Rimmed with low-lying mountains and sparsely settled highlands, the villages and the ancient capital, Hué, were open to easy infiltration. While President Eisenhower had pledged supplies and a few hundred military advisers to train South Vietnamese military units, he had avoided the commitment of American military forces to so disadvantageous a distant war.

The American commitment to the South Vietnamese government, driven by our fear of Communist control of the Pacific Rim and Southeast Asia, had followed our earlier financial and logistical support of the French colonial government after Japan's surrender in World War II. After the French were defeated in the battle of Dien Bien Phu, they, with the support of other great powers, gained the division of Vietnam between the Communist North and the non-Communist South. A promised election to decide reunification had not been held because the leaders of the two divisions could not agree on procedures. Freedom of election in the ruthlessly controlled Communist North seemed unlikely. South Vietnam declared itself a republic.

Its government, then headed by Ngo Dinh Diem, became increasingly autocratic and unpopular. While Buddhist priests immolated themselves to protest perceived pro-Catholic discrimination, peasants increasingly resented the neglect of their interests and favoritism shown Diem's fam-

2. *See also* B.W. Tuchman, op. cit.

ily and wealthy supporters. Communists and other opponents of the government, with support from North Vietnam, revived and expanded the guerilla forces that had previously opposed the Japanese and French. Renamed the Viet Cong, the forces destabilized the Diem government. President Kennedy established a U.S. Military Assistance Command, authorized the commitment of American counterinsurgency forces, and increased the number of U.S. military advisers and other personnel to several thousand, including aircraft pilots, technicians, and military support experts. As some participated in combat, the United States sustained its first casualties. In 1963, however, Diem's own military leaders turned against him. He and his brother were assassinated the day he was forced from office. After a period of military rule, a new government was elected, headed by President Nguyen Van Thieu.

The Viet Cong continued to be successful in clandestine attacks, controlling over half of South Vietnam and sending rockets into Saigon itself. The South Vietnamese army had at first withdrawn to fortified bases, but with increased military support and training by Americans, some divisions had improved and begun to conduct "search and destroy" missions to locate and exterminate enemy units. In response, North Vietnam increased its support of the insurgents. To try to preserve South Vietnam as a barrier to Communist expansion, President Johnson, with the authority of the Tonkin Gulf Resolution (an earlier congressional resolution authorizing the president to undertake warlike activities), ordered heavy bombing of Communist positions in South Vietnam and support facilities in North Vietnam. Johnson then sent U.S. infantry into the country, leading to war. With a fierce commitment to independence, a deep reverence for ancestral continuity, and a seeming acceptance of death, North Vietnamese soldiers excelled, matched only by American forces and those of our allies, South Korea and Australia. The North Vietnamese consistently held the initiative because U.S. policy, out of concern for possible intervention by China and the Soviet Union, prevented our military invasion of North Vietnam. Bypassing the demilitarized zone between North and South Vietnam, the North Vietnamese infiltrated forces and supplies through the Ho Chi Minh trail, a complex of jungle roads along the borders of Laos and Cambodia, to bases just within Cambodia from which they attacked our forces defending the cities of South Vietnam.

Until surprised by the 1968 Tet offensive of the North Vietnamese and the Viet Cong, our government had been misled by overly favorable reports from military and civilian agencies. The assignment of General Creighton Abrams as military commander and William Colby as local head of the CIA largely ended this problem. But the Tet offensive had shaken political support in the United States and undermined President Johnson as the North Vietnamese and Viet Cong captured and briefly held Hué, Vietnam's historic capital, and other strategic centers. While our armed forces had recovered this lost territory and the enemy had sacrificed many of its irreplaceable seasoned veterans, the antiwar movement in the United States flourished. A shocked President Johnson, after announcing that he would not seek reelection, had welcomed a French proposal for negotiation, appointing Harriman and Vance to head our delegation.

The North Vietnamese, however, continued to endure military and economic losses with fortitude and with support from the Soviet Union and China. They fully understood the unpopularity of our war effort and were unhurried and unyielding. After weeks of negotiations about preliminary procedures, the parties had just agreed on the shape and seating of the conference table. While the North Vietnamese had insisted on a four-sided table, giving the Viet Cong recognition comparable to South Vietnam and the United States, they accepted a circular table with equal seating in which the North Vietnamese and Viet Cong were set apart from the other parties by the stenographers' tables.

I tried to absorb Holbrooke's briefing and supporting material and even read Kissinger's book on nuclear weapons and foreign policy while at the same time arranging for the temporary disposition of my work for the firm. Davis Polk generously solved two essential problems, granting me both a leave of absence and a continuation of my share of the firm's earnings—Harriman and Vance had served without government compensation. Wives had accompanied the senior officers of the delegation. Mary decided to accompany me despite her pregnancy, but she delayed her trip to Paris a few days to permit me to get settled.

On the day before Nixon's inauguration, Lodge and I met with him in Washington. He was still using Statler Hotel suites as offices. Although Kissinger and Rogers were there, I did not spend time with them. Nixon was friendly but obviously toiling with a heavy schedule. The meeting was brief, more ceremonial than substantive. He stepped out of his office to talk with us. It was my first meeting with Lodge, who was cordial and generous. At his suggestion, Nixon agreed that I should arrive in Paris first. I preceded Lodge on a commercial flight from New York that evening. Lodge was to arrive by military plane the following day.

As I thanked the Air Force pilot who flew me back to New York from Washington, he provided me with a sobering moment when he said he was proud to help me in my effort to bring an end to the war. The earnestness of his expectation shamed my thrill of personal excitement in anticipation of a new experience. A close-mouthed Habib flew with me to Paris. Waiting for our delayed flight, I tried to learn a little more about routine matters of behavior. After an hour or two of uncomfortable sleep, I met the press as we arrived at Orly Airport. I had little to say, except to express my determined hopes. One reporter surprised me by asking me to say a few words in French. I avoided ridicule by responding that French was such a beautiful language it should be spoken only by those who spoke it well.

While my bags were taken to the Hotel Crillon, across the street from the American embassy, I was hurried to our embassy annex to meet Vance and then other members of the staff. Hurrying to no clear purpose seemed to be the rule. For the next several weeks, we always seemed to be hurrying from the early morning to the evening, answering cables and attending ceremonial meetings. This, however, emphasized our primary role—not spontaneous negotiation but supplying information and observations to policy makers in Washington and Saigon.

The next morning, Vance, Habib, and I, followed by others, greeted Lodge at the airport. Lodge contributed an impressive political stature that symbolized the importance of our delegation. With the exception of some career State Department officers, few others could match his experience in foreign affairs, for which he had been inspired by his grandfather, the elder Senator Henry Cabot Lodge. As an early organizer of Eisenhower's 1952 campaign, Lodge had sacrificed his own campaign for reelection to the Senate. He was defeated by John F. Kennedy. During the Eisenhower administration, he had been ambassador to the United Nations, with cabinet rank. Nixon had selected him as his running mate for vice president in 1960. Then, at President Kennedy's request, he had served as ambassador to South Vietnam during the political turmoil that preceded our ultimate military intervention. With Habib as his principal career assistant, he had been at that post when the assassination of the South Vietnamese president publicly exposed the disintegration of the South Vietnamese government. When he replaced Harriman in Paris, Lodge had been serving as ambassador to Germany, a key European ally. Able but occasionally temperamental, his independence had caused a problem or two in the 1960 political campaign. Rogers, of course, knew his history.

Governor Harriman had permitted Vance to manage the delegation. At the request of President Nixon, Vance stayed on for a month after my arrival, but he and Lodge more or less ignored each other. Vance made no attempt to break me in, but I attended his morning staff intelligence briefings and accompanied him on visits to the South Vietnamese and, with Lodge, to the Soviet ambassador to France, Andrei Vyshinsky. When Vance left, Habib became the central figure of our delegation and, with Lodge's acquiescence, not too gently pushed me aside.

Habib, unlike the public image of State Department officers, had entered the department from a rough-and-tumble background as a Brooklyn shipping clerk. His exceptional rise through the department reflected his shrewdness, industry, intelligence, and an expert poker player's ability to read his adversaries. Working long hours and with a Spartan lifestyle, he was intolerant of amateurs and other nonsense. His obvious affection and regard for Vance testified to Vance's professionalism. The young career staff that reported to Habib included three future important ambassadors and a future executive secretary of the department. Habib himself, after later serving as ambassador to South Korea, rose to the State Department's senior career post, under secretary of state for political affairs.

Our military advisory group, selected by the chiefs of staff, was equally outstanding. Headed by Lieutenant General Fred Weyand, later general and commanding officer of the U.S. Army, it also included Colonel Paul Gorman, who was later promoted to general and chief of the U.S. Southern Command. As Habib and Lodge fulfilled Kissinger's prophecy that I might be frozen out, I depended on our military advisers to avoid total exclusion.

My closest friend was Marshall Green, former career ambassador to Indonesia, who joined the delegation as a possible replacement for Habib. Except for Lodge's personal aide, he was the only state department officer with no prior attachment to Harriman and Vance. As the only partisan Republican besides Lodge, I was at first somewhat guarded because the peace effort was so subject to divisive political and public controversy. Even though Presidents Kennedy and Johnson had drawn us into the war, leaders of the Democratic party now attacked Nixon for not getting us out. I did not know what President Nixon's ultimate position would be or whether it would conform with the view of the Harriman-Vance staff. Few questioned the desirability of extricating U.S. forces from Vietnam. The problem was how to do it without exposing the South Vietnamese to destruction and betraying our allies, the Australians, the South Koreans, and others who had joined our fight against the expansion of communism into Southeast Asia. Whether or not more aggressive military activity would accelerate peace negotiations was a critical secondary question.

Our military advisers tended to support more aggressive military action than the State Department group. For example, the two groups differed regarding the bombing of North Vietnamese bases just inside Cambodia from which enemy regulars persistently infiltrated South Vietnam and attacked our forces. With no basis for a judgment of my own and with my obligation to Rogers to "push in," I could only raise questions as I would in preparing an expert witness. A lawyer questioning an expert does not have to pretend to be one but a delegation leader so questioning his staff appears irritating and even naïve. Never before had I stepped into a controversial government post so dependent upon policy advisers selected by a political opponent. Unlike Lodge, I had even failed to request a personal aide. This isolation became obvious after Vance left. While I took over his morning staff briefings, Habib ultimately declined to attend and conducted his own while the military group continued to assist me.

In the early formulation of recommendations for the president's position, our delegation contributed its views to be considered along with those of our ambassador to South Vietnam, Ellsworth Bunker. A few weeks after my arrival, the four parties began weekly, closed meetings at the Hotel Majestic, the site supplied by the French. Once the official four-party talks began in mid-February, Lodge's statements were the subject of lengthy cable traffic, with cables arriving early each day from Vietnam updating our information and expressing Ambassador Bunker's views and with cables from Washington arriving in the evening, commenting on the views expressed by Bunker and by us.

We sat around an immense circular table, the North Vietnamese and the Viet Cong delegates separated from the South Vietnamese and U.S. delegates by the stenographers' tables, which were placed at right angles to the circular table. At each session, the heads of the four delegations read prepared papers, the North Vietnamese and Viet Cong usually offering harsh statements addressed mostly to the South Vietnamese but also to us, demanding withdrawal of U.S. forces and the abdication of the South Vietnamese governing officials. Lodge's statement would include a few conciliatory sentences that would hopefully open a more constructive discussion. It was understood that the North Vietnamese were always to have the last word in the rebuttal, which usually followed a buffet lunch supplied by the French to each of the four delegations in separate dining rooms. While on two occasions I substituted for Lodge, I usually sat quietly next to him along with the senior members of our delegation. I had the responsibility to keep our allies advised of our position. Once a week I briefed the South Vietnamese in advance on our proposed statement. I also briefed the Australian ambassador who, although not a participant in the talks, was a careful observer.

Disappointed by the unyielding position of our enemies, our hopes rose when the North Vietnamese agreed to additional private two-party talks with us at their Paris headquarters. But these were no more productive than the four-party talks. Le Duc Tho, the real leader of the North Vietnamese delegation, although not so titled, took over the private meetings. He would pull a stenographer's spiral notebook out of his pocket and read off the North Vietnamese grievances against the Americans and South Vietnamese. Lodge would respond with his prepared statement, urging a constructive outcome. Then, after a brief rebuttal, the North Vietnamese would serve us tea and politely ask us about our families. Somewhat impatiently, I learned that in carrying out an unproductive diplomatic assignment, continued gracious private contact becomes an end in itself.

Probably the most important event while I was in Paris was President Nixon's visit to our delegation during his European trip in late February 1969. Marshall Green and I had drafted a proposed public position for him to use politically in riding out a diplomatic stalemate. It included a cease-fire under international supervision; simultaneous withdrawal of U.S. and allied forces from South Vietnam as the North Vietnamese withdrew theirs; and, following the cessation of hostilities, a free election in South Vietnam in which all factions would participate, to be conducted under the supervision of an international body. During the meeting of Lodge, Habib, Green, and me with the president, Rogers, and Kissinger in the "tank" (a room intensively protected against eavesdropping), the president accepted the proposed statement and later incorporated its substance in a public speech, his first statement in response to a harsh 10-point proposal by the North Vietnamese.[3]

At the meeting, I, of course, noticed a difference in President Nixon. While still cordial, he was somewhat stiffer in his relationship with Rogers, who had been his close friend. A joke by Rogers poking a little fun at him fell flat when the president did not laugh. I had also noted that Rogers did not stay with Nixon and Kissinger at the apartments for visiting heads of state at the Quai d'Orsay or attend Charles de Gaulle's dinner. Instead, he stayed at the Crillon Hotel and had dinner with me. I had already warned Rogers that Kissinger was bypassing him and communicating directly with Lodge and Habib. At one point in Nixon's

3. *See* KISSINGER, op. cit. p. 270.

meeting, I raised the question of whether all communications should not be routed through the State Department. While the others at the table listened, the president made no response. Accustomed to the practice in the Department of Justice where communications from the White House almost always went through Rogers or me, I was slow to appreciate that decisions in foreign affairs, particularly those relating to Vietnam, were to be constantly at the presidential level, with Kissinger dealing directly with our embassies and the president himself making the decisions. While in Paris, Rogers, on my advice, decided to select Green rather than Habib to be assistant secretary of state for Far Eastern affairs. I had advised this because Habib was in such ready contact with Kissinger, while Green adhered to departmental lines of communication.

Mary had arrived in Paris a few days behind me with the symptoms of a prospective miscarriage. A French physician attempted to reassure me by explaining that one out of every 10 pregnancies ended in a miscarriage—but for us, this was a very special pregnancy. Mary responded successfully by spending most of the next three months in bed. Lodge's wife, Emily, and Gay Vance and Lisa Green graciously made our suite a center of activity as they spent many hours with her. By late April it was clear that the negotiations were stalled and that it was time for Mary to return to New York. I accompanied her but then reported to Washington and continued on to Japan, Hong Kong, Thailand, and Vietnam to explain the president's position and describe the negotiations to our allies and to our military commanders.

In Washington, I reported to Rogers that Lodge, while carefully adhering to prepared positions written out by Habib, seemed to lack spontaneity and any promise for initiating a breakthrough of his own. I mentioned this as a descriptive fact, not as a complaint. I was surprised that Rogers had me report this seemingly obvious evaluation to Kissinger and that Kissinger, in turn, brought me to the Oval Office to report it to the president. None of them commented. Nixon was jovial and friendly. Months later, when I learned of Kissinger's direct negotiations with the North Vietnamese, I realized that the president had already been considering this possibility at the time of my visit.

My friends, our military advisers, arranged a remarkably comprehensive trip, visiting all four military corps areas, including an advanced post just south of the demilitarized zone. The low mountains appeared deserted, foreboding, and desolate. The post seemed hushed and alert. Thunderstorms during the return trip foretold the approaching monsoon and the end of the oppressive, humid heat. In Da Nang, I briefed the marine commander and spent the night at his headquarters. I also met William Colby, who had taken charge of CIA activities. In the highlands along the Laotian border I met with Montagnards and also spoke with local officials at Pleiku and Kantum where, in the early fighting, the Green Berets had established their reputation. Farther south, as I was flown to Tay Ninh near the "parrot's beak," the site of infiltration along the Cambodian border, I could see B-52s dropping their bombs on a parallel course. In a small helicopter without doors, flown personally by the director of our pacification program, I visited a South Vietnamese division headquarters and reviewed the honor guard that received me. With him, I also visited villages in the delta country that had just been "pacified" by ridding them of Viet Cong assassins. The local officials and residents seemed isolated and a little bewildered, but they welcomed this recognition and my assurance of support. More enthusiastically, in the fishing villages along the sea near Da Nang, the entire village populations turned out and applauded my extemporaneous speeches. I briefed Vietnamese President Thieu and the foreign ministers of Vietnam and Thailand regarding the Paris talks and the main points of the president's position. On the trip to Vietnam, I also updated our ambassadors to Japan and Thailand and our consul general in Hong Kong.

My schedule was intense, but I did see enough of Saigon to observe an almost carefree attitude among the population. Even though we heard artillery fire on the city outskirts every night, civilians seemed unapprehensive and busy, good-naturedly driving motor scooters, pedaling bicycles, or threading their way through congested traffic. I came away impressed by their graciousness. I liked President Thieu and the foreign minister and even the aggressive Vice President Ky, who had been an air force aviator. He and his beautiful wife at times entertained in Paris. He had been president first but he had given way to the slightly older and less flamboyant Thieu.

But most of all, I felt a deep admiration for our military leaders and a deep sense of obligation to the young officers who flew me to the front—uncomplaining, committed, exemplary young Americans entangled in a war in which they could only seek a stalemate. One of them, then a lieutenant, generously wrote me a letter of support 20 years later, when I was in public controversy, to remind me of our flight along the demilitarized zone through a thunderstorm as we returned from the forward command post.

I was unprepared for the social activity accompanying so short a trip. On the advice of my State Department associate, I brought the least possible baggage and my lightest clothes. In the daytime short-sleeved, open-necked shirts and khaki slacks were just right, but in the evening I was out of place with a light-colored suit when everyone else, including my State Department adviser, wore dark clothes. After lunch with our ambassador to Japan and the next day with our consul general in Hong Kong, one dinner followed another. First our ambassador to Thailand entertained the diplomatic corps and their wives. Then in Saigon, first the Vietnamese foreign minister and then my host, our deputy ambassador, had dinners for the ambassadors of our friends and allies. Finally, U.S. Ambassador Bunker had a small dinner for us; President Thieu had me for drinks; and General Abrams and I had lunch alone.

One policy that I had to explain to our military leaders and to our allies was the president's developing expectation for the "Vietnamization" of the war, the transfer of military responsibility from American forces to the improving military forces of the South Vietnamese. This was a hard sell. While the Vietnamese and Thais listened politely, I could tell in my private lunch with General Abrams that he regarded the policy as unrealistic. He had to set his jaw to keep silent. While our armed forces protected South Vietnam's major cities, the North Vietnamese and the Viet Cong still retained the initiative. While two of the South Vietnamese divisions were meeting the North Vietnamese on fairly equal terms, others were not. It was dubious that the South Vietnamese could survive alone. When I left by military plane for Hong Kong, there was gunfire as we landed before dawn to refuel in Da Nang, South Vietnam's second-largest city.

After flying without interruption from Saigon to Hong Kong to Tokyo to Seattle and then to Washington, I briefed the president on my trip and also, at his suggestion, the cabinet. I told him that I did not think that Vietnamization was being seriously accepted and that our military commanders did not believe it feasible. In the cabinet meeting he asked me what I thought of the South Vietnamese, and he seemed pleased when I expressed high regard. During our private talk he urged me to stay that night for his annual dinner for the Supreme Court, suggesting that I could borrow a tuxedo from Rogers. But I told him about Mary's pregnancy and my eagerness to get home for a day before returning to Paris. He then gave me a personal silver medallion about the size of a silver dollar as our daughter's first birth present.

The next morning, I read in the newspapers that my name had been floated by the White House as a possible replacement for Chief Justice Earl Warren, who was about to resign. While I appreciated the compliment, I did not take it seriously because there had been no discussion of the subject. Happily, Warren Burger received the appointment.

The trip to Vietnam was the high point of my ambassadorial experience. After Mary's return to New York, there was little for me to do. I continued going through the routines. Once, in Lodge's absence, I irritated several in our delegation as well as the North Vietnamese by replying extemporaneously to the North Vietnamese spokesman. On weekends I was able to walk around Paris and make trips to Chartres and other historic sites. While I was visiting a chateau on a Saturday afternoon, the owner learned who I was and invited me to have tea with his wife and him. They politely listened to my improved but still imperfect French. At other times, the Lodges took me with them. Chartres Cathedral, however, moved me as it has countless others. Subdued by its devout beauty, as the light of a spring afternoon illuminated its incomparable windows and softened its centuries-old stone, I found a seat midway down its central aisle and drifted into lengthy reflection, concern for Mary's pregnancy, and private prayer.

My personal decisions were more matter-of-fact. While a deputy with ambassadorial rank might be useful to share the meetings and the drafting incidental to active negotiations, I recognized that, in a stalemate, a restless amateur offered little and might even be detrimental. As a judge and as a lawyer I had been proud of my high rate of dispositions, and, in spite of Lodge's calming reassurance, I was not very adaptable to a seemingly nonproductive, ceremonial existence. Finally, after Lodge and Habib, without talking to me, had proposed something with which I disagreed, I sent a letter to Rogers through a visiting State Department official, telling him that I thought it was time for me to leave. Although I admired and liked Lodge and Habib, we had one too many cooks; I was not participating effectively in their decisions.

In early June, President Nixon convened Rogers, Kissinger, Lodge, President Thieu, and General Abrams on Midway Island to explain the need for Vietnamization of the war and the ultimate withdrawal of American forces. In flight, Rogers talked briefly with Lodge about me, and they both agreed that I could return to New York and keep up to date by reviewing cables once a week in Washington. Lodge and his personal assistant saw me off. Indeed, the rapidity with which they did it suggested that Lodge not only agreed with the proposal but that he welcomed it. I could not blame him for that. While trying to be loyal to him, my principal loyalty was to Rogers and the president. There was no round of farewells because I had not resigned.

I thereafter visited the State Department weekly and read cables. I met

Lodge when he visited the United States. In December, he resigned and I resigned at the same time. Rogers had told me that he anticipated Lodge's resignation and that if I wanted to replace him I could, but that in view of the lack of activity in Paris, he believed that the vacancy should be left open with Habib serving as acting head of the delegation. I realized that I lacked the political stature to be regarded as a true replacement for Lodge, and I thought Habib was actually an ideal choice. When Colonel Alexander Haig, Kissinger's assistant, called to tell me that Lodge was resigning, I had my letter of resignation ready.

In the meantime, in New York, Mary had given birth to our daughter Elizabeth. The war had depleted the Columbia-Presbyterian Hospital's staff. Predawn, while I was confined by a hard-jawed nurse to a cheerless waiting room and while the resident physician was apparently otherwise occupied, Mary and Elizabeth Porter Walsh proceeded unattended to a natural birth, which our obstetrician arrived barely in time to witness. Emily Lodge became Elizabeth's godmother.

The war had no such happy ending. While the Paris stalemate continued, Henry Kissinger in long, drawn-out private conversations with North Vietnamese representative Le Duc Tho, with President Nixon's approval, finally accepted an agreement for the unilateral withdrawal of American forces and those of all countries other than South Vietnam in return for a North Vietnamese promise not to invade. About a year after our forces withdrew, the North Vietnamese broke their promise, invaded, and supported the Communist overthrow of the South Vietnamese government.

Of my personal conversations with Lodge, one of the most memorable was his speculation about what Richard Nixon's life must have been like after his 1960 defeat by Kennedy—eight years trying to hold together support for a second try, unceasing travel, breakfast meetings in small communities, speaking to varied audiences, raising money, trying to practice law in a strange city, trying to show interest in private undertakings and maintain an appearance of assurance, while always keeping the goal of the presidency in sight. While recognizing the relentlessness of this strain, I have always believed that Nixon was a casualty of the Vietnam War. Kissinger's well-documented portrayal of Nixon's personal effort to manage the war and related negotiations exposes this overload. Neither he nor Kissinger were seasoned diplomats. Gifted though they both were, they were often addressing problems as new experiences. This contrasts with Eisenhower, who, like a professional athlete, absorbed the problems of the presidency and did not try to micro-manage any part of the job.

Chapter 15
THE CREST

If my career had a climax, it was the decade after I returned from Paris. Demanding extracurricular activities crowded in on me, along with leading corporations, including a new client, General Motors, as well as old clients for whom I had previously done little work, such as R.J. Reynolds. My work as chairman of the ABA Federal Judiciary Committee forced me to drop out of the line of succession to the presidency of the New York County Lawyers Association and the local Federal Bar Council. In spite of the overload, I did, at New York Chief Judge Fuld's request, accept appointment as counsel to the state court on the judiciary to investigate a corrupt state supreme court justice, even though this required me to create a new office and special staff to handle this assignment. After we filed our charges, the justice voluntarily retired.

After it seemed likely that I would be elected president of the ABA, I was also canvassed for the presidency of the Association of the Bar of the City of New York. I followed the advice of Fritz Schwarz reflecting the view of other senior partners that I decline. A little later, Schwarz's successor, Nelson Adams, wisely advised me not to accept the chairmanship of Columbia University's trustees. When General Motors' chairman sounded me out as possible corporate general counsel, I appreciatively declined, even though Schwarz regarded this as probably the most respected corporate law post in the country. Preferring to continue private practice, I recommended Ross Malone, a former deputy attorney general of the United States and former president of the American Bar Association, who was also under consideration, and he was appointed.

While lawyers outside the firm identified me as Davis Polk's "leading litigator,"[1] within the firm we did not compete for such recognition. If we had, we would have selected Hazard Gillespie. With recognized subspecialties, clients and corporate partners chose among us freely. Tag

---

1. Paul Hoffman, Lions in the Street 20 (Saturday Review Press 1973).

Whipple had largely withdrawn from litigation to follow Ralph Carson as the firm's principal adviser on antitrust matters. Gillespie, who had been with the firm longest, had trained under Mr. Davis and had served under President Eisenhower as U.S. attorney. Able younger partners, whom they had recruited, rapidly assumed the regular litigation of our clients. More often than not, the trials for which I was selected were out of town, presented a public controversy, and sometimes threatened a flood of litigation that might endanger the future of the client.

Each new major commitment to excel always raised a corresponding concern that I could meet the obligation—a long-accustomed "insecurity." My expanded responsibilities at times exacerbated the friction in the use of younger partners and associates and in demands I made on them. My family staunchly withstood the pressure. We did not socialize very much. On most Saturdays, we had dinner at Trader Vic's; on Sundays at the Carlyle. As the older children went away to school and college, Elizabeth established her self-assurance, first on a single city block and then as a steady customer of a friendly taxi-cab (later private car) company. Every two months, Mary and I left the children at home for a long weekend alone at the Cape Cod house whose spell somehow helped us solve our controversies and stay together. Each summer, while the older children were in camp or on a ranch, we spent a month on the island of Hawaii. During the rest of the year, except when out of town, I was usually home for dinner but started working in the early morning to follow up my younger partners and associates, whom I left to work in the office at night.

Introduced to "takeover" litigation as trial counsel for legendary expert Joseph Flom, who taught us to test every element of the deal he was opposing and also the value of using chauffeured cars instead of taxis, I temporarily delayed Kirk Kerkorian's hostile takeover of Metro-Goldwyn-Mayer by enjoining his financial backer, Transamerica Corporation. But after I won, my opponent, Arthur Goldberg, former U.S. Supreme Court Justice and former U.S. ambassador to the United Nations, gave me an unwanted education in negotiation as he shrewdly persuaded the judge to delete parts of my victory. Unfortunately, I could not complete the experience because of a conflict between MGM's contentions on other issues and previous opinions given by my firm to other clients.

I always welcomed maritime matters. R.J. Reynolds, one of Davis Polk's oldest clients, had acquired as a new subsidiary Sea-Land Service, Inc., the originator of the concept of container ships—ships into which large, prepacked containers were stowed directly from truck trailers.

Malcom McLean, who, had become Reynolds's largest individual stockholder by the sale of the company, had begun a trucking business with a horse and wagon in North Carolina. Progressing to trailer trucks, he surpassed his competitors by strategically locating pools of containers for quick delivery to a customer for loading and later pickup. Extending this strategy to ocean commerce, he first bought a few old cargo vessels, tore out their midsections, and expanded them to accommodate previously packed 35-foot containers. By avoiding government maritime subsidies, he was free to fix his own rates. Finally, he sold his old trucking company and developed Sea-Land into the largest ocean carrier in the world. But he always needed additional ships.

When he first came to me it was because his lease of new United States Line container ships had led a competitor, American Export Line, to claim an antitrust violation. Seeking a preliminary injunction, our opponent gave us short notice over Thanksgiving weekend. Working nights, on the following Monday, we caught their distinguished antitrust lawyer uncertain of the facts and having to read his argument while I argued extemporaneously and responded easily to the judge's questions. After the judge denied an injunction, the controversy settled satisfactorily. Thereafter, I represented McLean and Sea-Land in further controversies, including a bitter personal action brought by the Washington firm Williams & Connolly for the former United States Lines president, who claimed to have had a personal deal with McLean apart from a merger agreement between their companies. By winning the pretrial motions and after a younger partner [2] successfully deposed the plaintiff, we concluded the case with a token settlement.

AT&T and Western Electric called on me frequently, AT&T once sending me to Hawaii to prevent General Telephone & Electronics from drawing AT&T into its conflict with ITT. In the bitterest period of the Vietnam War, both General Motors and AT&T had me attend their annual meetings to deal with possible disruption. When General Motors was charged with polluting the Hudson River, I settled the controversy by a civil decree and nolo contendere plea for the company and its two local officers. General Motors then had Struve and me handle its litigation with its dealers.

The chairmanship of the ABA Federal Judiciary Committee absorbed one-third of my time. Deputy Attorney General William Kleindienst, as I had for Rogers, had initial responsibility for the selection and confirma-

2. Thomas P. Griesa was later appointed a federal judge and is now chief judge of the U.S. Court for the Southern District of New York.

tion of federal judicial nominees. An Arizonan, jovial, quick, shrewd, and bright, he wanted our committee's support, not its opposition. He and I became friends. President Nixon never nominated a federal judge not found qualified or better by my committee. Most achieved higher classification. Others were quietly dropped after an adverse report. But the work doubled in intensity, difficulty, and controversy when dealing with a Supreme Court vacancy. Friendly but a little cynical, a hard-boiled municipal bond lawyer rather than a litigator, Attorney General John Mitchell would not let the committee investigate before the president announced the appointment for fear that our investigation would cause premature publicity, publicly embarrassing to the prospective nominee and offensive to the Senate. This seriously reduced our effectiveness because, once an appointment was announced, lawyers tended to become less candid.

President Nixon's effort to appoint a southern judge to the Supreme Court provoked the ultimate in bitter controversy. The South had supported his presidential candidacy. The resignation of Justice Tom Clark when his son became President Johnson's attorney general and the advanced age of Justice Hugo Black could leave the South unrepresented on the Court. Many respected southern judges had been slow in overturning old patterns of discrimination. While realistic civil rights groups somewhat tempered their opposition, labor unions and organizations opposing the appointment for other reasons used these early decisions to rationalize their opposition. In these cases, the good relationship Kleindienst had established with my committee served him well.

First was Clement Haynsworth, the chief judge of the U.S. Court of Appeals for the Fourth Circuit (Maryland, Virginia, West Virginia, North Carolina, and South Carolina). While Haynsworth was well liked and able, an early decision of his had retarded school desegregation in a rural Virginia county. My committee nevertheless reported him well qualified and I testified for him before the Senate Judiciary Committee, acknowledging the one erroneous ruling. But opponents professed concern that he had traded in the stock of a company while it had a case before his court. The stock transaction, one of his frequent trades, was small and not materially affected by the court decision, for which the opinion was written by another judge. Nevertheless, those concerned with his conservatism used this technical misstep to defeat his nomination even though the Senate's Judiciary Committee had reported it favorably.

President Nixon then nominated George Harrold Carswell, a young federal district judge from Tallahassee, Florida. I liked him because, when

I was deputy attorney general, he was one of the few southern U.S. attorneys who would cooperate with our policy of enforcing desegregation. Chief Justice Earl Warren had selected him as a young southern addition to a judicial conference committee. A Roosevelt-appointed, respected, midwestern chief circuit judge had suggested his nomination. Serving as a trial judge in the essentially rural Northern District of Florida, Carswell had relatively few complex cases and little chance to show above-average ability. The local bar approved him. With one exception, the appellate judges who had reviewed his work commended him. Civil rights lawyers spoke of him as courteous and fair in demeanor, even though he frequently ruled against them. His weakest spot was his open antipathy for federal habeas corpus proceedings to review state court criminal judgments.

My committee had no advance notice of the nomination before it was sent to the Senate. When the Senate Judiciary Committee required us to rush our report, we refused to specify degrees of qualification and simply found Carswell qualified. In other words, we did not oppose him. We did not affirmatively recommend him and I did not testify for him. While we were criticized for straddling, the Senate committee reported the nomination favorably. Then Carswell had to admit that, in his testimony before the Senate committee, he had falsely denied once being a director of an all-white private country club created to acquire the property of a desegregated public golf course. Liberal groups, newspapers, and several bar associations, including that of New York City, demanded that my committee then oppose the nomination. By a vote of eight to four we declined. The false testimony was given after we had filed our report. We did not want to set a precedent for modifying our report as each new fact developed. We believed the Senate Committee could make its own evaluation of this false statement. Many erstwhile supporters criticized us. Led by Senator Edward Brooke of Massachusetts, the Senate rejected the nomination.

To restore the reputation of the committee, I proposed changing our standards for Supreme Court nominees. I was less concerned with Carswell's false statement than with his mediocrity.[3] We had been applying the same standards for Supreme Court appointees that we applied to the lower courts. After a full day's meeting, we unanimously agreed that

3. When Carswell was attacked in the Senate as mediocre, Senator Roman Hruska of Nebraska lightened the debate when he argued that mediocrities were entitled to representation on the Supreme Court.

we would more severely test Supreme Court nominees. We clarified our grades of qualification, differentiating between those we would recommend as "one of the best available" and others merely "not opposed" or "not qualified," We filed a special report with the ABA House of Delegates, and I appeared personally before the board of governors to explain our position. At the next meeting of the House of Delegates, Attorney General Mitchell praised the work of the committee and announced that future proposals for Supreme Court appointment would be sent to the committee for investigation before the president announced the nomination. Judge Harry Blackmun of the Eighth Circuit, the first nominee investigated under the new system, received our highest rating and won easy confirmation.

The next two nominees, Herschel Friday and Mildred Lillie, were not so lucky. Returning by ship from an ABA meeting in London, the Chief Justice and the attorney general were impressed by a well-liked lawyer from Arkansas and an intermediate state appellate court judge from Southern California. The attorney general proposed them to fill two new Supreme Court vacancies. Realizing that these nominations would probably test our new standards, my committee was dismayed. Pursuing exhaustive investigations, one member of the committee reviewed every brief written by the Arkansas lawyer and another reviewed every opinion written by the judge. The committee concluded by a vote of eight to four that neither prospect was qualified. I voted with the majority.

Kleindienst was stunned when I telephoned him at the end of our daylong meeting. While our committee members and the former chairmen who had joined us were committed to secrecy, the following morning *The Washington Post* carried an exclusive story reporting our action. A *Post* reporter who did not ordinarily cover the Justice Department was seen leaving the department in the evening after I had informed Kleindienst of our decision. Attorney General Mitchell, professing outrage at the leak, revoked his promise to let my committee investigate proposed Supreme Court justices before the president announced their nomination.

The night of the *Post* report, Mike Wallace invited me to appear, live, on his CBS "60 Minutes" program. Warned that he could be severe, I prepared for extemporaneous responses, as I often did, spending most of the afternoon sitting in Battery Park talking out my explanation aloud but to myself. As I arrived at the CBS studio, Mitchell announced the president's nomination to the Supreme Court of former ABA president Lewis Powell and Assistant Attorney General William Rehnquist. Wallace questioned me sympathetically for the full hour as I explained the need for candor, which could only be gained by permitting the committee to screen nominations before they were announced. I denied the committee's responsibility for the leak but explained that leaks in the course of investigations would be inevitable and that they would actually be beneficial because it would be better for the president to learn the worst about a nomination before sending it to the Senate rather than afterward. I predicted that the committee would support both Powell and Rehnquist. In a much earlier private conversation with Mitchell and Kleindienst, I had already suggested Powell, and when they asked about Rehnquist, I had forecast probable approval.

As seems often to be the case, public controversy was not detrimental to my practice, but beneficial. Corporate counsel, particularly those like Ross Malone of General Motors, understood the responsibilities of my committee and respected its independence both in rejecting excessive public criticism of a proposed appointee and in standing up to the president of the United States. Leon Jaworski, then president of the ABA, its Board of Governors, and its House of Delegates, strongly supported us. The leader of the most important bloc of state delegates asked me to accept his support for the association's presidency. With his guidance, two years later, I was elected unopposed.

My friendship with Mitchell and Kleindienst was central to the rumors that I used government relationships for my clients.[4] In fact, I did not. I always dealt with the Department of Justice at the career level, not just for propriety but for effectiveness. I knew many of the career lawyers personally. We trusted each other. Moreover, I knew that they would be consulted if I went to a higher officer. The one exception was my intercession on behalf of a long-standing firm client, ITT. In the 1970s, ITT, with its foreign subsidiaries, was a leading producer of favorable foreign exchange for the United States. But because its foreign commitments were both vulnerable and extensive, Harold Geneen, its hard-driving, ambitious, committed chairman, commenced a program of diversified acquisitions in the United States. As he succeeded, he aroused the opposition of the antitrust division of the Justice Department. In 1971, it opposed ITT's acquisition of the Hartford Insurance Group; the Grinnell Corporation, a large fire alarm manufacturer; and the Canteen Corporation, a large prepared-food vending company.

Even though the antitrust litigation was being handled by a Washing-

---

4. Hoffman, op. cit. pp. 179-88; ANTHONY SAMPSON, THE SOVEREIGN STATE OF ITT 221, 246-48 (Stein and Day 1973).

ton firm, Fritz Schwarz was ITT's principal outside counsel. At his invitation, I met with Geneen. While engaging and attractive, he wasted no time. He wanted to appeal to the president. Instead, I proposed that I try to get Mitchell to agree to join in a meeting with a cabinet subcommittee and the secretaries of treasury and commerce to review the antitrust division's position. I advised Geneen against a direct appeal to the president for fear of arousing opposition by Mitchell, who was the president's friend and former law partner. My plan was frustrated when Mitchell surprisingly disqualified himself, apparently because of prior dealings with ITT, and turned ITT matters over to Kleindienst, who, I feared, did not have the stature to convene a cabinet-level review of the strong-willed antitrust division. Nevertheless, Guy Struve and I prepared a memorandum to him, which Struve delivered. By telephone, I urged Kleindienst to persuade Mitchell to reconsider his decision to disqualify himself. As an incidental and immediate objective, we sought to delay the Supreme Court review of a lower-court decision approving one of the three challenged acquisitions, the Grinnell acquisition. Kleindienst simply referred the memorandum to the head of the antitrust division and a day or two later denied our request.

A few hours after I had reported failure to ITT's general counsel, Kleindienst again telephoned to tell me that the solicitor general would request a postponement of the Grinnell case. He was actually laughing, saying, "You can never tell what will happen next around here. . . . If you want to see one mad solicitor general . . . . " Puzzled but pleased, I again passed the information to ITT's general counsel. The mystery was forgotten until President Nixon, months later, nominated Kleindienst to replace Mitchell as attorney general. Mitchell had resigned in June 1972, to become chairman of Nixon's reelection committee. When Kleindienst was asked during his confirmation hearings about the Grinnell postponement, he credited my intervention. I was called to testify before the Senate Judiciary Committee to the facts I have just related. A year later, however, after he had resigned during the Watergate investigation, Kleindienst admitted that his testimony was false and that he had acted at the personal direction of President Nixon. Another representative of ITT, contrary to my original advice to Geneen, had presented our memorandum to President Nixon's assistant, John Ehrlichman, and the president himself had directed Kleindienst to get a postponement in the Grinnell case. After acknowledging the falsity of his earlier testimony, Kleindienst had pleaded guilty to misleading the committee.

After Mitchell had become chairman of the Committee to Re-elect the President, employees of the committee were arrested as they burglarized the headquarters of the Democratic Party campaign committee located in the office annex of the Watergate Hotel. They were convicted, and during the following year some of them incriminated John Dean, counsel to the president. He in turn testified against Mitchell and two important members of President Nixon's staff, H.R. "Bob" Haldeman and John Ehrlichman. Elliot Richardson, whom Nixon had appointed to replace Kleindienst as attorney general, appointed Archibald Cox special prosecutor to investigate the Watergate crimes and a broader group of crimes involving possible corruption. As one aspect, a year later, I testified before the grand jury about the adjournment of the Grinnell case.

In 1972, the Columbia University Board of Trustees was again drawn into controversy. *The New York Times,* in June 1971, had published *The Pentagon Papers*, a classified study of the mistakes of the Vietnam War. The scholarly committee that selected recipients of Columbia University's Pulitzer Prize for excellence in journalism selected *The New York Times* stories on *The Pentagon Papers* for its 1971 award. Within the board, controversy erupted as to whether the selection should be rejected because of its unauthorized publication of classified material. The admired William Paley, chairman of Columbia Broadcasting System, led the defense of the award, but the outcome was in doubt. I finally united all but one or two trustees with a resolution that the board of trustees should not second-guess the merits of its expert committee's selection and should follow the recommendation, unless it was objectionable for some reason other than a disagreement as to the merits. Mr. Paley and I had been friendly, but thereafter he occasionally consulted me on personal matters.

In August 1972, as I completed my fourth year as ABA committee chairman, I was elected to the ABA's Board of Governors, the executive committee that oversees the association between the semi-annual meetings of the House of Delegates. In 1973, while serving on this board and under observation for the ABA presidency, I tried and lost my most interesting case.

Two groups of insurers disputed liability for the destruction of a PanAmerican 747 aircraft hijacked by the Popular Front for the Liberation of Palestine (PFLP), one of the two most violent Palestinian terrorist groups, a group committed to harass and ultimately destroy the state of Israel by, among other means, interfering with its national trade and ultimately fomenting its invasion by Arab forces. Hospitable to displaced Palestinians, the neighboring country of Jordan had for several years tolerated the assembly of PFLP and other quasi-military groups known as "fedayeen" (commandos), permitting them to walk through the streets carrying machineguns and other arms. King Hussein was, however, considering imposing restraints. The fedayeen challenged not only Israel but, by their insolence, the sovereignty of the Jordanian government.

Angered by the acquiescence of Jordan and Egypt in Secretary Rogers's Mideast peace initiatives, the PFLP hoped to "explode" a revolution by which it would draw all of the fedayeen into a common effort to dominate the government of Jordan or, at least, gain control of its policies toward the fedayeen and Israel. To spark this explosion and to suck in the largest and most conservative fedayeen group, El Fatah, the organization of Yasser Arafat, the PFLP hijacked three foreign passenger aircraft on Labor Day 1970, planning to land them on an abandoned airstrip in northern Jordan, destroy them, and hold the passengers hostage to demonstrate the impotence of the government of Jordan. Two of the aircraft, Boeing 707s belonging to Swiss Air and TWA, were safely landed but the third, the PanAmerican 747 aircraft my clients had insured, was too heavy to land there. After it had been seized by three PFLP "commandos" while in flight from Amsterdam, it was redirected to Beirut, Lebanon, and then, under PFLP control, refueled, laced with explosives, and flown to Cairo still loaded with passengers. There it was blown up to embarrass President Gamal Abdel Nasser for his support of the Rogers peace accord. The passengers were given 15 minutes to escape through emergency exits. One passenger broke his arm. The others were uninjured.

The next day the PFLP seized a British Airways aircraft to replace the too-heavy 747 and landed it on the Jordanian airstrip. While the world watched, the passengers, under armed guards, were taken to Amman and held prisoner. The aircraft were blown up. Led by the PFLP, and aroused by this dramatic achievement, all of the fedayeen, including El Fatah, joined in an uprising that captured parts of Amman, the nation's capital, established roadblocks, and controlled the movement of its population. Finally King Hussein had to call out the army and bombard and invade his own capital in order to regain control.

Was the seizure and destruction of the PanAm 747 a war risk excepted from PanAm's all-risk policy? The all-risk group, through Fritz Schwarz, retained me and I drew in Henry King and a young associate, Chris Crowley, a former reporter for *Time* magazine. A little later, for critical legal analysis, I called on Guy Struve.[5] The war-risk coverage was divided between Lloyds' war-risk syndicate and the U.S. government. These insurers were represented by well-known New York trial lawyers and the Department of Justice. The all-risk group had the burden of proving that the destruction was excluded from its policy. The war-risk exclusion did not expressly mention sabotage or hijacking but only a "war-like operation" or an "insurrection" or a "riot." The war-risk insurers claimed that the Amsterdam hijacking was too remote to be attributed to the events in Jordan, however characterized, and that neither it nor the fedayeen uprising was an insurrection, riot, or warlike operation.

Surprisingly, PanAm, the insured, instead of merely interpleading the two contesting insurance groups and remaining neutral, sided with the war-risk insurers against my clients. Although the all-risk coverage was slightly higher than that of the war-risk policies, we quickly offered to settle out this small difference. PanAm's partiality proved an increasingly formidable obstacle as the litigation progressed because, although we seemed usually able to prevail against the war-risk group, the court was more sympathetic with PanAm, our insured.

A shadow issue, never quite formulated but always overhanging the case, was the reluctance of anyone to characterize the PFLP as anything more honorable than "terrorist." Israeli policy condemned fedayeen activity as criminal terrorism. We decided against a jury trial because a New York jury would include not only Israeli sympathizers but also others abhorrent of the PFLP tactics. The case was assigned in regular rotation to Judge Marvin Frankel. While Judge Frankel had visited Israel and could be expected to react strongly against PFLP outrages, I did not suggest that he recuse himself because most other judges would also be sympathetic to the Israeli view. I decided to count on Judge Frankel's unquestioned intellectual strength and independence to be as dispassionate as any judge between two conflicting groups of insurance carriers.

While our clients perceived these difficulties and an officer attended every court session, they had determined to take a stand against the war-risk group, which, they believed, consistently litigated away its liability. Any settlement would have had to be substantial. Our early legal research suggested a fair prospect. We won most of the pretrial motions, but this,

5. On a Saturday, after explaining to his young son, Andy, how to use a computer for legal research, Struve was surprised and we were amused that Andy produced a relevant citation we had missed. He had simply typed in the words "hijacking" and "airplane."

we knew, did not promise ultimate success. Matters worsened when PanAmerican took the lead against us.

Chaim Herzog, a former Israeli military intelligence officer, later to become president of Israel, joined us as Israeli counsel. Our Lebanese lawyer helped us identify witnesses both within the PFLP and from the community to portray PFLP's activities and objectives. By inviting PFLP officials to use our case to explain PFLP objectives, Henry King arranged to take the deposition of a high-ranking PFLP officer, but the night before his scheduled deposition the witness was murdered. A general of the Palestine Liberation Army later agreed to testify at the trial and explain the purpose of the hijacking. Unable to minimize the horror of the PFLP, we deliberately portrayed it to demonstrate the PFLP's determination to isolate Israel.

My American Bar Association activities kept intruding. Just before the trial began, while attending the association's midwinter meeting in Cleveland, I simultaneously prepared our opening witness, the president of the Jordanian Bar Association, who was to explain the status of the fedayeen at the outbreak of the Jordanian insurrection. When he insisted that he, as a lawyer, did not need to be prepared for trial, we compromised as I had *him* prepare *me* by responding to my mock cross-examination. While he was a good trial witness, I was never quite sure how he would answer my questions—a little like playing Russian roulette.

While I was in Cleveland, an officer of our client, cleaning out his desk a few days before trial, produced a folder of rough notes regarding the drafting of the war-risk exclusion that suggested a more precise exclusion of hijacking had been considered. Pursuant to discovery orders, this should have been produced earlier. We, of course, immediately gave copies to our delighted opponents, who happily complained about our delayed production. Earlier production might have effected a possible settlement between the two groups of insurers, but after PanAmerican took the lead against us, settlement became more difficult.

In the crowded courtroom, the trial went relatively well. Our witnesses unflinchingly looked into the array of hostile counsel who surrounded us. PanAm's lawyers sat between us and the witness, behind them Justice Department counsel, behind us war-risk trial counsel, and in the jury box, the war-risk syndicate's original counsel. Judge Frankel indulged our use of hearsay evidence to establish the background and objectives of PFLP. The PanAm flight crew and a few passengers dramatically described the hijacking and the destruction. Passengers from the other destroyed aircraft told of being held for two days in their sweltering, crowded aircraft without water and without decent sanitary conditions, then watching the destruction of the three aircraft, and finally being bussed to Amman and confined by the fedayeen.

Judge Frankel's personal feelings broke through rarely. Once, during the testimony of a Beirut reporter describing PFLP terrorist attacks on civilian air passengers; once later, when one of our witnesses falsely denied on cross-examination that he expected to receive compensation as an expert for his testimony even though I informed counsel and the judge in chambers of the facts and that the witness feared an honest answer might endanger his life; and once again, when the war-risk insurers introduced Israeli government documents characterizing PFLP activities. At first, Judge Frankel admitted them in spite of my objection but then, after hearing the testimony of an Israeli official, he struck it all out, saying irritably, "Why do I need this?" Our opponents did not contradict our evidence of PFLP objectives and activity. They concentrated on our clients' failure to broaden the language of the war-risk exception and the physical separation of the PanAm 747 destruction from the events in Jordan.

After receiving extensive post-trial briefs, Judge Frankel decided against us with damaging findings of fact and his opinion on the law. Among the findings that hurt the most were those denying that the uprising in Jordan amounted to an insurrection. Unable to characterize it as anything else, he described the events in Amman as "unique," "rather uniquely unsettled," a "perilous game of challenge and response," "generally precarious," "severely unstable and in an uncomfortable measure anarchic," and "severe unrest in what was probably an unparalleled situation."

A year later, I argued the appeal. Because a trial judge's findings of fact must be accepted by the appellate court unless clearly erroneous, I did not use my time to contradict them. We had already exposed their weak points in our brief, which I knew the court had already read. Instead I used my 45 minutes to argue two points of law: First, to the surprise of my adversaries, I began with the last point in our brief, that assault and destruction by three armed hijackers and the additional Lebanese group of explosive experts, under legal precedents and insurance usage, constituted a "riot" and that the trial judge, as a matter of law, was bound to apply this definition rather than resort to commonplace understanding. On the strength of Struve's research and analysis, I then used most of my time to argue our dominant claim that the activity of the PFLP, discreditable or not, was, under the prior court decisions, "warlike" and that it was part of PFLP's continuing effort to isolate Israel just as, in our precedents, warlike attacks on neutral vessels isolated a combatant.

Our opposition's surprise and disarray showed even though, at the close of my argument, the court allowed them a one-hour luncheon recess. The lawyer who answered my argument on "riot" lacked a working knowledge of the precedents. The PanAm lawyer who started to defend Judge Frankel's findings of fact was stopped by one of the judges, who pointed out that, in my oral argument, I had not challenged them. When asked to respond to my arguments on the warlike nature of the PFLP acts, he had to fall back on a generalized argument that I had overstated the precedents without having in hand precise distinctions. Fritz Schwarz, our client's usual outside counsel, and one of the judges used superlatives to compliment my argument. Another of the judges told a third person that Struve's brief was the best appellant's brief he had ever read. While I welcomed these comments, I was always slightly superstitious about judicial praise. Too often, it only softens a disappointing result. It proved so in this case as the court unanimously affirmed the judgment of Judge Frankel. The failure of the all risk companies to exclude terrorist hijacking in more precise terms had been fatal.

Winning and even losing—this was the side of my profession I enjoyed most, but just before I argued the appeal, in February 1974, the state delegates, acting as the nominating committee of the American Bar Association, selected me, unopposed, for the presidency of the American Bar Association. This meant almost a two-year full-time commitment, the first year as president-elect, the second year as president.

The Watergate scandal had already aroused the public. Six months earlier, on a Sunday morning in October 1973, Chesterfield Smith, the then-president of the American Bar Association, had awakened me to discuss the "Saturday night massacre." Watergate special prosecutor Archibald Cox had subpoenaed White House tapes of the president's relevant personal conversations regarding the Watergate burglary and cover-up. President Nixon had ordered Attorney General Richardson to fire Cox. Richardson had refused and resigned. Nixon then repeated the order to the deputy attorney general, William Ruckelshaus, who refused and was fired by Nixon. The third-ranking officer of the department, Solicitor General Robert Bork, then carried out the president's order. Should the American Bar Association act? And if so, how? I advised Smith to denounce the president and call for a new special prosecutor. Either then or a little later, we discussed a new law to protect a special prosecutor from arbitrary removal. With the approval of the board of governors, he appointed a special committee to develop and advocate the legislation, which became known as the Independent Counsel Act. Smith's statement that Sunday was carried prominently by the media.

Nixon reacted quickly and had Bork appoint former ABA president Leon Jaworski to replace Cox. During the following months of controversy, Nixon produced the tapes a few at a time to Jaworski and to congressional committees investigating the scandal. A special committee of the House of Representatives recommended Nixon's impeachment. As more tapes were produced, the pressure for impeachment mounted. Finally, on August 9, 1974, Nixon resigned. Vice President Gerald R. Ford, who then became president, had succeeded to the vice presidency as Minority Leader of the House of Representatives after Vice President Spiro Agnew had resigned to face criminal charges. Within a month, Ford granted a pardon to President Nixon for any federal crimes he might have committed. This led to widespread attacks and demands to know whether Ford had made a deal with Nixon in advance of his resignation. Ford at first declined an answer and then denied such a deal.

Between Nixon's resignation and pardon, the ABA House of Delegates elected me president-elect to serve under the new ABA president for one year and then succeed him. On Labor Day I debated constitutional law expert Professor Philip Kurland of the University of Chicago Law School and defended Ford's pardon. I argued that the pardon power was intended to be used at just such a time as this, to rid the country of an embarrassing president by making a deal if necessary. I urged President Ford to issue a white paper that would explain, step by step, any negotiations leading to Nixon's resignation, including the possible promise of a pardon. President Ford never did this. Two years later the pardon hurt his chances for reelection. I believed that a concurrent, formal, and forthright statement of facts would have been better than trying to defend his action amidst election controversy.

While sharing speaking assignments with the ABA president, my year as president-elect was devoted principally to developing plans for my presidency and getting the necessary board of governors' approval for my proposals. As Mary and I were about to leave for Montreal to assume the presidency at the 1975 annual meeting, our son was hospitalized for a serious illness. He had been sent home from Dartmouth where, after an excellent first year, he had enrolled in extra literature courses for the summer session. He and his sister, Sara, had enthusiastically and loyally taken the brunt of my public activities, particularly during the Vietnam War, when my association with Nixon and the continuation of the war was not fully understood by young people. I believed the illness in part reflected this stress.

While brooding in Montreal's impressive cathedral about this ironic coincidence and the stress in the lives of many lawyers, I thought back to a colleague on the deputy attorney general's staff, Frank Chambers, the chief of the section on legislation. Considerably older than I, he had years before resigned as an associate of the prestigious Cravath firm to take a government job. With regular hours and little tension, he had been a successful parent whose son had won scholarship after scholarship in preparatory school, college, and law school. Who was the more secure? Whose achievements the more important? Brushing aside these reflections, I had to get my projects off the ground.

Chapter 16
COMMON FAITH AND COMMON LAW

". . . for, as you know, it is not in books that the law can live, but in the consciousness of the profession as a whole. Judges, dressed with their brief authority, may seem to speak more finally, but it is only for the moment. In the end they must take their cues from the bar and the great schools . . . which slowly form the molds."

—Learned Hand[1]

As a still largely self-regulated profession, the bar has depended on it own organizations for governance. For centuries, the Inns of Court on the outskirts of the old city of London have supervised the education and discipline of barristers and judges, while the Law Society of England and Wales has carried a similar responsibility for solicitors. In the United States, with a much larger number of lawyers, undivided between barristers and solicitors and scattered over thousands of miles, local bar associations have assumed responsibilities for discipline and law schools for education. In 1906, however, following a memorable address by Roscoe Pound, dean of the Harvard Law School, on the reasons for the public dissatisfaction with the administration of justice, the then-small American Bar Association began the formulation of nationwide canons of ethics and later took responsibility for accrediting law schools. These canons and standards have become a national guide adopted by state and federal courts.

At first somewhat a "gentleman's club," the ABA became more broadly representative of the profession and a more important influence in pub-

1. Quoted in Irving Dilliard, The Spirit of Liberty 88-89 (Alfred A. Knopf 1960).

lic affairs, leading the fight against Franklin D. Roosevelt's effort to pack the Supreme Court, and later against the isolationist "Bricker Amendment." As the association grew and diversified, the presidency became less an honorary title and more a demanding office. Leading lawyers like Joseph Choate, Elihu Root, William Howard Taft, Charles Evans Hughes, and John W. Davis were followed by sometimes less notable lawyers who worked their way up in the organization.

Like a temporary mahout on a galloping elephant that has already determined where it is going, the association president spends nearly two years executing the policies of the association, which he may guide but does not control. During his year as president-elect, he formulates his objectives for his presidential year. He hopes that his successor will continue the programs he could not complete. In large part, however, his energy is absorbed by long-established routines—reviewing recommendations of association sections and committees, explaining and advocating association policies, and improving relations with state and local bar associations and with the public.

With more than 250,000 members at the time of my presidency, the American Bar Association was the largest professional association in the world. Over two dozen very large, self-governing, specialized sections and divisions served the differing needs and interests of its members, restrained only by the need for approval of the Board of Governors or House of Delegates before stating an association position. Sixty or more smaller units, standing and special committees of the association, addressed professional problems and made recommendations through the Board of Governors to the House of Delegates. A large headquarters professional staff under a full-time executive director attended to these units and, in consultation with the president, discharged the association's day-to-day responsibilities.

On the Board of Governors, the president and the other five association officers each had only one vote, the same as the 30 governors. While the president received considerable deference, he had to advocate his proposals to the board's satisfaction. Most of the association officers and governors began as active members of the Young Lawyers Division, with friendships that had tightened over years of constant association. Several had been elected state delegates by the lawyers of their state. A president lacking these early relationships, somewhat like a partner making a lateral entry into a law firm, needed their support. Fortunately, several of them elected with me to the Board of Governors became fast friends and guided me as I dealt with the latent rivalry of the chairman of the House of

Delegates, the president-elect, and the immediate past president. As president, I divided the board into committees to facilitate individual participation and to improve its general efficiency. These committees have been continued ever since.

Traveling to speak to state and local bar associations, one week I had every dinner in flight. On a scorching Fourth of July in San Antonio, I began by bringing greetings to the Texas State Bar Association only to hear its president denounce the ABA because of its failure to support former Texas Governor John Connally while he was under charges for alleged misconduct as secretary of the treasury. Usually, however, I outlined current professional problems and the association's response to them.

Because my year as president would coincide with the 200th anniversary of American independence, I began early to prepare for my annual meeting. Taking my theme, the "Declaration of Interdependence" of American and English legal professions, Columbia's professor of legal history, Harry Jones, who was also president of the American Historical Society, enlisted a number of scholars to deliver papers at the meeting expounding the concept "Common Faith and Common Law." In the course of 10 trips to London, Mary and I gained the support of English judges and lawyers for a related program, "English and American Approaches Compared." The lord chancellor, lord chief justice, master of the rolls, chairman of the Bar Council, president of the Law Society, and the attorney general all joined in the program.

The English visits were, in themselves, an inspiring education. At the invitation of Lord Denning, master of the rolls, Mary, Sara, and I participated in a ceremonial commemoration of the Magna Charta at Bury St. Edmonds, one of four locations associated with the charter, honored in annual rotation. In a small procession of English lawyers, we followed Lord Denning to the cathedral as he displayed to onlookers one of the four original copies of the Magna Charta. In the cathedral service, I read the lesson of Jesus responding to the interrogation of a lawyer by relating the parable of the Good Samaritan. After the service, the rector commented on the emphasis of my reading, saying that he had never heard it read quite that way before. I hoped this was a compliment, not a caution.

I readily fell under the spell of our English hosts as they had us to their homes, their clubs, and the Inns of Court themselves, always with the (to us) indefinable blend of informality and formality that graces English entertainment. Once Lord Denning unexpectedly included our teenage son, Dale, then spending a year at school in England, as a guest at a dinner for me at Lincoln's Inn to become better acquainted with the judges and lawyers who were to guide me. Dale's house master and fellow students assembled a very creditable dinner suit and he held his own as, after dinner, the port passed round and round the table.

A year later, during my presidency, Mary and I were honored guests for the Westminster Abbey ceremony marking the opening of the courts after the summer recess. Deeply impressed, I felt the moving aspect of a ceremony almost free of speeches as the judges and barristers in their handsome robes and wigs of ancient tradition, wearing military decorations, proceeded down the central aisle of Westminster, in a simple service dominated by the boys' choir and the overpowering presence of the abbey itself. After the service, while Mary joined the wives of the judges, I attended the lord chancellor's breakfast in the House of Lords, a jovial buffet for the bar, at which the lord chief justice told me where to find the coldest beer.

As the year passed, I dined with the benchers of Lincoln's Inn and heard a moot argument at the weekly dinner of prospective barristers at Gray's Inn, where the master spoke movingly of the contributions of American lawyers to replace the inn's stained-glass windows after they had been destroyed by World War II bombs. Lord Peter Rawlinson, former attorney general and chairman of the Bar Council, became my most frequent host, each occasion giving me a new insight: Whyte's, the club where in past centuries an aristocrat could, in one evening, gamble away his fortune; the hall of the Inner Temple, restored from World War II destruction; the Horse Guards Parade, to witness a review by the Prince of Wales and to talk with him briefly afterwards; and, after flying all night from the ABA midwinter meeting, to be the only outside guest at the bar's dinner for the queen in the centuries-old hall of the Middle Temple. On other occasions, Rawlinson and I were both guests of the American ambassador, first Elliott Richardson, then Anne Armstrong.

My presidency began with the profession on the defensive. The Supreme Court had sustained an antitrust attack upon the advertising restraints of the pharmaceutical association. Because pharmacists rarely compounded medications and, in most cases, repackaged compounds delivered ready-made by pharmaceutical manufacturers, the court concluded that the denial of publicly advertised price information was not justified by a need for professional restraint. While the legal profession had better arguments for its restraints on advertising, the decision forecast their vulnerability. My responsibility was twofold. First, I had to alert the profession to the danger, then I had to defend the ABA from government antitrust attack. After retaining defense counsel, I produced and circulated to state and local bar associations a videotaped address outlining the threat and the related problem of publicized claims of specialized competence, newly permitted in some states.

Both controversies derived from the perpetual problem of delivering legal services at reasonable cost to all who need them. Privately supported legal defense organizations and the government, through the Legal Services Administration, had provided for the indigent but not the exposure of persons with moderate means to rising legal costs and the problem of finding a lawyer. While a few groups had experimented with insurance plans comparable to insurance for medical care, many local bar associations offered legal referral services. Listing of professional specialists in public directories was also intended to assist the public but, with advertising legalized, extravagant claims seemed inevitable.

To defend the association, I spent a morning presenting our arguments to Attorney General Edward Levi. Unfortunately, he then disqualified himself. In his place, the deputy attorney general, former Judge Harold Tyler, a friend of mine who had not heard my presentation, authorized a civil suit against the American Bar Association to enjoin its restraints on professional advertising. Before our litigation ripened, however, the state bar association of Arizona, in a suit raising similar issues, reached the Supreme Court, which then extended its permissive view of advertising to our profession. We negotiated a settlement with the Department of Justice.

Controversy over judicial nominations continued. While president-elect, I had led the Federal Judiciary Committee to oppose the appointment of Governor Thomas Meskill of Connecticut to the federal court of appeals because certain charges of state contract irregularity had been brushed aside without full answers. The Senate nevertheless confirmed the nomination; he proved to be a good judge, to whom I later publicly apologized. As president, I did not want additional judicial appointment problems. Most concerned for the likelihood of a new Supreme Court vacancy, I sought a chairman of the ABA Federal Judiciary Committee who had been through the process of selecting federal judges, who knew the members of the Senate Judiciary Committee, and who would be at ease dealing with the attorney general. Estranging some of my own ABA supporters, I bypassed the existing committee members and selected as chairman Warren Christopher, former U.S. deputy attorney general under President Johnson.

Even those most critical ultimately congratulated me after Attorney General Levi actually turned over to me, and through me to the committee, the evaluation of several possible Supreme Court nominees. Christopher was surefooted. The committee soon admired him. Making a difficult choice between two excellent contenders, in December 1975 we recommended John Paul Stevens, who was easily confirmed. Having practiced as a partner in a Chicago law firm and then sitting on the Court of Appeals for the Seventh Judicial Circuit, which included Illinois, Indiana, and Wisconsin, Judge Stevens was highly recommended by the lawyers and judges of his own circuit and, because of his prompt dispositions, by those pursuing court reform.

The following March, I arranged a two-day conference at Vanderbilt University on judicial selection. Professor Elliot Cheatham, who had befriended me at Columbia and was then teaching at Vanderbilt, had given me a forum during the most difficult period of the Carswell controversy to explain the ABA committee's mistakes and its new recommendations. (Also, our daughter, Sara, was then a first-year student in the law school.) While participants were largely drawn from organizations concerned for better judges, former Attorney General Herbert Brownell was a speaker, and commentators included the deputy attorney general, Senate staff members, federal judges, and respected law school professors. As the speakers advocated requirements of experience and merit and candidly reviewed the composition and procedures of the ABA committee, the meeting strengthened and expanded professional support for the ABA committee, while also emphasizing the profession's broader objectives of judicial selection based on merit, with longer terms and better salaries for state judges and more adequate salaries for those in the federal courts.

My second and more demanding undertaking, conceived by Chief Justice Warren Burger, was a three-day April conference on long-term professional goals, commemorating the 70th anniversary of Roscoe Pound's speech in St. Paul, Minnesota, in 1906, during which he challenged the ABA and particularized the reasons for the popular dissatisfaction with the administration of justice. Attacked at the time by judges, leading lawyers, and bar associations, his telling indictment of the profession led to its gradual improvement as bar associations adopted canons of professional ethics and slowly addressed the responsibility of all lawyers for the administration of justice. With Chief Justice Burger's leadership and support and that of the president of the Association of State Chief Justices, I obtained funding from the Board of Governors and attracted an outstanding group of lawyers, judges, and scholars to develop a reform agenda for the last 25 years of the century.

Speaking in the legislative chamber in which Pound had spoken, the chief justice delivered an eloquent challenge to the participants. During the next two days, they responded impressively. Some recommendations were sweeping: the abolition of the diversity jurisdiction of the federal courts; the establishment of a national institute of justice comparable to the National Science Foundation; the elimination of lawyers in uncontested probate and divorce proceedings; and, among the most important, the concept of a multidoor courthouse—a courthouse offering many services in addition to trials, such as mediation, arbitration, and fact finding. Could no-fault auto insurance and contingent-fee control reduce litigation costs? Was it time for the United States to follow England and give up jury trials in civil matters? Other recommendations were more mundane, such as controls for the abuse of discovery and the pretrial process. Almost all expressed concern for the overload on courts continuously confronted with fresh statutes creating new crimes and areas of liability in complex and demanding social, economic, and environmental areas, even at times requiring federal judicial continuing supervision of state institutions. While former U.S. Judge Simon Rifkind asked whether we were not demanding too much of our courts, U.S. Judge A. Leon Higginbotham, Jr., urged new priorities for human rights.

Lost in the welter of impressively presented recommendations was the assessment of Dr. Laura Nader, a social scientist, who noted that lawyers were making recommendation after recommendation without adequate data. Another nonlawyer, President William McGill of Columbia University, decried the splintering of our society into warring, litigious groups. I warned of the inevitable future danger of weapons of mass destruction falling into the hands of terrorist groups and the accompanying need to anticipate government infiltration into these groups, notwithstanding the constitutional right of freedom of assembly. (As president-elect, I had previously persuaded the Board of Governors and the House of Delegates to create a section on science and technology in the hope of a fruitful dialogue between lawyers and scientists.)

West Publishing Company published the presentations. Three respected past ABA presidents characterized the conference as successful in "the identification of major problems and the generation of enough corrective ideas to start the great ball rolling toward our most critical goals" and "arousing a new spirit of zeal for fundamental procedural reform, a new optimism about the possibility of creative innovation in the administration of justice."[2] Chaired by former attorney general Griffin Bell, a follow-up committee of judges and lawyers distilled an impressive list of specific recommendations to be addressed. My successor, Justin Stanley, took a first step and devoted much of his year as president to the improvement of small-claim courts and the more efficient handling of the clutter of minor disputes.

After the Pound conference, Mary and I moved through the remaining Board of Governors meetings. As we approached our August annual meeting in Atlanta, Chief Justice Burger, who had been consistently supportive, and the entire Court greeted the Board of Governors at a reception in the courthouse itself. Mary developed an outstanding arrangement of accompanying social activities. Discriminating use of flowers and colors briefly softened the austere marble of the courthouse.

Finally, we flew to Hawaii for a month's rest before the annual meeting. We flew back, however, when Queen Elizabeth invited us to a small dinner on the royal yacht *Britannia*, in New York Harbor. The queen, marking the 200th anniversary of our independence, had visited the United States, and, in her amazingly gracious way, reconquered New York, moving through the city with the ease and openness so characteristic of her public appearances in London. Hundreds of shoppers pinched themselves to be sure they were not dreaming as she casually rode department store escalators. She personified, as no meeting could, the joint heritage and the interdependence of the United States and Great Britain.

Mary curtsied to the queen as she received us. The queen seated me at her table opposite her and next to Mrs. Averell Harriman. Also at the table was our ambassador to Great Britain, Anne Armstrong. After dinner, on deck under the summer sky, the queen and the Duke of Edinburgh informally talked with us all and with a larger group that arrived a little later. Mary and I had traveled the farthest to be there. Next was Leontyne Price, the opera prima donna, who made a round-trip from England. Mary and I returned to Hawaii the next day.

In August, on the eve of the Atlanta meeting, I acted at a Columbia University convocation for the vacationing university president as I awarded honorary degrees to the lord chancellor, the lord chief justice, the master of the rolls and, at the same time, to the chief judge of New

2. Foreword by former ABA presidents William T. Gossett, Bernard T. Segal & Chesterfield Smith, *in* The Pound Conference: Perspectives on Justice in the Future (A. Leo Levin & Russell R. Wheeler eds.) (West Publishing Co. 1979).

York, Charles Breitel, and Chief Justice Warren Burger. Dean Michael Sovern of the law school presented the degree recipients.

While the annual meeting culminates a president's achievements, most of the 10,000 in attendance have their own special interests, and a much smaller number concern themselves with "the president's program" if it extends beyond the traditional events of his "assembly program." The assembly consists of all of the ABA members at the meeting, and it has the power to join or modify action by the House of Delegates, but this rarely happens. Traditionally, the assembly program consists of the prayer breakfast, the opening session of the meeting, one later session, and the final banquet. Each of these meetings is protected from competition and is addressed by speakers selected by the president. While the president also organizes assembly luncheons for each day, these must compete with those of other units. Each evening finds the president appearing and sometimes briefly addressing receptions and dinners of association divisions or allied professional groups. For most presidents this is enough. With occasional press conferences and trying to "touch all the bases" in meetings scattered in several hotels, he or she frequently resembles a late commuter running for a train.

On top of these traditional activities, however, I tried to impose a serious, multisession intellectual program that expounded the thesis of the meeting—the interdependence of the American and English legal professions. While it was only modestly attended, every meeting registrant took home an attractively bound set of the papers. Mary and the association's able meetings director arranged a series of luncheons and receptions stretching from the first meeting of the Board of Governors, before the formal meeting began, until the final banquet after it was all over. Guided by an eager Atlanta host committee responding to its first ABA annual meeting, entertainment was scattered in beautiful settings that included a museum, a cathedral, Emory University, and each of the major hotels.

The prayer breakfast, addressed by the president of the Law Society of England and Wales, went well. A Sunday afternoon opening service at St. Phillip's Episcopal Cathedral presented in abbreviated form the beautiful Westminster Abbey ceremony of the opening of the courts with the English judges and law officers in their robes, gowns, and wigs. While the service was executed perfectly, I had regrettably allowed the staff to persuade me to limit invitations to avoid overcrowding so that the cathedral was not full. As I spoke briefly before Chief Justice Burger and Lord Chancellor Elwyn-Jones, I emphasized that we were giving thanks not for a long-ago event but for two centuries of national consolidation in which Atlanta was second only to Gettysburg in tragic contribution and during which the law had held together a population of inherited stubbornness, each person the descendant of an ancestor who left his home in search of freedom. The choir sang a rousing, favorite English-Welsh hymn, *Jerusalem,*[3] and the lord chancellor, a Welshman, stood and joined them.

The opening assembly, addressed by Chief Justice Burger, after greetings from the president of the Law Society and chairman of the Bar Council, in Atlanta's largest state meeting hall, was packed and successful except that, through an acoustical oversight, those of us on the speakers' platform could not hear the speeches and my introductions could not supply continuity. The traditional Wednesday morning meeting of the assembly also overflowed, as it was addressed by former governor and future president Jimmy Carter. The three traditional assembly luncheons, while in competition with others, were also complete sellouts, as we listened to the lord chief justice, awarded silver gavels to the media, and then concluded with an address by U.S. Ambassador Anne Armstrong.

While my various introductions were commended, unexpectedly, the most rewarding praise followed my introduction of Ambassador Armstrong, which touched on the theme of women in the professions. After gaining laughter for a professed exaggerated concern for their disadvantages, I shifted to the tableau of the queen's dinner on the *Britannia*. Behind the queen as she sat at table, fastened to the bulkhead, had towered an immense, naked, up-thrust, two-handed broadsword. I recalled that her ancestor, King Edward III, had been the "first knight in Christendom" and that to him, this sword was no mere symbol of authority, it was a weapon he used well. But I suggested how useless such masculine skills might be today and, in contrast, I noted the queen's recent diplomatic conquest of New York and, indeed, the United States by her own incomparable skill in fashioning the relationships by which two great nations were now drawn to each other. My concern for professional women, I said, dissipated as I noted, sitting a few places from the queen, the ambassador to whom our country had entrusted its most

---

3. By C. Hubert H. Parry with words by William Blake:

Bring me my bow of burning gold! Bring me my arrows of desire!
Bring me my spear! O clouds unfold! Bring me my chariot of fire!
I will not cease from mental fight. Nor shall my sword sleep in my hand,
Till we have built Jerusalem In England's green and pleasant land.

important international alliance—the cornerstone of its foreign policy, our speaker, our ambassador to the United Kingdom, Anne Armstrong. "What an introduction!" she responded. While I, of course, recognized the intensity of the standing response and greeting to the ambassador, I was moved when several English wives asked me afterward whether I had realized that I had brought tears to their eyes.

That night our final banquet concluded the meeting. Led by Payson Coleman, Davis Polk's new managing partner, many partners joined in a reception for Mary and me and those attending the banquet, as did Mary's mother and her brother and his family. The English lawyers and their wives formed a consistent, ever-present block that never wavered while, through the week, many American lawyers returned home, so that, as usual, the banquet did not have as large an attendance as the other affairs. The lord chancellor spoke for the English lawyers and presented the ABA an ancient crystal goblet. Mary had selected for us to give them a Steuben crystal eagle, identical with one we also gave our Supreme Court, one of a numbered, limited production of 200, commemorating our country's 200th anniversary. As we made the exchange, I suggested that our gifts marked our mutual support but that the crystal also symbolized the fragility of that union. The banquet closed as Justin Stanley, my successor, took office and fulsomely thanked Mary for her contribution during the year of our presidency.

Chapter 17
GOOD-BYE NEW YORK

After representing the ABA, addressing the International Bar Association meeting in Stockholm, and dropping off a handsomely bound set of the *Common Faith and Common Law* papers for the Buckingham Palace library, Mary and I enjoyed a few days on the *QE2* and then returned home to stay. I had become Davis Polk's senior partner, a ceremonial post from which I supported Payson Coleman, the managing partner of the firm. Mary and I felt a particular loyalty to him and to his wife. They had generously used their personal advantages and relationships to support us in our American Bar Association duties and at other times when my public activities squeezed us financially. For example, after the 1972 presidential campaign, when I received a request to raise a contribution from the firm to offset the campaign deficit, he took the responsibility from me and, with the help of David Lindsay, John Lindsay's brother, and a few others, quickly raised the amount requested. When the younger members of the firm protested that the senior partners were too remote on our office's upper floor, he moved to the middle floor and asked me to take the office next to his. At his request, I became chairman of the firm's committee to study the desirability of a Washington office. The firm approved our recommendation and opened one.

Due in part to the ABA presidency, Mary and I decided to sell our cherished Cape Cod house. Spending our summer vacations in Hawaii, we had been able to use it only for long weekends during the rest of the year, but even this became impossible during the ABA presidency. After a summer rental had proved unsatisfactory, we became concerned about leaving the house unoccupied. Rather than accept a price below its value, we decided to give it to Columbia as a summer home for the president of the university. This actually supplied an important need, guaranteeing an August escape from a then-increasingly contentious job. Two successive presidents told me that the mysterious, magic spell of the house continued to ease family stress and tragedy. Semi-isolated on Bound Brook Island in the Cape Cod National Park, it offered the pain-absorbing combination of quiet simplicity and thoughtful design in an entrancing setting, a setting of natural beauty deepened by the ever-present wind and sea and the trace of sadness of the unspoiled shadows of an abandoned community of long ago.

While ABA president, I had missed out on at least two important cases that went to other firms because I could not handle them personally—an antitrust case for General Motors and an opportunity to participate in AT&T's resistance to the government breakup of the Bell system. For several years, as a Columbia trustee, I had sat next to the president of AT&T. He surprised me when he told me that the company had regretted my acceptance of the ABA presidency, that they had counted on me when they had needed me most.

Nevertheless, as a director of Cities Service Corporation, he retained me as counsel to his board committee to investigate possible illegal foreign payments by company personnel. At this time, government agencies were concentrating on such payments that had previously been accepted as normal business practice when dealing in countries where they were tolerated. Other new matters quickly filled my time. The Cravath firm brought me in to defend the independent directors of its client, Allied Chemical, in a derivative stockholders' suit. We obtained a dismissal of the case and the affirmance of this decision on appeal. Henry King had me argue a successful appeal for International Paper before the U.S. Court of Appeals for the Fourth Circuit, a particular pleasure because Chief Judge Haynsworth presided. At the end of the argument, in accordance with the court's custom, the three judges came down into the well of the court and shook hands with counsel on both sides, reflecting the continuing fraternity between the practicing lawyers and the judges of that circuit. Judge Haynsworth also invited Mary and me to the highly regarded Fourth Circuit judicial conference, which alternates each year between two well-known hotels, the Greenbriar in West Virginia and the Homestead in Virginia. While it followed the pattern of other judicial conferences (each judge in the circuit invited two lawyers with spouses and the chief judge invites a few more), the Fourth Circuit conference not only presented the usual informative lawyers' programs, it excelled in conviviality, led by the Haynsworths, who danced together like professionals.

Extracurricular activities resumed. The Liberian Maritime Commission appointed me chairman of a five-person investigatory commission to determine the cause of the stranding and loss of the steam tanker *Argo Merchant* and its full cargo of fuel oil off Cape Cod. The ugly question was whether the aged, rundown vessel had been deliberately stranded. From Cape Hatteras, its course seemed predestined for destruction on Nantucket Shoals, well inside the protective lightship. Its ill-trained and inexperienced watch officers and crew, the failure of the gyro compass recorder at the helm, the miscalculations of the deviation of the magnetic compass used as a substitute, the reliance on current flow data for the wrong month, and disregard of the shoaling depth of water accurately reported by regular soundings supported an alternative hypothesis of incompetence. Most incriminating, however, was the failure to salvage either cargo or vessel during the three days of good weather between the stranding and the breakup of the vessel, a period when responsibility was evaded by the owners, their agents, and the ship's master. After hearings in New York, London, and Rotterdam, we found the ship's master at fault. His license was revoked by the Liberian government. The controversy between ship owners, cargo owners, and insurers was resolved in federal court.

Throughout the ABA presidency, I had continued my membership on the board of trustees of Mutual Life Insurance Company of New York (MONY) and the board of directors of Richardson-Merrell, Inc. After my return to practice, President Carter appointed me chairman of his committee to recommend nominees for the Second Circuit Court of Appeals. The other six committee members were divided between lawyers and lay persons, including a New York City councilwoman and a New York City official. Leonard Garment, President Nixon's former private lawyer, was elected vice chairman. Judith Kaye, who a few years later was elected to New York's highest court and then New York's chief judge, became our best-known member.

Three major matters filled my remaining time. Struve and I defended R.J. Reynolds and its subsidiary, Sea-Land Service, Inc., from an attack by the Pacific Far East Lines, the successor of the old Dollar Line, for which I had worked two summers while going to college. Confronted with the government crackdown on foreign payments by American companies, Reynolds had requested Davis Polk to conduct an extensive investigation of these activities. Reynolds then made public this candid report. It disclosed that, in the Pacific trade, Sea-Land had given rebates to compete for cargo. Pacific Far East Lines, a Sea-Land competitor, had fallen under the control of the sons of San Francisco Mayor Joseph Alioto. Well known as an aggressive trial lawyer as well as a politician, Alioto and his sons believed that the confessions of R.J. Reynolds had given them an unbeatable case. They filed an antitrust suit in San Francisco claiming that Pacific Far East was entitled to recover triple damages for its loss of cargo due to rebates granted by Sea-Land. In fact, the trade in the Pacific was permeated by rebates granted by all steamship lines in order to price their carriage below the rates fixed by the steamship conferences. We responded that those who, themselves, rebate may not use the antitrust laws to recover damages for rebates by others.

Pacific Far East then falsely denied its rebating practices. In his deposition, an overconfident John Alioto, president of Pacific Far East, personally denied them. After first disdaining our discovery requests, its lawyers disregarded the specific orders by the judge to make their files and those of their agents available for inspection. The firm and Pacific Far East's officers were ultimately drawn into denials they knew to be false. In an unusual development, one document they did produce accidentally revealed their duplicity. An officer had handwritten a note cryptically describing a rebate. While someone destroyed his note, he had unthinkingly written it on top of an unnoticed, unrelated form that included carbon paper, which provided a copy of the destroyed incriminating memorandum. After a series of bitter hearings in the San Francisco federal court spread over nearly four years, the judge, on evidence presented by Struve and me, found that Pacific Far East had rebated and lied to conceal its rebating. As a sanction, the judge dismissed the case. On appeal, handled by Struve, these judgments were affirmed.

Even more demanding was the defense of Richardson-Merrell from claims that Bendectin, its very successful medication for morning sickness during pregnancy, caused birth defects. A physician-turned-lawyer in Miami had advanced the claim without any support in the scientific literature. Realizing that 10 percent of all children were born with birth defects and that the causes of most birth defects were unknown, he used a few equally reckless pharmacologists and physicians to spin out an incriminating rationalization. Then he obtained the support of an acclaimed Australian physician, Dr. William McBride, who had been honored for his part in the exposure of the fearful teratogen, Thalidomide.

The case was dangerous, not only because of the emotional appeal of an innocent, handicapped infant, but also because of the difficulty in testing drugs for use in pregnancy. Ordinarily, after extensive animal studies, a new medication is given to one group of volunteer patients, while another group unknowingly receives an inert placebo. Scientists then compare the results of the two groups to decide the effectiveness of the medication, its appropriate dose, and its possible side effects. But it is unethical to deliberately test a new drug on a pregnant woman.

Accordingly, Bendectin's safety had been established by heavy doses in animals and then used in very moderate doses in women. A retrospective study of mothers whose children had had birth defects showed that there was no statistically significant difference between the incidence of birth defects in children whose mothers had received Bendectin and those who had not. After the litigation started, an English scientist conducted a more impressive retrospective study, analyzing the extensive records of English medical care agencies, which register the prescriptions given and the results of the pregnancies. This large-scale study again showed that there was no statistical difference between those using Bendectin and those who did not.

Prospective studies of mothers, which follow them through their pregnancies and then compare the incidence of birth defects, were difficult to conduct because, to be statistically significant against the normal 10 percent rate of birth defects, it would be necessary to control a very large group of women and minimize other variables in their conduct. Fortunately, a Finnish scientist had conducted such a large, prospective study, looking at all possible causes of birth defects. Among many factors, it showed no statistically significant difference due to the use of Bendectin.

The trial was set for Orlando, Florida, then a relatively small city, three days after I completed the climactic hearing in the Pacific Far East Lines litigation. Arriving in Orlando late on a Friday night, I spent an exhausting weekend absorbing background infromation provided by the company scientist-lawyer and my principal associates. Trained as a prosecutor of persons in jail awaiting trial, I never requested a postponement. As we appeared in court, however, good fortune gave me a needed respite. Melvin Belli, one of the country's foremost personal injury lawyers, was to lead the team against us, but he was unprepared and claimed another engagement. The court reluctantly postponed the trial to accommodate Belli's schedule and then his planned Italian winter vacation. It fixed a January trial date, which gave me ample time for full preparation. In addition to a team of other Davis Polk associates, I was assisted by Miriam Cedarbaum, who had returned to full-time practice as a Davis Polk senior associate.

When January came, however, Belli rejected the case, and the furious parents of the plaintiff went to trial depending on their Miami firm. Once again, I was confronted with a long case in which I did not want to wait until the end of the plaintiff's case before focusing the jury on the merits of our defense. Instead of using adverse personal information in hostile cross-examination of the plaintiff's experts, I dealt with them in a complimentary fashion, inviting them to explain the various studies that supported our defense. This actually worked. While I had to overcome the transparent hostility of the plaintiff's least-qualified witness, each of his other experts acknowledged, in turn, an important study suggesting the innocence of Bendectin.

When I came to the final expert, McBride, the Australian physician, I knew that he was dangerously facile and articulate. While showing him the respect he deserved for his part in the exposure of Thalidomide, I did not ask him anything that could hurt us. Instead, I had him expound on the difficulty in identifying teratogens due to the high percentage of unaccountable birth defects. I suggested 10 percent as the probability among mothers who did not take any medication. He answered, "That's just the tip of the iceberg." I immediately thanked him and terminated my examination. My surprised adversary groped for something to use on redirect examination and then requested a postponement until the next day.

Our defense brought scientists from England, Finland, and Germany as well as the United States. All opined that there was no statistical connection between the use of Bendectin and birth defects. Our most prominent witness was Dr. Widukind Lenz, the true investigator of Thalidomide, who, in Germany, had forced its recall from the market. Throughout the trial of several weeks, the jury stayed with us. The jurors showed their disgust as the plaintiff's physician-lawyer harshly cross-examined one of our expert witnesses, who was suffering from cancer of the bone marrow. At one point, when I was leading the jury through the records of an animal study, I momentarily lost my place. Three jurors simultaneously called out, "Page X, line Y."

The verdict was a surprise, however, as the jury awarded $19,000 for the plaintiff (my third verdict in that exact amount). One juror, a former part-time judge, had urged them to give the plaintiff enough to go to college. The plaintiffs glumly claimed victory, but I was content to let the verdict stand. I could not assure our client that on retrial we could get a better result, and I did not think so small a verdict would encourage other litigation. The trial judge, however, on his own motion, set the verdict aside, holding that if the plaintiff was entitled to a recovery, the recovery was inadequate, and if he wasn't entitled to a recovery, it was an inappropriate gesture by the jury. The plaintiff's counsel then tried to escape the responsibility to retry the case, claiming incompatibility with the plaintiff's mother, but I supported the mother and opposed delay. The court forced them on. After I tried the case a second time, the jury returned a defendant's verdict. The jurors asked to keep their individual books of exhibits as mementos. A few months later, the court of appeals affirmed our trial court victory.

My last new case for Davis Polk was for the state of South Carolina, which was engaged in a boundary dispute with the state of Georgia over the eastern shore of the Savannah River, opposite the city of Savannah. An early compact between the two states had ceded all islands in the river to Georgia. As time passed, accretions on the inner curves of the river had developed into bars, then islands, which ultimately attached themselves to the South Carolina side. At times in high water, they might be flooded, and they were often separated from the river bank by small, shallow streams. By the time Georgia commenced its action, they had been firmly affixed to South Carolina and were, indeed, valuable waterfront property.

Family correspondence and other historical documents told of pre-Civil War rice fields cultivated by owners who lived in Savannah and spent summers on their South Carolina plantations across the river. Throughout a sad history of pestilence, war, and hurricanes, they persevered, maintaining intricate canals for the periodic flooding of the rice fields, until they succumbed to competition from Louisiana. They had gone to Beaufort, South Carolina, to pay their taxes and to register their documents of title. Early maps showed these areas as part of South Carolina.

Each state retained experts. Ours included a geographer, an expert on the meanders of rivers, and a historian who specialized in the southern seaboard of the United States. Walter Hoffman, a federal district judge from Norfolk, served as special master appointed by the U.S. Supreme Court, which has original jurisdiction of litigation between states. After my colleague from Columbia, South Carolina, cross-examined the Georgia experts, I presented the testimony of ours. The special master ruled in our favor, following a precedent established by Chief Justice John Marshall, that similar islets, set off by rivulets along the edge of the Ohio River, were not islands *in* the river, not being within the stream of the "mighty Ohio." Without hearing arguments, the Supreme Court affirmed his decision.

This was to be my last case for Davis Polk. Following the example of Fritz Schwarz, each partner retired from active partnership without quite waiting until he was 70. I had the choice of becoming counsel to the firm and ceasing to practice or continuing to practice with another firm not in competition with Davis Polk. With the approval of Payson Coleman and other interested partners, I had decided to move to Honolulu as counsel to a leading firm of that city. One afternoon in Honolulu, as I had watched the great white clouds piled up by the trade winds, I had asked myself why we were going back to New York. Unable to answer, I telephoned the Hawaii member of the ABA Board of Governors to inquire about teaching at the University of Hawaii. He was enthusiastic. He also suggested that I meet Marshall Goodsill, the managing partner of the city's leading firm. Goodsill and I immediately liked each other and after a day of meetings with other partners, we agreed that I should become counsel to the firm when I left Davis Polk. Mary and I started househunting and interviewing at schools for our 12-year-old daughter, Elizabeth. But this was not to be.

A most dangerous Bendectin case had started in Washington, D.C., brought for a child born without three limbs and with a fourth that was defective. The attractive mother, a nurse, had retained the California law firm that had successfully recovered over $1 million in one of the few successful Thalidomide cases in the United States. Richardson-Merrell's insurer had selected for the defense a Baltimore firm that practiced regularly in Washington. I had briefed that firm's partners as I prepared to move to Honolulu. But after a few weeks, the new firm concluded that it could not be ready in time to try the case, then scheduled for February the following year. At the request of that firm and the client, I agreed to take the case but this meant that we could not move to Honolulu. It would have been too far for me to commute and keep control of preparations, the pretrial proceedings, and the trial.

Reluctantly, Goodsill and I canceled our agreement. Instead, I became counsel to my present firm in Oklahoma City, Mary's hometown. The firm's managing partner and I knew each other because he had been president of the Oklahoma State Bar Association when I was president of the American Bar Association. He also was a college friend of Mary and Mary's family members were clients of the firm. With his sponsorship, the firm accepted me as counsel and agreed to support me in finishing the Bendectin case for which I had become responsible.

There were few occasions when Davis Polk partners and their wives all dined together. A farewell to a retiring partner was one. Traditionally, it was lighthearted with an underlying note of admiration and respect. My farewell dinner was the only one held downtown. At my request, we selected India House, my favorite spot in New York. Built in the middle of the nineteenth century as the New York Cotton Exchange, on the reputed site of Captain Kidd's former home, it had become a center of the maritime fraternity. Four floors were adorned by oil paintings of nineteenth-century sailing ships and beautiful ship models, including one ivory scale model of a British ship of the line built by French war prisoners during the Napoleonic wars, exact to each plank and spike.

Bob Fiske spoke for the firm. After serving four years as U.S. attorney for the Southern District of New York, appointed by President Ford and continued by President Carter, he had succeeded me as a partner likely to be sought for dangerous and controversial cases. He presented Mary and me with the traditional silver bowl inscribed in Latin, "One quality only—his best." Because Payson Coleman had been feeling pressure from one or two of our brightest partners, chafing for greater recognition as they were sought as general counsel by clients, I spoke of the remarkable lack of discord in a firm in which every one of us worked under continuous personal tension and extraordinarily demanding responsibility. No longer consulted for run-of-the-mill legal problems, we were each constantly called upon to forge solutions of utmost difficulty. It was, therefore, remarkable that there was so little contention and friction among us. This, I said, was due to the skill and effort of Payson Coleman and even more to the basic confidence of each of us in each other, our assurance that if we did our best, "this Firm, this mighty Firm" would swing in behind us and see us through.

I turned over to the firm's new senior partner three symbols of office, Francis Stetson's silver desk calendar, John W. Davis's cane, and the key to an ancient clock that had been in the firm's office since its founding. I attributed a superstitious power to each. To Mr. Davis's cane, I credited my unbroken success, since it was kept in my office. For the clock, I recounted Irish folklore, which I first heard from Frank Hogan speaking for the district attorney's staff in its farewell dinner to Governor Dewey: That in the still of the night, with the wind from the sea keening around a cottage's eaves and chimney pots, if one was very quiet, a clock would speak. While I realized that our office at One Chase Manhattan Plaza might seem unlike a cottage by the sea, I claimed that when the office quieted down at the end of the day and the lights of the city came on, I could hear the clock speak to me, that it seemed to say, as the pendulum moved back and forth, "Our beloved firm. Our beloved firm."

The partners responded with the warmth we rarely had time to show for each other. One partner who had been my associate when I received my first client, though dying from cancer, made the trip downtown to be with us. Others with whom I had sometimes disagreed and even fought were particularly warm in their farewells. To continue to practice law, I was leaving a near-family association. Concerned only for the loss of my most valued comradeship, I treasured the bowl's inscription, "One quality only—his best."

Chapter 18
OKLAHOMA

When, in the fall of 1981, I told Lord Peter Rawlinson during his visit to New York that I was moving to Oklahoma, he was unbelieving. He repeated the name hesitantly, as though speaking of a strange, distant, foreign land. No antecedent, no publicly known activity suggested a destination so far from New York, so far from a metropolitan center, and so far from the sea. A few New York lawyers and judges were critical, others simply regretful. The most obvious explanation and the one most quickly accepted was that Oklahoma was Mary's family home, but actually I had been attracted to Oklahoma even before I knew Mary. As deputy attorney general, I had been asked to speak at an Oklahoma City luncheon in honor of the 25th anniversary of the appointment of the chief judge of the Tenth Judicial Circuit, Alfred Murrah, the youngest federal judicial appointee since Justice Joseph Story.

Judge Murrah's history had been unusually interesting. Without funds, he had ridden a freight train to Oklahoma during the early oil boom. Quickly mastering the skills necessary to register lease claims, he became a busy and then prosperous lawyer. Befriended by Oklahoma's powerful senator, Robert S. Kerr, he was one of the first appointed by President Franklin D. Roosevelt to the newly created Tenth Judicial Circuit. As the federal courts modernized themselves, first with new rules of procedure, then by an aggressive effort to eliminate antiquated calendar systems, Murrah became a leader in advocating individual calendars for each judge, rather than central calendars for a multijudge court. He was best known for his advocacy of early pretrial action by the judge assigned to the case, requiring the judge to promptly sift out the issues and insist that the lawyers address them, complete discovery, and move to a prompt disposition. When I was a young federal judge assigned to a national judicial conference committee on supporting personnel, I participated in joint meetings with Judge Murrah's committee on pretrial. It was upon Murrah's recommendation that Chief Justice Warren appointed me to a new, select committee to establish procedures for the trial of long and complex cases.

Arriving in Oklahoma City for the Murrah ceremony, I received, literally, a red-carpet treatment. Descending from the propeller aircraft to a long red carpet, I was greeted by Chief Judge Stephen Chandler of the local federal court and several state court justices. Taken to the city's leading hotel, I was assigned not one but two large suites, comprising the hotel's entire top floor. Entertained so steadily that I was afraid I could not prepare my extemporaneous luncheon talk, I looked out from a club on the top floor of the city's highest building across miles of seemingly unbroken land under a vast sky. But it was not until after my well-received talk, during a late afternoon visit to Judge Chandler's home, that I happened to look across a nearby golf course at the sky itself. Its immense unbroken sweep diminished an observer as the sky at sea and its great clouds resembled those of the Pacific. In some subconscious way, I believe I had then reserved the possibility of return. I liked the Oklahomans I met. Without swagger or exaggerated claims, they personified the sober self-confidence of an enterprising community. As my first bond to the state, a few weeks later, Senator Kerr arranged for Judge Chandler and the chief and supporting committee of the Kiowa Tribe to come to Washington to initiate me as an honorary chief.

Twenty years later, when I did move to Oklahoma, Judge Murrah had died, and in his honor a new federal office building had been named for him. This name is now imprinted in the headlines of every country in the world as the site of one of our country's most cruelly devastating bombings.

Bill Paul, later the president of the American Bar Association, was then chairman of my new law firm, Crowe & Dunlevy. He took over my indoctrination. The state's chief justice, Marion Opala, satisfied himself as to my credentials and admitted me to the Oklahoma Bar. Shortly thereafter, the local federal court assigned me as spokesman for a group of lawyers newly admitted to its bar, and I began to experience the unlabored cordiality between the bench and the bar of my new community.

The pressure to get ready for the trial of the Bendectin case I had undertaken cut short further indoctrination. It was clear that I would need a combined team of New York and Oklahoma lawyers. Crowe & Dunlevy, an outstanding litigation firm and the largest firm in the state, gave me a nucleus of both experienced and young lawyers, including Pat Ryan, who subsequently became the U.S. attorney for the Western District of Oklahoma and co-counsel for the trial and conviction of Timothy McVeigh, the Murrah Federal Building bomber, and Rick Ford, who became my closest friend in my new firm. Although my old Davis Polk group had been dispersed, Struve agreed to work with me part-time and a new young partner, Ogden Lewis, assumed management of our temporary office in Washington. As Washington counsel, we selected Hogan & Hartson partner Vincent Cohen.

On the way to Hawaii for our 1981 vacation, Mary and I bought a house not far from her parents' home.[1] An escalating oil boom put houses in such demand that on the day this house was first offered we unhesitatingly agreed to pay the asking price, even though I had not seen the house. As Mary left, cars of other would-be purchasers lined the street. We then expanded and remodeled it and added a 44-foot swimming pool in which I could swim laps from March until December. But these improvements were not completed on schedule, so Mary, Elizabeth, and I spent six months in a furnished apartment.

The Crowe & Dunlevy lawyers merged easily with those from Davis Polk. Our Washington counsel proved impressive both as a guide to juror attitudes and as an intermediary to the close-knit District of Columbia bench and bar. But the case itself kept me awake nights. According to jury selection experts surveying representative community residents, the sight of a child with all four limbs disabled was more shocking and aroused a more sympathetic response than blindness, deafness, or other terrible handicaps. While we had essentially the same scientific evidence with which we had won the case in Florida, we were dealing with a more sympathetic child, a more attractive mother, and a much more formidable opponent.

---

1. In Oklahoma City, we had the advantage of Mary's family's community leadership. While her father had died before I met Mary, he had been a pioneer in the oil fields of Kansas and Oklahoma. Descended from English and Pennsylvania coal miners, he was the nephew, executive assistant, and successor of Robert Watchorn, an organizer and the first secretary of the United Mine Workers of America, who, after a brief period in politics and after serving as U.S. Commissioner of Immigration and Naturalization, had successfully turned to oil exploration and, later, philanthropy. Her mother, a descendant of early Kansas settlers and a benevolent matriarch, consistently held children and grandchildren together, keeping them during vacations and funding their education.

To test the reaction of potential jurors, our jury experts selected two panels of 12. Pat Ryan, acting as plaintiff's counsel, and I, for the defense, delivered opening addresses to the two groups. Our jury experts then listened as the two panels independently discussed their mock verdicts. Although one panel would have returned a defense verdict, the other was divided. Some comments were both amusing and telling. For example, without thinking, I had worn a blue suit with a white shirt. Some jurors distrusted me as a banker's lawyer. When we repeated the performance 10 days later, I did a lot better with a more forceful presentation and with a blue oxford shirt and a soft grey suit. At that time, both jury panels returned defense verdicts, but success in the absence of the plaintiff and her mother was no assurance that I could repeat the result in a courtroom with both present. I invited my adversary to dinner and for the first time in a Bendectin case, I opened discussion of a generous settlement. Although I made no offer, he laughed and brushed aside a very large hypothetical figure. He was confident that he would not only secure a large verdict in this case but that it would lead to his being retained in a string of similar cases. We proceeded toward a February trial.

Then came a break. The plaintiff's mother had become pregnant and the pregnancy would be obvious before the trial was over. At the very least, this would suggest to a jury her confidence that her child's disabilities were not the result of heredity. The trial judge, Norma Holloway Johnson, agreed that it would be unfair to require us to try the case under these circumstances, so she postponed it for a year. This gave us time to reorganize and gain the initiative. That fall we moved to the office building connected with Washington's Watergate Hotel, and most of our staff lived in the hotel.

We had the benefit of new scientific studies. To put plaintiff's counsel on the defensive, I had Struve prepare an extensive motion for summary judgment. Even though it was unlikely that a judge would grant summary judgment in a personal injury case, Struve's excellent set of motion papers angered the plaintiff's lawyers and forced them to devote themselves to the difficult preparation of answering papers at a time when they would rather have been working on other aspects of the case. But my real purpose was to educate the judge about the strength of our scientific evidence. Even though she denied the motion, she recognized the good faith of our position and questionable nature of the scientific claims of the plaintiff.

Then our overconfident opponent became reckless. A few days before Christmas, a secretary employed by his firm quit and revealed to my associate, Miriam Cedarbaum, that our opponent had invited the plaintiff's mother to strengthen her testimony. While the limbs of an unborn child develop rather early during pregnancy, the mother's first prescription for Bendectin was dated significantly after the plaintiff's limbs should have been formed. The plaintiff's counsel had suggested to her that earlier in her pregnancy she used Bendectin left over from a previous pregnancy. Notwithstanding Christmas, we sent Pat Ryan to Los Angeles to question the secretary and other appropriate witnesses and to make certain that they were testifying freely and responsibly. We had the secretary's statement before our adversary learned of our activity. His complaints about our action and our complaints about his led to motions and cross-motions as the case moved toward its February trial.

Then, after the jury panel members had been notified to report to the courthouse, our opponent committed his final folly. He released to *The Washington Post,* in a story about the upcoming trial, photographs of 12 deformed children accompanied by a statement that their mothers had all taken Bendectin. The *Post* published the pictures and the statement, even though those called for jury duty would almost certainly read it. The truth was that 10 percent of all children were born with birth defects whether or not their mothers took Bendectin. Ten equally disabled children whose mothers did not take Bendectin could have been photographed. The coincidence of birth defects with the ingestion of Bendectin was never proved to be statistically significant. More important, the court had already ruled the photographs inadmissable. Plaintiff's counsel had deliberately published, and thus released to the jury panel, prejudicial, inadmissable evidence.

We asked the trial judge to disqualify him and his firm as trial counsel. She was receptive. She again postponed the trial and ordered hearings on our opponent's conduct. To minimize the danger of my own possible disqualification as trial counsel, I did not conduct the hearings myself but turned them over to our able Washington counsel. After several days of hearings, the judge reserved decision; then, after receiving extensive briefs, she disqualified plaintiff's counsel. The U.S. Court of Appeals for the District of Columbia Circuit reversed her decision. I then obtained review by the Supreme Court, which, in turn, after questioning me extensively during argument, reversed the Court of Appeals by a vote of eight to one, holding that it lacked jurisdiction to reverse the trial judge's ruling.

While these tactics were essential in dealing with a case dangerous both because of its sympathetic appeal and because of the willfulness of plaintiff's counsel, our efforts were also expensive. Twice we had established Washington offices with most of our personnel living in a hotel at the expense of our client. During the pendency of the motion to disqualify plaintiff's counsel, we had kept open our Washington office in case we lost, continuing a meticulous preparation of our own expert witnesses and developing material for the cross-examination of hostile experts. Because of the cost of litigation, Bendectin had already been taken off the market, even though it had been the best medication for morning sickness. While I held off the most dangerous single case, our client decided on a master stroke.

In Cincinnati, its home city, an excellent defense counsel with a medical degree and a respected plaintiff's lawyer skilled in personal injury cases persuaded an aggressive and intelligently daring federal district judge to consolidate most of the outstanding Bendectin cases for the trial of the single issue: whether Bendectin was a teratogen—whether it caused birth defects. We turned over our extensive files to defense counsel. The court established procedures to prevent undue prejudice by requiring the disabled children and their parents to watch the proceedings on videotape out of the presence of the jury. The case ended with a jury verdict in favor of our client. It was affirmed on appeal. This decision took the wind out of the sails of most plaintiffs. A plaintiff's verdict in one other case tried by other defense counsel was reversed on appeal. In Washington, at the request of the client, my associates and I had again moved for summary judgment in our case, but by then Mary and I had made a heavy commitment for an around-the-world trip. New plaintiff's counsel opposed advancing the motion before my departure and our client was unwilling to await my return, so Ogden Lewis argued the motion. It was first denied but later granted after the affirmance of the Cincinnati judgment.

During the intervals when I returned home from Washington, I had worked on a few local cases. Some came to me and I requested my firm's assistance; others were firm cases in which my assistance was requested. The first referral I received, a dispute between a passenger and a steamship line, which was settled, came to me as the only Oklahoma member of the Maritime Law Association. Another, for example, was a product liability case defending the manufacturer of a baby's automobile seat after a family tragedy in which an uninsured driver ran a red light, killed the family's father, and injured the mother and the child as their car was broadsided. Like the Bendectin cases, it posed the danger of an emotional jury verdict because my client was the only financially sound source of recovery for the bereaved family. Fortunately, unlike the Bendectin cases, plaintiff's counsel and the family were reasonable and the case was settled without establishing a pattern that would embarrass the car seat manufacturer.

Working on the firm's cases was less inviting because the firm properly insisted that one of its active partners maintain control. I did, however, learn a little about oil and gas law, particularly when the property was owned by an Indian tribe. After an auction of a lease, the highest bidder, our client, had assumed it had won the lease, but the Indian tribe claimed a governmentally protected right to negotiate privately with an unsuccessful bidder who was willing to match or exceed the bid of the company successful at the auction. After I handled the depositions, the case was ultimately settled. I really did not enjoy the litigation. I did not mind using harsh tactics against the lawyers who were, in my mind, inappropriately exploiting the vulnerability of Bendectin, but I did not like using these tactics against an aggressive young lawyer from my own modest-sized community.

On our 20th anniversary, June 14, 1985, Mary and I gave each other a trip around the world. All of the children were now away from home. Elizabeth was the last to go off to school. Six months later, on a darkening, freezing January afternoon, I stood almost alone near the stern of the *Queen Elizabeth 2*, to watch, perhaps for the last time from shipboard, the receding lights of the city of New York as the great ship rapidly passed under the Verrazzano Bridge, through the Narrows and dropped its pilot. The voyage would only slightly overlap my previous travels. First picking up passengers in Miami and allowing a day among the Mayan ruins of the Yucatan, the *QE2* became the largest ship ever to traverse the Panama Canal. After hot, dusty visits to Lima, Valparaiso, and Santiago, the beautiful Chilean lake district refreshed us. For most of a day, notwithstanding fog, mist, and drizzle, I watched from the open deck beneath the bridge as we made the desolately beautiful passage through the Straits of Magellan.

In Montevideo, U.S. Ambassador Malcolm Wilkey, my former Justice Department associate, joined us for lunch on board and then took us to his residence. In Rio de Janeiro we witnessed the annual carnival. After crossing the South Atlantic to Cape Town, our shipboard tablemates entertained us in their home. Rounding the Cape of Good Hope to Kenya, we flew from Mombasa to Nairobi and then by small plane over the Great Rift Valley to spend two days enjoying a luxurious photographing safari on Kenya's western plateau. After other brief ports of call, we flew from Bombay to Agra to spend an afternoon at the Taj Mahal and the following day, a few hours away, in the abandoned seat of earlier Mogul rulers. While the remainder of the trip retraced my former voyages, the vast growth of the Pacific Rim made the cities unrecognizable. Singapore, Hong Kong, and Japan reveled in their prosperity. The Raffles Hotel and other important sites of earlier times were dwarfed. Bangkok was almost clogged with crowded streets and waterways. We left the ship at Nagasaki and rejoined her in Yokohama after visiting Kyoto and Tokyo and spending a night across the lake from Fujiyama, which was sparkling after a snowfall.

Shortly after flying home from San Francisco, I once more undertook the kind of work I most enjoyed. The Kansas Gas and Electric Company (KG&E), a utility serving Wichita and southern Kansas, had joined with another utility to construct the Wolf Creek nuclear power plant. The success of other nuclear plants had justified the decision. Even though disappointed that the general contractor had unexpectedly assigned its most experienced team to another job, they nevertheless went ahead. With construction half completed, the Atomic Energy Commission abruptly suspended work because of the tragic meltdown of a nuclear plant on Three Mile Island, Pennsylvania. The commission promulgated severe regulations retroactively applicable to unfinished construction. They forbade minor variations from approved plans—even matters of inches. They also required a record of the history of each part installed. Confronted with these harsh requirements and the absence of many newly required records, the two companies and their contractor faced financial catastrophe.

KG&E undertook the immediate supervision of continuing construction. A vice president moved to the site. Heartbreakingly, some construction had to be torn down because of slight variations or simply because records did not exist showing the source of each individual component. Disputes arose over responsibility and accuracy. Construction costs mounted and the company came under increasing criticism. Rate increases would obviously be necessary for the company to recover its costs and even to enable it to carry its heavy financing. Customers, stockholders, and government officials joined the attack.

The board voted to appoint three new directors to serve as an investigatory committee to report to the board and ultimately to the stockholders and to the public regarding the crisis. In addition to me, the board elected a San Antonio banker who had been through a similar problem with a Texas utility and a respected retired Kansas Supreme Court justice. The banker and I both agreed that the former state justice should be the chairman of our small committee. The banker brought to us his business judgment. I had had the most experience in complicated investigations.

Given a free hand, my colleagues accepted my insistence that the only satisfactory solution would be a hard-hitting, unquestionably thorough investigation. This, we agreed, would prove most valuable to the officers and the company, even though there would be periods when it would cause them distress. With the aid of a leading Wichita law firm and supplemental assistance by Crowe & Dunlevy, we sifted through the records of the company and the contractor. We questioned, sometimes repeatedly, every officer who had any part in the relevant decisions, including our chairman and chief executive officer and some officers of the general contractor. Ultimately, after many sometimes sharp discussions among ourselves, we produced a report fully supportive of the company's management and board of directors and so thorough and persuasive that it ended the public criticism and the danger of commission, stockholder, or customer litigation. The possible controversy between the company and its general contractor was referred to the company's general counsel and settled constructively. The new plant has impressively and consistently proved first or second in efficiency among all of the plants in the country.

Before we had finished this work, however, I received an unexpected phone call that drew me back to Washington and away from the professional activities of Oklahoma City. President Ronald Reagan and his National Security Council staff had come under investigation for trading arms to Iran to recover American hostages seized by Iranian sympathizers; for the disregard of congressional restraints on the sale of weapons to a foreign country; and for the secret financial support of a counterrevolutionary group in Nicaragua, the Contras. Worse, the two efforts had been linked as the price of the weapons to Iran had been inflated by 300 percent and the excess diverted from the United States Treasury to the private Swiss bank accounts of those secretly arming the Nicaraguan Contras. High-ranking government officials were suspected of crimes—even President Reagan himself. Each effort to allay the concerns of the press had backfired. Attorney General Edwin Meese, perceiving a conflict of interest that disqualified him and the Department of Justice from undertaking a criminal investigation, called for the appointment of a statutory independent counsel. Two of the three judges responsible for this appointment telephoned me to ask me to accept the post. I agreed to start immediately but with the understanding that I would also complete my work for KG&E.[2]

2. I have previously related the full story of the Iran/Contra investigation in FIREWALL, published in 1998 by W.W. Norton & Co.

Chapter 19
INDEPENDENT COUNSEL

On December 19, 1986, after being sworn in as independent counsel for Iran/Contra matters, and after meeting with a large group of reporters on the courthouse steps, I sat alone in the stale chambers of a long-inactive federal judge, the office that had been lent to me by the chief judge until I could organize my own.

Briefly uninterrupted, I thought back many years to a conversation in the New York district attorney's office. An investigation of mayoral candidate William O'Dwyer by others in the office had failed. My own bureau chief criticized those responsible as too cautious. He would have put O'Dwyer before the grand jury at the outset instead of trying to work up to him through his subordinates. Politically, O'Dwyer could not have afforded to claim his privilege against self-incrimination. Even though he denied guilt, his answers regarding details would likely produce admissions or prosecutable misstatements.

I had been impressed by my bureau chief's argument, but now I was in somewhat the same position. Would I boldly demand an early interrogation of the president or would I work up to him through his subordinates? Even anticipating the public impatience that would accompany a conservative course, I knew instinctively that I would choose it. Unlike the brash handling of a flamboyant city politician, I did not think the public or Congress would tolerate provocative treatment of a popular president, the country's one officer who is never off duty and has no real letup from his awesome responsibilities. I could not question him repeatedly. Public respect would require confidence in my fairness and thoroughness.

That afternoon, I called on FBI Director William Webster, an old friend, and met the two senior members of the FBI team that had begun the investigation for which I had become responsible. Then, to speed the completion of the KG&E investigation, I caught the last flight to Wichita and met with my committee and then with lawyers and company officers. Reporters pursued me, friendly but persistent, as I continued recruiting by phone from Oklahoma City and during a visit to New York. With the guidance of Bob Fiske and Leon Silverman, I acquired a full-time staff of four who had served recently as assistant U.S. attorneys. I added two associates from Davis Polk and a lawyer from the criminal division of the Department of Justice. Struve, Rick Ford of Crowe & Dunlevy, and former senior prosecutors promised part-time assistance. A retired Department of Justice lawyer assembled the administrative side of the office. To expand my full-time staff, I began to recruit judicial law clerks, inexperienced top law school students who had for a year assisted a federal judge.

On Christmas Eve, in Oklahoma, the head of the FBI team briefed Ford and me. Following advice from Washington experts, after New Year's Day I met with Speaker Jim Wright, House Minority Leader Bob Michel, and Lee Hamilton and Dick Cheney, the chairman and ranking minority member of the House committee investigating Iran/Contra activities. Within two weeks of my appointment, our office was in action. The chief judge lent us a second set of judicial chambers; the FBI assigned us basement space; and the General Services Administration began its search for a permanent office that would satisfy the intelligence agencies as a depository of classified information. Two important witnesses began to cooperate in return for immunity. After the full FBI team briefed our first staff meeting, we subdivided, assigning lawyers to cover the White House, the National Security Council, the CIA, and the departments of State, Justice, and Defense.

We were, however, in conflict with others investigating the same misconduct. Slighted in their oversight responsibility, both houses of Congress had established special committees to learn and expose the facts. Unlike my staff, they did not have to meet the high standard for criminal prosecution—proof beyond a reasonable doubt. Even as we first met, Hamilton and Cheney pressed us to move faster and to share information. Then Hamilton warned us that the committees were considering a grant of immunity that might prevent the prosecution of the most vulnerable and immediately important subjects of our investigation. A presidential commission to investigate the National Security Council, headed by former Senator John Tower of Texas, also clamored for information. I quickly doubled my staff.

We perceived a complicated, interlocked, three-part conspiratorial activity of the president's National Security Council staff and the obvious ultimate question of whether these activities were approved or supervised by cabinet officers and by the president himself. Until 1984, the CIA had covertly assisted the Contras, the Nicaraguan counterrevolutionary group. While the agency ostensibly sought to prevent arms traffic from Russia through Cuba and Nicaragua to other Central American countries, Congress suspected a second purpose—to overthrow the Communist-dominated government of Nicaragua. Shocked by some extreme CIA activity, such as mining harbors and damaging neutral ships, Congress shut off funds and forbade personnel of the CIA, the Department of Defense, or any other "intelligence entity" to support the Contras. The National Security Council, as overseer of intelligence activity, was an intelligence entity.

President Reagan decided to support the Contras surreptitiously. Through the intercession of his national security adviser, Robert McFarlane, Saudi Arabia provided them with funds. To replace the CIA as liaison with the Contras, McFarlane assigned a National Security Council staff member, a marine in active service, Lieutenant Colonel Oliver North. Guided by CIA Director William Casey, North developed a clandestine private supply organization directed by a retired Air Force major general, Richard Secord, a logistics expert, who was in turn aided by arms dealer and former CIA agent Thomas Clines and by Iranian-born, international wheeler-dealer Albert Hakim.

At about the same time, President Reagan also decided to try to free eight American hostages seized by a radical Islamic group in Lebanon. One of them was the CIA chief of station. Although giving lip service to our national policy, and that of our allies, not to traffic with hostage takers, the president approved an Israeli scheme to permit Israel to sell U.S. arms to Iran during the Iran-Iraq war with the expectation that the Iranian government would persuade the hostage takers to release the Americans and that the U.S. would sell arms replacements to Israel. As the Israeli delivery to Iran ran into a logistical snag, North was assigned to solve the problem. He secretly drew in Duane Clarridge, the CIA official who had preceded him as liaison with the Contras, and, through him, a CIA-controlled airline. But the Iranians rejected the Israeli weapons as outdated and marked with the Star of David. Fearing retaliation against the hostages and fed up with Israeli bungling, the president authorized direct arms sales by the United States to Iran through private intermediaries, and Admiral John Poindexter, who had succeeded McFarlane as national security adviser, turned the program over to North and his private associates.

These activities violated several laws: (1) the 1984 congressional restrictions on aid to the Contras, the Boland Amendment; (2) the National Security Act, requiring presidential notice to congressional leaders of new CIA foreign covert activities; and (3) the Arms Export Control Act, requiring presidential notice to Congress of the sale of arms to foreign recipients and of the transfer of U.S. arms from one foreign recipient to another. None of these statutes carried express criminal sanctions, but under Supreme Court decisions, the deliberate, illegal misuse of government personnel and resources could amount to a conspiracy to defraud the United States.

Exposure began two months before my appointment when one of North's Contra supply aircraft was shot down over Nicaragua. The scandal exploded three weeks later when a Lebanese magazine published the story of the Iranian arms-hostage transactions. Aroused congressional committees and journalists pursued the secretary of state, the director of the CIA, and the president's national security adviser to learn the facts. This led to a third part of the conspiracy—a conspiracy to cover up the other two parts.

The president's chief of staff, Donald Regan, alerted to the danger of inconsistent testimony by administration witnesses, had President Reagan call in Attorney General Meese to develop a "coherent" administration position. At a meeting of the president, vice president, the secretaries of state and defense, the director of the CIA, and the national security adviser, Meese told them that if the president had authorized the Israeli arms sales to Iran without notice to Congress, it would have been illegal, but that the president did not know about them. Each person in the room knew that this was false; the president knew about them in advance. Realizing that Meese was indicating the necessary line for the president's defense, no one spoke. Then Meese told the president and Regan privately that his assistants had found a copy of a memorandum from North to Poindexter, which disclosed that North and Secord had secretly inflated the price of arms sold by the U.S. through them to Iran by 300 percent and that they had diverted the extra proceeds to Swiss bank accounts to buy arms for the Contras. Regan and Meese decided to charge the National Security Council staff with a "runaway" conspiracy. Informed of the impending investigation, North shredded hundreds of

National Security Council documents and Poindexter destroyed an incriminating presidential finding.

President Reagan denied knowledge of the diversion of the arms proceeds. He returned North to the Marine Corps and accepted the resignation of Poindexter, yet his confused denials and explanations of other aspects of the arms sales raised suspicion of his own participation. The scope of my investigative assignment, while specifically focused on North, included all persons involved in these activities. Thus, I became the first post-Watergate independent counsel to investigate a president for official misconduct.

Dealing with experts in covert deception, we first had to obtain the relevant documents with which to confront them in order to prevent evasive and dishonest answers. The truth lay in thousands of disguised cables and memoranda, as well as financial records. The chief judge of the federal court quickly impaneled a special grand jury, but, confronted with the pressure of the congressional committees, I did not want to use grand jury subpoenas to government agencies for fear of inviting litigation delays. Instead, I used informal document requests and reserved subpoenas to deal with noncompliance. Delays nevertheless persisted. Clearance of my staff to receive top-secret classified information, in some cases, took weeks. The CIA, for example, held back documents until threatened with subpoenas, then flooded us with thousands of documents, faster than we could absorb them. Even though I was a government prosecutor, I was obviously being treated as a government adversary. Switzerland was a special problem. Under its laws, it could not release any records until after lengthy appeals to its supreme court. Israel was also a problem. It would not permit us to examine Israeli financial records or question Israeli witnesses.

The congressional committees investigating Iran/Contra unrealistically committed themselves to complete their investigations in six months and thus avoid a presidential election year. Poindexter, North, Secord, and Hakim had claimed the privilege against self-incrimination and refused to testify. Unable to compel production of Swiss banking records, the committees gave immunity to Hakim to get them from him. Later, they gave immunity to North and Poindexter so that they would testify. A witness granted immunity may still be prosecuted but his testimony, so induced, cannot be used against him. The courts have been zealous to prevent even indirect use of such testimony by prosecutors. I opposed these grants of immunity because they would endanger our prosecutions and because I did not believe that North and Poindexter would be candid until prosecuted and confronted with imprisonment. After negotiating for two months and appearing before both committees, the committees agreed to withhold public immunized testimony for 90 days so that I could at least assemble evidence against North and Poindexter free of any claim that we learned about it through their immunized testimony.

Senator Tower's commission filed its report. It had questioned President Reagan. His recollection of operating details had proved even worse than I had assumed. He gave three inconsistent answers as to whether he had personally authorized the Israeli-Iranian arms sales. First, he testified that he had. Then he returned to testify that he had not. Then he wrote the commission that he simply did not remember. I concluded that when the time came for us to question him, we would have to use written interrogatories to get firm answers even though he would, of course, be aided by his staff in answering them and we would have to sacrifice spontaneity and surprise.

Two of those helping North solicit and transmit substantial American contributions to the Contras, notwithstanding the congressional restriction against his participation in this activity, pleaded guilty to a conspiracy to defraud the United States, named North as a co-conspirator, and agreed to testify against him. Others testified to his criminal destruction of National Security Council files and his false statements to a congressional committee. But while the Swiss financial agent of Secord and Hakim, in return for immunity from prosecution, relayed through his American lawyers information exposing the North-Secord-Hakim diversion of United States arms proceeds and even a $200,000 personal Swiss investment account set up for North, he could not talk with us or testify until after the Swiss courts released the financial records. Unwilling to give immunity to Hakim or to ask the grand jury to proceed on hearsay reports of Swiss activities, I decided not to be pushed into a fragmented indictment of North and his collaborators by the pressure of the congressional committees. Rightly or wrongly, I chose to rely on precedents suggesting that if my staff and I rigidly insulated ourselves from his immunized testimony, we could still prosecute him.

The congressional committees then bungled their interrogation of North. In reckless haste, they gave North immunity in spite of his refusal to give a proffer of his testimony or to testify privately in advance of his public testimony. They questioned him before a television audience of millions not knowing exactly what he would say. Committee counsel and chairmen could not restrict him to relevant answers or effectively cross-examine him. Intensively prepared, North dominated the hearing with impressive, self-serving speeches. A poll of Americans asked to identify the 10 most respected persons in the world placed President Reagan number four, North number five, and the Pope number six. We were left to prosecute an immunized national hero.

It was December, almost a year after my appointment, before we could utilize the Swiss financial records and witnesses. We were particularly interested in the $200,000 transferred from the Swiss depository of the Iranian arms sales proceeds through Hakim's personal account to a personal investment account for North, ostensibly to cover the education of his children, and another indirect transfer of $18,000 to pay for a security system for North's home. Mrs. North had supplied family information to the Swiss financial manager who set up the investment account, but she could not be compelled to testify against her husband. This Swiss witness, however, could not testify that North was party to the arrangement; he had acted at the direction of Hakim. We could, however, prove that North accepted the home security system as a gift and falsified records to conceal the transaction.

With the Swiss evidence and the testimony of former national security adviser McFarlane, who had pleaded guilty to withholding information from Congress, our grand jury indicted Poindexter, North, Secord, and Hakim for a conspiracy to defraud the United States and for diverting from the U.S. Treasury part of the proceeds of the sale of American arms. The indictment charged individual false statements to Congress and other acts to obstruct the congressional investigations. It also charged North with the destruction of National Security Council records and the acceptance of the illegal gift of his home security system.

For almost a year, we fended off motions by the defendants attacking the indictment. Because Congress had given immunity to Poindexter, North, and Hakim, the trial judge required us to try each of the defendants separately to permit one defendant to utilize the immunized testimony of another. This ruling more than doubled the time and expense necessary to complete the trials. It also made necessary separate teams for each trial because the exposure of a trial team to defendants not on trial would make it ineligible to try any of those defendants.

The intelligence agencies then protested that certain evidence necessary for trial could not be used without endangering national security. Under the law, the judge could not evaluate these claims, only the attorney general. Because of one such claim by the National Security Agency, we had to drop the two central counts of the indictment, the conspiracy to defraud the United States and the diversion of the arms sales proceeds. This seriously jeopardized the outcome because, without those central counts, the charges of isolated individual misconduct had less apparent significance and less jury appeal. Nevertheless, we convicted those who did not plead guilty. John Keker, a highly regarded San Francisco criminal defense lawyer and Vietnam marine veteran, tried North and convicted him of three felonies. Dan Webb, a former Chicago U.S. attorney, tried Poindexter and convicted him of five. Secord pleaded guilty to a felony and Hakim to a misdemeanor.

We had required President Reagan to answer written interrogatories to reduce the danger that he might be a defense witness. He denied authorizing the diversion of the proceeds of the Iran arms sales, North's clandestine Contra supply activities, or the false statements to Congress by North and Poindexter. While we had sacrificed spontaneity, we had obtained clear-cut denials. The value of this tactical decision unfolded when President Reagan was deposed as a defense witness by Richard Beckler, the lawyer for Admiral Poindexter, and cross-examined by my associate, Dan Webb. Every time the former president tried to help Poindexter, he ultimately backed off and emphatically confirmed the truth of his written interrogatory denials. The president's deposition was videotaped for the trial and then broadcast to the general public.

After convicting North and Poindexter, we began our investigation of the government departments that had supported them. While Dan Webb had skillfully used North as a witness against Poindexter, we had no direct evidence that President Reagan had authorized the criminal activity of Poindexter or North. The District of Columbia Circuit Court of Appeals, with Chief Judge Patricia Wald dissenting, eliminated any possible inducement for their cooperation by reversing their convictions, holding that even though my associates and I, in accordance with previous court decisions, had successfully insulated ourselves from their immunized testimony, the trial witnesses had been exposed to its broadcasts, and that even though neither North nor Poindexter specified any misuse of their testimony, we had to prove a negative beyond a reasonable doubt—that not one witness gave testimony affected by the immunized testimony. We could not meet that test. While the first witness to be examined, McFarlane, could not specify any effect, he could not give assurance that his answers were not subconsciously responsive to North's testimony.

Occupied for over three years by the cases against McFarlane, Poindexter, North, Secord, and Hakim, we nevertheless proceeded with our investigation of the CIA, the State Department, and the personal staffs of President Reagan and Vice President George Bush. Contrary to the final report of the congressional committees, the National Security Council staff had not conducted a "runaway" conspiracy. North had not operated alone. He had regularly conferred with CIA Director William Casey and he reported his activities to a restricted interagency group (RIG) representing several government agencies. He was more intimately supervised by a much smaller group, the "Riglet," including Alan D. Fiers, chief of the CIA Central American Task Force, and Elliott Abrams, the assistant secretary of state for inter-American affairs. While North was the most exposed, he had carried out the strategy of Casey, Fiers, and Abrams. Casey had died shortly after I was appointed. Confronted with cables, and North's notes and testimony, Fiers and Abrams pleaded guilty to misdemeanors. Fiers then testified against Clair George, the CIA director of operations who, under Casey, had been the senior officer in charge of all of the CIA's clandestine operations and who had lied to congressional committees to avoid, as he said, "turning a searchlight on the White House." My deputy, Craig Gillen, tried and convicted him of several felonies.

After our grand juries had returned their first 13 indictments, 11 defendants had been convicted, two convictions had been reversed on appeal, and one indictment had to be dismissed because the CIA refused to release nonsecret, widely known classified information. No defendant was acquitted. The indictment of Clarridge, North's first CIA colleague, awaited trial.

Having been too long preoccupied with Poindexter, North, and the central conspirators, we belatedly found that Secretary of State George Shultz had not produced to Congress or to us all of his notes, that he had omitted those showing knowledge of arms shipments to Iran, and that he had given testimony to congressional committees that was incomplete. Because we could not allocate fault between him and his executive assistant, to whom he had dictated the notes and who jealously kept possession of them, and because they had both opposed the arms sales, and both, at the time of his testimony, were under extraordinary pressure trying to regain control of our embarrassed foreign relations, we did not ask the grand jury to indict either of them.

From the extensive notes Shultz had dictated, we learned that Defense Secretary Caspar Weinberger had also kept notes. We finally found hundreds of pages of them, in his own hand, in a restricted (but unclassified) deposit in the Library of Congress. To us, and under oath before the congressional committees, Weinberger had denied having notes while, in fact, he had over 700 pages relating to Iran/Contra, including conversations with President Reagan in which Weinberger told him that the transactions were illegal. His notes, if disclosed when he was first questioned, would have illuminated the investigations of Congress, my office, and the grand jury. Five years later, however, the statute of limitations had reduced their usefulness.

In June 1992, our grand jury indicted Weinberger, charging him with the obstruction of our investigation and that of Congress and with specific acts of perjury. We also found that Donald Regan, the president's chief of staff, had withheld extensive, relevant personal notes but that he had avoided lying about them under oath. We decided to use him as a witness against Weinberger rather than prosecute him. Before we obtained Weinberger's incriminating notes, the statute of limitations had run out on Meese's efforts to protect the president by developing "coherent" testimony by cabinet officers and other top presidential assistants. Even though he gave prosecutable fresh denials of his false statements to the president's foreign policy advisers, which Weinberger and Regan had recorded, we believed that, to a jury, the passage of five years could raise a reasonable doubt that these new lies were deliberate and thus jeopardize a successful prosecution.

Shortly before the 1992 presidential election, the Weinberger trial judge dismissed the central count of his indictment—the charge of obstructing a congressional investigation. He held that the charge should have been perjury. Confronted with a trial irrevocably scheduled for January and with extensive pretrial hearings throughout December, Weinberger's counsel and the judge pressed us to replace the missing charge before the end of October. We agreed to do so. After the denial of an additional week, on October 30, four days before Election Day, we replaced the obstruction count with a perjury count, which contrasted Weinberger's testimony under oath with quotations from his notes.

One note placed Vice President Bush at a meeting of President Reagan, Shultz, Weinberger, Casey, Meese, and Poindexter when President Reagan decided to authorize direct arms sales to Iran. It recited that Poindexter, Casey, Meese, and Bush favored this action, while Weinberger and Shultz opposed it. Bush's participation in that meeting had long been public knowledge. Poindexter had disclosed it in his congressional testimony. Yet the Clinton presidential campaign and the press picked up the quote as documentary refutation of Bush's frequent claim that he had been "out of the loop." To my surprise, this fresh recital of old information received extensive attention, and an angry Bush blamed it as one reason for his election defeat.

On Christmas Eve, President Bush, knowing that he himself had not yet produced his own diary for the Iran/Contra period, notwithstanding our document request, granted Weinberger an in-advance-of-trial pardon, a pardon that blocked the trial and left forever undecided Weinberger's guilt or innocence. The pardon also eliminated the public trial that would have exposed the full facts regarding the Iranian arms sales, a trial at which Bush had been told that he might be called and cross-examined as a defense witness. While general grants of amnesty had long been sustained, the pardon power had not been intended to prevent a court from deciding guilt or innocence of an indicted individual. Traditionally, in individual cases, pardons had been used as acts of mercy alleviating punishment *after* conviction.[1] The drafters of our Constitution regarded this concept as so well established that they did not believe the Constitution needed such a specific reservation.

To divert attention from his self-interest, Bush also decided to give a pretrial pardon to Clarridge, the other untried indicted person, and to pardon several who had pleaded guilty or whom we had convicted. This action was the ultimate cover-up, the culmination of a series of cover-ups that, particularly as to Weinberger, had delayed our work and now made its completion impossible. While I considered further action against Bush, my staff was unanimous against prolonging our activity. To compel him to testify, we would have had to subpoena him before a grand jury. With an indictment unlikely, such a use of a grand jury could be questionable and would have appeared retaliatory. In a larger sense, his election defeat had reduced any activity by us to an anticlimax. Accordingly, after reporting these events to Congress, we ended our investigation and completed our comprehensive final report. Notwithstanding motions by former President Reagan, North, Meese, and others to suppress it, the court ultimately released our report to Congress and to the public.

---

1. Before there were immunity statutes, the pardon power was sometimes used to encourage a person to testify as a witness but not just to block a trial.

Throughout our investigation, individual senators and congressmen and a succession of Reagan and Bush attorneys general and their assistants criticized our activity. Within two months of my appointment, an assistant to Edwin Meese complained to a congressional committee of our expense and the incongruity of the office of independent counsel. Within three months, the chairman and ranking minority member of the Senate committee investigating Iran/Contra matters jointly complained that I was moving too slowly and suggested I limit my investigation to North's destruction of records. A month later they renewed their public attack, but we then immediately released an interim report explaining the full importance of the crimes we were investigating and explaining the problem of the Swiss records and other delays. Some congressmen, particularly those from the conservative right wing of the Republican party, showed their support for North by public statements and even by attending his trial.

These attacks were dwarfed by those that followed our indictment of Weinberger. Republican Senate leader Bob Dole denounced us as hired assassins. The ranking Republican member of the House Rules Committee began an investigation nitpicking our expenditures, hoping to find some technical violation. Senator Dole and a majority of the Republicans on the Senate Judiciary Committee wrote the attorney general urging him to request the appointment of an independent counsel to investigate us. The General Accounting Office was pressed to expedite its audit of our accounts, even though we had previously been guided by the Administrative Office of the Courts. The public integrity section of the Department of Justice had the FBI also investigate our travel expense. The FBI, at the request of the deputy attorney general, investigated our chief file clerk and me for the loss of a classified document packed in the clerk's stolen suitcase. Bush's attorney general denounced our indictments as cases were about to go to trial. Nevertheless, we had staunch defense by some very important members of both houses of Congress, including the chairmen and other members of the Senate and House Intelligence committees, the chairman of the House Committee on Government Oversight, and the chairman and ranking minority member of the Senate Committee on Government Operations.

As we rounded out our investigation and prepared for the Weinberger trial, I took former President Reagan's deposition at his Los Angeles Century City office. It was to be our final opportunity to have him respond to the questions we had accumulated. As we sat around a conference table in a pleasant room next to his private office, my associates and I were shocked to find that he had sustained a serious loss of memory. Careful testing regarding both relevant and irrelevant matters convinced us that his memory loss was genuine. Perhaps most dramatic was his lack of recollection that Poindexter had resigned and his having forgotten whether his close friend and former assistant, Mike Deaver, had been on his staff when he was governor of California. He grasped at fragments of memory, such as his successful private fireside conversation with President Mikhail Gorbachev at their first Geneva meeting, which led to further top-level meetings. He also recalled an earlier conversation with Margaret Thatcher, before she became prime minister. He seemed embarrassed by his lapses and anxious to please, anxious to find a subject unencumbered by his disability. During one recess he took me to a window to point out Los Angeles points of interest. He offered all of us licorice jelly beans. A little later, his public disclosure that he was suffering from Alzheimer's disease confirmed our judgment. In my final report, I stated that we did not have credible evidence that President Reagan deliberately violated a criminal statute but that his disregard of other laws enacted to limit presidential action created a climate in which subordinates felt emboldened and compelled to circumvent those laws.

The North case did not reach trial until two years after my appointment. The trial of Poindexter followed a year after that. Nearing 80, I reluctantly turned our trials over to younger lawyers. When I returned to Oklahoma four years later, I looked forward to a role as mediator in civil litigation, but conflicts of interest flowing from my affiliation with the largest local law firm and one of the largest national firms diminished my availability. The devil, seeking work for idle hands, then tempted me to write this book.

INDEX

B

C

D

E

H

I

J

K

N

O

P

T

U

V

W

Y